W9-AUU-216

BONNIE GREER

A Parallel Life

Arcadia Books Ltd
139 Highlever Road
London W10 6PH

www.arcadiabooks.co.uk

First published by Arcadia Books 2014

A catalogue record for this book is available from the British Library.

ISBN 978-1-909807-62-4

Typeset Typeset in Berling by 2H Design
Printed and bound by CPI Group (UK) Ltd, Croydon CR0 4YY

Arcadia Books supports English PEN *www.englishpen.org* and The Book Trade Charity *http://booktradecharity.wordpress.com*

Arcadia Books distributors are as follows:

in the UK and elsewhere in Europe:
Macmillan Distribution Ltd
Brunel Road
Houndmills
Basingstoke
Hants RG21 6XS

in the USA and Canada:
Dufour Editions
PO Box 7
Chester Springs
PA 19425

in Australia/New Zealand:
NewSouth Books
University of New South Wales
Sydney NSW 205

BONNIE GREER

A Parallel Life

DEDICATION

For my parents. For Judith. And for David.

EPIGRAPH

Those are the same stars, and that is the same moon, that look down upon your brothers and sisters and which they see as they look up to them though they are ever so far away from us, and each other.

Sojourner Truth

PART ONE

BLUES PEOPLE

1948–1963

ONE

I was born in Chicago, city of the blues.

I grew up on the South Side, one of the blues' seedbeds.

I'm the eldest child of plain-speaking people who came from people who, like them, worked hard, often for less than they were worth, and many times for nothing at all.

They partied on Saturday night and went to church on Sunday.

They raised their children to live better and longer than they did and to die wealthier.

And always to be 'proper' and to love the Lord.

They had no horizon other than the 'better' and they stayed amongst their own. Even if they didn't want to do that all of the time, they had no choice, so it was best to make a virtue of it.

Education was basic and brief, but they aimed for more for their children, telling them to never forget 'mother wit'.

They may not have completely approved of me, but would not have been surprised.

They were what the late poet Amiri Baraka called 'Blues People'.

These 'Blues People' took the big trains up from the cotton fields of the South to be with kin and start anew.

I come from a people who always moved, once they were freed from being a part of the land. From being the land.

The great blues singer Howlin' Wolf said: 'Never forget your inherit.'

And with these moving people, you always had to call them by what they called their 'right name', the name you call yourself. Not the name given to you by others.

And the names?

'Coloured'; 'Negro'; 'black'; 'Black'; 'African American'.

The words that have been used in my lifetime to describe me. I've used most of them myself.

But these words never came close to describing me, nor that parallel life – the one that sustains me, the one that propels me forwards. The one that has always directed me the other way, made me look on the other side.

It is *'sans foi ni loi'* – 'lawless.' It is touched by nothing and no one. Not even me.

It has its route, and sometimes makes itself known, leaving me with the task of deciphering its language, learning all over again its codes, its rules, its terrain.

Still.

But it merges more often now.

This 'parallel life' holds my arboretum, my mythology, my landscape, my story. If I am lucky, it will be this parallel life that will be with me at the very end.

Words for me are rooted in music – sound and images. I remember people and events and eras that way. Words exist in images, colours, sounds.

Take the word 'Negro'.

That word always had a grey, metallic colour in my mind. The sound of it was like a scouring brush on an old frying pan: harsh, hollow, ugly.

Its music is one of those soppy, sentimental harmonicas that always accompanied Sidney Poitier when he used to die in the movies a lot.

Never liked it. Never used it.

Which was funny because as a child growing up in the late 1950s it seemed to be the name *du jour*, a name that made people actually happy or invoked serious discussion on TV; the name screaming from the covers of magazines in the shops in our neighbourhood ('Negro Discovers the Secret of the Universe!') on the West Side of Chicago, Lawndale, the Badlands.

When Muhammed Ali asked once on TV: 'Negro? Where is "Negroland"?' I jumped up and down with glee. Somebody had finally said it.

Of course, I learned later on that 'Negro/negro' came from the Spanish. That was no excuse.

But it did give me something.

It was the word 'Negro' that gave me one of the first signs of my synaesthesia, that gift/curse – part of the so-called 'primitive brain', the in utero state – that can cause an individual to see sound. A note can be seen as an object, for example, or a word can conjure up an entire film. Or a word like 'Negro' was and is ugly in my mind's eye.

I don't care for 'Black', nor 'African American' nor 'BAME'.

They're not as bad as 'Negro', but they're like a flat desert.

'African American' looks like one of those hair ads from the 1970s with the man seated in a high-backed wicker chair, a palm tree draped over the top of it, and his lady leaning towards him in a tiger-skin, off-the-shoulder gown.

I prefer 'black' to describe me.

Just plain 'black'.

When I was a child, to call someone 'black' was an insult, a curse word, something that made you fight.

But to me it contains all of the history of oppression and resistance, of being close to the soil and the sky, of plain speaking. Of The Journey.

In the '70s, I had to work my way through university, so one of my jobs was waitressing at a legendary blues club.

One night a big, tall, what folks would call a 'country' black woman, dressed in farmer's overalls and with a guitar, climbed up onstage. Everybody stopped what they were doing.

She surveyed the audience and said: 'Hello. I'm Big Mamma Thornton. I wrote "Hound Dog" and this is the way you supposed to sing it.'

She slowed it right down to the level of a menace to life. A truth-telling woman recounting a statement from another truth-telling woman to a man who messed up her life. Through her voice I saw a free woman, down on her land, a woman who knew how to kill her own chickens, hunt her own possum, cut her own cotton, fix her own roof, make her own whiskey, walk in her own shoes, and speak her mind, tell her own story.

A black woman.

Ready for the journey.

The Journey.

TWO

There is an irony in the American search for roots.

With the important exceptions of Americans descended from enslaved Africans, the peoples once called 'Indians', and those whose ancestors were part of the work cargo 'imported' from China in the nineteenth century, enslaved in all but name, Hispanic Americans and indentured Europeans – the majority of those who became Americans arrived more or less voluntarily, eager to forget their roots, or at least the unpleasant bits. This can make for startling discoveries.

I once met, in the South of France, an Italian American airline pilot named Sal. Sal had the profile of a Roman coin; he could be nothing but an Italian. He was perfect.

Sal sat in total amazement when, over several small glasses of spirit, my husband and I talked about Rome. And Renaissance Italy.

Suddenly he said, in a small voice: 'Did Italians do all that?'

He then explained to me that his parents and grandparents told him nothing about Italy. Nothing. They'd wanted to forget it. Forget the Old Country. They wanted to be new. They wanted to be Americans.

But the official erasure of any existence before enslavement – as if black Americans did not exist before the yolk and the chains and the whip – has always created a passion for us. Black people need to find out. We have to find out Who We Are. And Where We Come From.

Records were kept in some cases, but they were – to the minds of the record keepers – stock inventories, records of pedigrees. Nothing to do with people.

Human beings – to them – did not exist within the pages of plantation records.

We had to find our own humanity, our own roots.

In 2011, in of all places the lobby of the Royal Opera House, Covent Garden, while waiting to begin rehearsal for an opera whose libretto I was writing, I allowed a swab to be taken of my cheek cells.

I had been asked by a newspaper to take part in a human genome study. Dad was dead by then, and anyway, I had always felt – with the exception of Aunt Bernice – closest to Mamma's family. So I chose to learn about my deep ancestry on the maternal side.

Eighty thousand years ago.

Like every human being on earth, I'm descended from what the human scientists call the 'African Eve', or 'Mitochondrial Eve', the most successful human being in history in terms of human generation.

She is the common ancestor of every member of genus *homo sapiens sapiens*, that is to say, modern human beings. This fact, of course, makes racism not only stupid and unscientific, but a reduction of wonder.

The report from IBM came back a few weeks later.

I've read the report over and over because it never fails to move me.

It begins very simply – like the Homeric tale that it is:

Your Branch on the Human Family Tree

Your DNA results identify you as belonging to a specific branch of the human family tree called haplogroup L3.

Haplogroup L3 contains the following subgroups: L3, L3*, L3d, L3e, L3f, L3g.

The most recent common ancestor of everybody in your haplogroup L3 is a woman who lived around 80,000 years ago.

An individual in L2 underwent a mutation in her mitochondrial DNA, which was passed on to her children. The children were successful, and their descendants ultimately broke away from the L2 clan, eventually separating into a new group called L3.

While L3 individuals are found all over Africa, including the southern reaches of the sub-Saharan region, L3 is particularly known for its push northward.

Your L3 ancestors were significant because they are the first modern humans to have left Africa, representing the deepest branches of the tree found outside of that continent.

Why would humans have first ventured out of the familiar African hunting grounds and into unexplored lands? It is likely that a fluctuation in climate may have provided the impetus for your ancestors' exodus out of Africa.

The African Ice Age was characterised by drought rather than by cold. Around 50,000 years ago the ice sheets of northern Europe began to melt, introducing a period of warmer temperatures and moister climate in Africa.

Parts of the inhospitable Sahara briefly became habitable.

As the drought-ridden desert changed to savanna, the animals your ancestors hunted expanded their range and began moving through the newly emerging green corridor of grasslands.

Your nomadic ancestors followed the good weather and plentiful game northward across this Saharan Gateway, although the exact route they followed remains to be determined.

Today, L3 individuals are found at high frequencies in populations across North Africa.

From there, members of this group went in a few different directions.

Some lineages within L3 testify to a distinct expansion event in the mid-Holocene that headed south, and are predominant in many Bantu groups found all over Africa.

One group of individuals headed west and is primarily restricted to Atlantic western Africa, including the islands of Cabo Verde.

Some of the other L3 individuals kept moving northward, eventually leaving the African continent completely.

These people currently make up around 10 per cent of the Middle Eastern population, and gave rise to two important haplogroups that went on to populate the rest of the world.

The first of these groups, M, was the result of the first great wave of migration of modern humans to leave Africa.

These people likely left the continent across the Horn of Africa near Ethiopia, and their descendants followed a coastal route eastward, eventually making it all the way to Australia and Polynesia.

The second group, haplogroup N, also consisting of L3 individuals, moved north rather than east and left the African continent across the Sinai Peninsula, in present-day Egypt. Faced with the harsh desert conditions of the Sahara, these people likely followed the Nile basin, which would have provided a reliable water and food supply in spite of the surrounding desert and its frequent sandstorms.

In addition to being the first to leave Africa, and producing the groups that went on to populate the rest of the world, L3 is an important haplogroup because it is also found among many Americans of African ancestry.

Most of the L3 lineages found in the Americas are of West African origin, with some lineages representative of west-central and south-eastern Africa also being found at lower frequencies.

L3b and L3d individuals are mainly West African, with a few types shared with eastern and south-eastern Africans.

Occasionally L3b and L3d individuals can be found in southern Africa, though these are largely the result of the Bantu migrations that brought derived lineages into these ancestral southern territories.

Members who [like myself] are L3* fall within the L3 haplogroup, but are not L3b or L3d, which is determined based on your genetic sequence.

L3* individuals include some of the more common and widespread African-American mtDNA lineages, and most likely derive from West Africa between Angola and Cameroon, or from south-eastern Africa in Mozambique.

> These lineages are also found among the São Tomé and Bioko in the Gulf of Guinea in West Africa.
>
> However, the transfer of slaves from Angola and Cameroon in the eighteenth century to work the sugar plantations of West Africa, and the subsequent transfer of slaves to the Americas, is responsible for the wide geographic distribution of L3s in western Africa and the Americas and makes pinpointing their geographical origin difficult.
>
> This is where the genetic clues get murky and your DNA trail goes cold.
>
> Fortunately, collaborative sampling with indigenous groups is currently underway to help learn more about these origins.
>
> Your initial results shown here are based upon the best information available today but this is just the beginning.
>
> With more genetic information from Africa, our anthropologists may be able to untangle the complex L3 landscape and begin pinpointing the origins of specific lineages.
>
> Our goal is to bridge the gap that was created during those transatlantic voyages hundreds of years ago.
>
> Although the arrow of your haplogroup currently ends across sub-Saharan Africa, this is not the end of the journey for haplogroup L3.

'The gap that was created during those transatlantic voyages hundreds of years ago.'

That gap is the matrix of 'Saudade' – The Longing, I think, that all Africans in the West have, that is at the root of the blues and jazz and soul and rap. If you listen you can hear it, elusive, fleeting, full of melancholy anger.

It was in our family, too. It was the filter through which I saw everything as a child. I could not defend myself against it. I didn't want to.

When I first saw that word 'saudade' in a book about Brazilian music, I felt an instant attraction to it.

I wanted to know precisely what it meant, so I did something that would probably be considered by many to be a bit too corny even in pursuit of knowledge: I listened again for the umpteenth time to 'The Girl from Ipanema'. This song embodies, in many ways, 'saudade'. And you can hear in it the 'quilombos', the settlements created by those who ran away, who revolted against enslavement, and there's also the slave owners, and the sailors and the indentured and the Church which blessed it all.

The music of Cabo Verde, Cape Verde.

This brings me back to the IBM report, and the fact that moved me the most: that my deep ancestry – the ancestry of all black people in the so called 'New World' – may have passed through those islands thousands of years ago. They may have settled then, and then left, or were brought back east, and eventually to the ships that would take them across the Atlantic on the Long Voyage where they would become me.

This word 'saudade' is considered to be the constant desire for something that does not exist and cannot exist. 'Saudade' is deeper than nostalgia.

I think that it is the condition of all of us taken away.

By the light of 'saudade' – a greenish blue for me like twilight over the Atlantic – I studied the IBM map of my ancestry.

I watched it snake from East Africa, to the west and the south, then to the edge of the Sahara, where the report states, 'The trail runs cold.'

It has to be at this point where 'saudade' begins, the condition of a people who may have been enslaved many times, may have even been a slave caste.

As a child, I heard people on their doorsteps and the corners talking about stolen royalty, that we were all descendants of kings and queens.

This never made sense to me. I never bought it.

But I could buy (and indeed have bought) the idea, the feeling, that my deep ancestors – we L3*s – may have been enslaved all of our lives, that the Atlantic Slave Trade, as insidious and unique as it was, could have been a continuation for us.

Most of the literature on Cabo Verde says something like this: 'Except for a few vague and questionable accounts of unknown islands by passing Phoenician or Arab sailors, the Cape Verde Islands were as yet undiscovered and uninhabited when the Portuguese arrived in the 1460s.'

Pliny the Elder in *Historia Naturalis* gave Cape Verde the name 'Gorgades', home of the Gorgons.

But my ancestors could not slay the Gorgons that engulfed us.

Daddy would say to me: 'There is always another story. They tell you to believe one thing. But there's always the other side. You always have to know the other side. Every story has one. There's always the other side. Buck Bonnet, you always have to know the other side.'

'Buck Bonnet' always looks for that other side.

THREE

In this age in which all secrets can be known, one of the last bastions of secrets is the family.

My brother-in-law Harry, my sister Lelia's husband, in the search for her ancestors, of course also researched mine.

It is always a dangerous and poignant thing for a black person to look back and to see.

I think sometimes: Is it possible to imagine these people, to dream about them?

It was Harry who found these people, to my surprise, people I cannot imagine, strangers as far away as those eighty thousand years ago:

> Green McKissick; North Carolina, 1803, and Patsy McKissick, 1805, who wound up in Tennessee. On both sides of the family, there were marriages in the 1820s: a person born in Virginia; a housekeeper in Tennessee in the 1870s. In 1890 a man named Ben Greer Sr married Lelia Putnam and they had children.

My sister Lelia was named after her.

I think I was between three and four when, with my sister, my baby brother Ben, and Mamma and Daddy, I travelled down South to see her.

I was to learn later that the train from Chicago became officially racially segregated (as opposed to 'de facto' segregated) when it entered the South.

Black people had to, by law, sit in the often dirty, cheap seats no matter who they were and what they were prepared to pay. The only black people allowed in the dining car were those who worked there.

I can still remember the smell of cold fried chicken in the shoebox on Mamma's lap. Our seat was cramped and the smell of Mamma's chicken made me very hungry. She struggled to feed us in the crowded car.

And what would she have done if Benny needed his nappy changed, or any of the number of the things that a mother has to do while travelling with three young children?

My next memory of that trip down South is of a dusty yard with chickens running all around and the quiet composed demeanour of Grandmother Lelia.

I can recall her bedroom full of afternoon shade. She was tall and slender and moved gracefully. She showed me the things on her bedroom dresser, delicate, fragile things, miniature glass objects, her own glass menagerie.

From my brother-in-law Harry:

> Census Report from 1870 of Maury County, TN shows your most distant ancestors Green and Patsy McKissack born in 1800 in North Carolina and 1805 in Virginia, respectively. They show up with their son Augustus and his wife, Caledonia, farming land and keeping house in Columbia, Tennessee just southwest of Nashville.
>
> By 1880 they are still there, but Augustus and Caledonia

have added 3 children – Willie (female), Annison (male) and Gustin (male).

Another 1880 Census of Madison County, TN which is just northwest of Nashville shows the Boone (or Boon) family. Samuel Boon (52) is head of household with his wife, Selah (40) and his mother Rachel (70) along with 9 Boon children, 5 boys and 4 girls. Sam Boon is 9 yrs old. He will go on to marry Willie McKissack on Feb. 15, 1894 and give birth to Nora Boone, your maternal grandmother on July 4, 1908. She is one of 6 girls and 3 boys as well as what appears to be an adopted brother and sister. Willie McKissack-Boon(e) raised them as a widow, although it is not clear exactly when Sam passed away.

The 1900 Census in Maury County, TN, shows Boones and McKissicks/McKissacks living next door to each other.

In 1920 the census shows Willie McKissack (48) as a widow with 6 girls, 2 boys and 2 wards. Your grandmother, Nora, was 11 years old.

The Ancestors

Samuel Boone (1870–?); William McKissick (1871–1938); Ben Greer Sr (1890–?); Johnnie Boone (1899–?); Mazey Boone (1899–?); Eliott Boone (1902–?); Ida Boone (1905–?); Syntha Crutcher (1910–?); Nora Boone (1908–1956); Lelia Putnam (1900–?);

Obituary

Mrs Donie Huddleston was born in Springhill, Tennessee to the union of Samuel S. and Willie Boone on January 29, 1895. She departed this life on Sunday, January 23,

1994 at 12:15 p.m. Donie was the sixth child born to this union. At a very young age, Donie joined tabernacle Baptist Church in Nashville, Tenn. In 1945, she moved to Chicago. Later she moved to Idlewild, Michigan, where she joined New Hope Baptist Church where she was a faithful member until stricken with ill health.

FOUR

That litany of names, carved in the wood of the world, the memory of ordinary folks. Nothing fancy. Had one of them known someone who had heard the Emancipation Proclamation read on the day it was issued, 1 January 1863?

The day the Diaspora had begun. The day the Great Migration had commenced:

> Some man who seemed to be a stranger (a United States officer, I presume) made a little speech and then read a rather long paper – the Emancipation Proclamation, I think. After the reading we were told that we were all free, and could go when and where we pleased. My mother, who was standing by my side, leaned over and kissed her children, while tears of joy ran down her cheeks.
>
> – from *Up From Slavery,* the original 'pull yourself up by your bootstraps' manual published in 1901, a book that divided the black community written by a man who divided the black community.

I saw a photo in one of the books that Dad puchased by mail order to enhance his limited formal education and fuel his dinner-table orations.

The picture was simply captioned: 'Some of the colored men of the 369th (15th N.Y.) who won the Croix de Guerre for gallantry in action.'

They were open-faced young men, recently out of boyhood, leaning into the camera, confident, free. Did they come back?

Or did they stay in Paris to become one of the founts of that legend of the 'African American in Paris', something still pursued almost a century later.

James Baldwin pursued it and left for Paris the month I was born, November 1948.

Dad, Ben Greer Jr, was born on Saturday, 7 June 1924, outside of Greenwood, Mississippi, the youngest son.

Mamma, Willie Mae Randolph, was born on Friday, the 22 July 1927, in Nashville, Tennessee. The oldest child and eldest daughter. Like me.

The difference between the bathtub-gin era, champagne bubbles and hot jazz of the year of Dad's birth –1924 – can be read in Langston Hughes' first collection of poetry *The Weary Blues* (1926). This book was championed by Carl Van Vechten, one of the white people who found a haven in Harlem, and one of those who created the 'Harlem Renaissance' brand which was for black people a kind of escape valve from the broken, war-weary West.

The poem 'Weary Blues' was a revolution.

The piano-player subject of the poem is called 'Negro', a word not often used in art at the time.

There was language, hard to read, but easy to hear. And that's what mattered to Langston the most: 'Mellow croon'; 'Ain't got nobody but ma self. I's gwine quit my frownin'… I ain't happy no mo'.'

'Improper' language.

The black-and-white keys of the piano are the symbols of the forbidden alliance of black-and-white, a battle against the grand-mal segregation that Dad was growing up under: 'separate but equal', which actually meant the exclusion of black people from the privilege of the citizenship they were entitled to at birth.

The Weary Blues laid out all of Langston's great themes of patriotism not only to America, but to black America: direct, uncomplicated, humorous in the face of adversity.

While Dad was growing up a black boy in the most dangerous state in the Union to be both black and male, Bessie Smith and Ma Rainey were presenting a diamond-encrusted blues, high-living and truth-telling, rolling through the South in its own train under its own steam. And black people were on the move. Their blues was a woman's blues, not the doom-laden Depression-era masterpieces that were popular in the 1930s, mostly composed and sung by men. In 1926, when Dad was a two-year-old in the Delta, a treacherous and beautiful place, the blues was a woman…

It was the Great Migration. The War had loosened the soil of their being, the soldiers came home with postcards of the Eiffel Tower, pictures of themselves smiling and free beside the Seine.

But by the time Mamma was born – 1927 – the glory of heading North to freedom was dying.

'Up North' became a statement that said things were no different on the South Side of Chicago and in Harlem then they were in Mississippi. It was just bigger and dirtier, more crowded and colder.

Langston published *Fine Clothes to the Jew*, a title that got him in more trouble than he bargained for.

The title practically killed the book, a book in which Langston laid out the reality of the North that Mamma and her family would soon move to: a place of disappointment and death.

'Song for a Dark Girl' (1927) begins with the words 'Way down South in Dixie'. In this masterpiece of compassion and compression, Langston documents the pain of a black escapee from the concentration camp that was the rural South after the Great War.

1924 – black people as light of the new post-war world.

1927 – then darkness descends in the cold world of the North Star.

Nobody thanked Langston for this poem, for this collection. The title was offensive, insensitive, maybe even racist. And there was too much information for the black elite and those in the clergy who wanted to keep it all clean and correct.

And the poem tells the pain of a dark-skinned girl, one of Langston's beauties.

But Mamma wasn't a 'dark girl'.

She was light-skinned and had ash-blonde hair. I remember her baby picture – wide-eyed, her head covered in a flapper's bonnet, a baby version of the Roaring Twenties.

There is another family photo – a jaunty one – a bit like a black Nora Charles flanked by two Nick Charleses, a black version of Dashiell Hammett's elegant sleuths from the '30s.

My mother's father – my grandfather – William Randolph, and his brother and sister, James and Lillian. They are dressed in slouched hats and trench coats, my ultra chic Aunt Lillian in a fur jacket, all of them haughty and magnificent, defying the Depression, defying being black in those times.

Aunt Lillian was always extremely elegant and so was my Uncle James, Mamma's favourite uncle. I thought that Aunt Lillian looked down on us a bit. But Uncle James was a boulevardier, and very friendly.

He and Mamma were very close up until the day he died in his Washington apartment decades later.

Mamma told me that Dad met Uncle James for the first time when, home unexpectedly from work to the shared house I was brought home to from the hospital, he came into their little bedroom to find Uncle James, in from D.C., asleep in their bed, Mom and me asleep next to him.

Grandpa William, I was told, illustrated shoes for newspaper ads. He died in his mid-thirties, maybe from diabetes. Maybe from alcoholism. Or maybe from being a black man with dreams bigger than the life he was allowed to lead.

There is another old photo, lost in one of the floods in our second home: Mom is standing with all of her brothers and sisters. She looks about eight or ten years old. She's scowling in the sun and the light is shining through her fine, fair hair.

Her little brother Marvin, who later died a toddler, is on her hip. She was already a woman taking care of children. A mother.

And that little girl's face is essentially the face she would have all of her life.

Behind her in the photo is what looks like an alley. It is the West Side of Chicago, the tenements, the black community, the 'ghetto'.

The freedom destination.

FIVE

Old people used to say that there were two groups of folks who didn't lose out in the Depression: poor black people and the Kennedys.

The Kennedys because old Joe the patriarch pulled out before the Crash. And black folks because we had nothing to lose.

Dad's little sister. Bernice, born in April, 1928. Our beloved Aunt Bernice.

A tiger, she suffered and suffers no fools. She helped Mamma take care of me when I was a baby and I would sometimes be mistaken for her child because I resembled the Greer side when I was little.

Mamma's youngest sister, Ernestine – who also took care of me before she had a family of her own – was born in 1932 on 9 November, born on the day that Franklin Delano Roosevelt was elected to his first term. Which meant that she came into the world to the sound of Roosevelt's 'Happy Days are Here Again'. Aunt Bernice and Aunt Ernestine. My other mommies. Still.

There was one more child, but he died. Grandma Nora needed to feed and care for her kids somehow. This left Mamma, at about fifteen, having to take a job to help, and soon she found a flat of her own and lived on Chinese food – it was plentiful and cheap – as she worked in a factory, eventually making parachutes for the war effort.

After work she would go to the movies with her girlfriends, putting herself in the place of Bette Davis and Joan Crawford and Olivia de Havilland – all honorary black women. Especially Bette.

I imagined her at night dancing at the Club DeLisa, the interracial nightspot on the South Side of Chicago. There was a floor for black customers and one for white customers and one where they all mingled together.

They would have liked her. She was a very pretty girl. And she loved to dance.

She still does.

On the day of Aunt Ernestine's birth, Dad was eight years old, growing up, without doubt, understanding the meaning of the poem that Langston Hughes wrote in protest against the treatment of the wrongly accused Southern black boys called 'The Scotsboro Boys'.

There is a *Life* magazine photo of a little black girl on a street in Greenwood, Mississippi, near the town where Dad was born.

The little girl is barefoot, standing in the dirt street, dressed in a kind of short romper suit.

Her hands are playfully folded on her head the way kids do when they are answering a question from an adult. Her belly thrust forward like a child's, too firmly rooting her on the ground.

She is standing like a child stands, as if the ground belongs to her. As if she knows the earth intimately.

But her head is bowed as she stands in a kind of deference in front of an old white man, dressed in overalls and wearing a white hat, bending over to talk to her.

Her upraised hands resting on her head in relation to him now look like a kind of submission, a kind of proof that she knows even at this young age to assume a posture of surrender.

Behind her, a little way off, is another white man, dressed in overalls and a cap, his hands on his hips, watching her as if he had just released her from somewhere and was waiting to claim her and take her back.

This picture was taken by the great documentary photographer Margaret Bourke-White, who took most of the classic Dust Bowl photos and this one, too.

She knows this child, not much younger than my own father, is at the mercy of these two men. Her entire family is.

The title of the photo: 'Plantation Child'.

Dad had come North by the middle of the 1940s, first to Waterloo, Iowa, to family. Legend had it that he talked too much for a black boy and had to leave.

He enlisted in the Army. A racially segregated Army.

He arrived in England as part of the D-Day invasion that happened the day before his twentieth birthday.

He never forgot the United Kingdom.

He saw black men.

He wasn't relegated to unpacking crates and making amphibious landing craft – the work of most of the black men in the US Army.

Yes, he romanticised England. Who could blame him? White people did not run away from him. They said 'hello' to him. He was a human being to them.

Michael Powell honoured these black GIs in his classic film *A Matter of Life and Death*, made in 1946. They are in the audience, part of Powell's unfolding tale. One of them is on the Heavenly Jury.

Sometimes I look for Dad in that film. And in the newsreels. Maybe he's there. Maybe.

Daddy had grown up in the Mississippi of the '20s and '30s and had seen the worst that humans could be.

He had survived the last German offensive called by the Allies, the Battle of the Bulge; he had been a soldier in the Ardennes in a bitterly cold winter.

He and the other black GIs were formally given guns a little before then. Previously, they were not routinely armed, used mainly as support. (Patton had said that he didn't care if the men were green as long as they could fight.)

In other words, a black man with a gun was a bigger threat than a German soldier.

He told me, from time to time, about a concentration camp he had seen, a vague and imprecise tale that made me wonder if he actually had. But hearing about them, listening to witnesses had to be traumatic in itself, a feeling he kept, even though as a boy he had been taken to a lynching in the Mississippi woods.

He kept his soldier's French all of his life, most of it full of phrases to get a lady into bed, but edited, of course.

Dad was at war but he was also away, abroad. People fascinated him, unlike Mamma, who liked the tried and familiar and staying close to home.

He would have stayed in Europe, in England, if he could.

He'd seen Something Else.

Soon he was back in the US.

Back to Chicago.

Back to the status quo for young black men.

But unlike post-First World War: the script had flipped.

Southern boys like him back in the 1920s and '30s would have had heard the tales of the soldiers who had returned home from the Great War, full of Paris with the photos to prove it, too, only to find themselves – if they were lucky – run out of town.

If unlucky, their destiny was much worse.

Lynchings were also big news, a deterrent.

But the sons of these men had fought on Iwo Jima; been burned alive in their hundreds in a naval disaster in San Francisco; treated like dirt while German POWs were treated with deference; watched black servicewomen sexually harassed by white servicemen; sat enraptured by the translucent Lena Horne, singing alone against a pillar in those MGM musicals so that she could be cut out when the picture played in the South.

But they saw that she was just for them alone.

Black GIs like Dad and black servicewomen, too, who had entered the military as 'coloured', 'Negroes' and worse – and came out Americans.

And they wanted the lot.

Most of the new homes being built were not allocated to them. So they fought at housing sites, wearing their uniforms and medals – the ones lucky enough to be given them. Many were never medalled even though they had earned them.

One vet told me – as part of a radio documentary I was making for the BBC: 'I saved this captain from a burning Jeep, but they didn't give me a medal. They told me that "Negroes don't get medals".'

Then he burst into tears, still hurt and angry and humiliated sixty years later.

In some cases, German prisoners-of-war were given more privileges than the black soldiers who guarded them.

Black vets revolted.

They were new.

They took jazz, which had become cosy and swinging and homogenised, and blew it apart.

Theirs was the generation who understood best the most influential three minutes or so of music of the twentieth century: the Charlie Parker Quintet's epoch-making rendition of the Gershwin song 'Embraceable You', featuring a very young Miles Davis on trumpet.

These three minutes of music had been released from another plane and that plane was 'hip', was bebop.

Bebop aimed for the speed of light, to be faster than the white man, faster than the black man who stood back and accepted it all.

These new Black people had their movie, too: *Home of the Brave,* whose protagonist had originally been Jewish on the stage but became a black man portrayed by the great James Edwards, a man who prefigured Sidney Poitier and Denzel Washington. An actor who carried in himself what Dad and others like him were.

Dad loved that film because it told everything about the discrimination, the racism, the cruelty of the service.

It was the first film since *The Emperor Jones,* a decade before, to use the word 'nigger'. The real deal.

Dad found a job in a factory and was introduced to Mamma by Aunt Bernice, whose friend she was.

She called herself 'a little piece of leather that's well put together'.

They went out dancing. She was a very pretty girl, just twenty, free and happy. She was fascinated by the Royal Family. She and her girlfriends – those black girls free and working in factories, earning their own money – watched the newsreel of the wedding of Princess Elizabeth and Prince Philip.

And soon, Mamma and the future Queen became pregnant at the same time.

Except the Princess was married.

And Mamma was not.

SIX

They were married in May, Mamma, Joan Crawford-glamorous in a white-shouldered coat, her hair piled on her head.

Dad looks radiant, as if he has won the biggest prize of all. His face is beautiful and he is impeccably dressed in a dark suit and tie.

They look full of promise, full of the future.

Mom is two months short of her twenty-first birthday. Dad will turn twenty-four the next month.

Kids.

There was some sort of contest somewhere for the mother who gave birth when the then Princess Elizabeth, Duchess of Edinburgh, did.

It was a year's supply of free nappies.

My parents needed those nappies.

Mamma couldn't work while pregnant with me and money was tight.

Unfortunately, I was born thirty-six hours after Prince Charles, a little after 12:16 p.m. GMT (6:17 a.m. CST) in Chicago.

I was given some kind of baptism by nuns in the delivery room, and my exact time noted, which Mamma said meant something but she never told me what.

I was named 'Bonnie', a fashionable name at the time, because apparently the infant Prince Charles was called 'Bonnie Prince Charlie.'

My name has always given me a great affinity for Scotland.

Decades later, it was Scotland that first allowed me an artistic life in the UK. It was Scotland that welcomed my work first.

Mamma got her revenge on me for being late: on every one of Prince Charles's birthdays, I had to celebrate it, or at least remember it.

He's always been in my life, in a strange way. When I finally met him and told him that I was named after him, his eyes grew as large as saucers and Camilla howled with laughter.

Dad called his sister 'Bonnie' and 'Bon' and he called me 'Buck Bonnet'. I think he named me.

He loved me, and he loved his wife.

When Dad was dying at the end of the nineties and the heat had to be kept up full blast and Mamma walked around wearing a T-shirt as she nursed him after he shrunk to almost nothing, I could feel his passion for her and hers for him. Even then they needled one another.

Daddy had given up cigarettes long ago, yet he was dying of cancer, and Mamma, a two-pack-a-day chain-smoker, was going strong.

He said to her one day: 'You know, you shouldn't be smoking around me.' Mamma looked at him and said: 'Afraid I'll give you cancer?'

The look they exchanged, something with a complicity and understanding that totally locked me and everyone else out, was something I will never forget.

I must have sensed this bond, too, as I slept between them in the first few months of my life.

Just as I knew their poverty, too, very early on.

My first home was living in one room in a shared house.

There was a photo of me – a few months old, in front of that brownstone. Mamma, like a South Side Madonna, had me perched on one hip, her belly already round with my sister.

At night I lay between them in their bed in their tiny room.

Mamma had to tiptoe into the kitchen in the dead of night to heat up my bottle when I woke up.

Mamma said that the landlady was harsh and strict.

This was the South Side – the 'ghetto' – not a place of romance but, for many, a place of poverty and the only place they could live.

They were not allowed to live elsewhere.

White landlords would not rent to them, not even to a hardworking, charming young black GI with 'mother wit', who had fought for his country in the worst war humankind had ever known and who had a young wife and new baby and had a job sweeping up at a factory.

That room gave me my next word after 'Mamma' and 'Daddy' – 'rat hole'.

Mamma's brother, Uncle Don, brought back a miniature Japanese kimono while on leave from Japan.

He was a bebop man, a hipster, and called everybody 'Man'. There was another picture: me in that little kimono, looking like Dad and probably being addressed as 'Man' by my uncle.

I was told that Grandma Nora took one look at my chubby legs and announced that I would be short, no doubt about it.

She was a prophet.

Mamma had a painted porcelain lamp on the dresser, a kind of belle époque thing that belonged to her mother.

She carried it with her to the places we moved to.
To me she is that lamp, delicate, sturdy, weathered.

SEVEN

In Euclidean geometry, two parallel lines do not intersect. But there are other mathematical systems, other realities in which these parallels do connect.

In the limit to Infinity.

Speak memory.

The biggest influences in my life were and still are my parents. Two people who lived parallel to one another. And yet, at the same time, found their conjunction. Every day.

Even now they still fascinate me, perplex me. I will never know them and yet I know everything that is important about them. I knew where they came from. Not their hometowns nor their people but who they could have been if they'd been allowed.

I felt the price they paid for not being there.

I learned from them the profound cost of discrimination: the diminution of human potential and the cheating of the human species – of history and progress itself. They both taught me by their being to mourn this. To fight this.

And, also, when I think of them in my life, their influence, their guardianship, even now, I see Velázquez: *Las Meninas.*

The man at the top of the painting. Is he coming inside? Or is he leaving? Is he an aspect of me?

The people in the background, in the shadows ... one is a nun, her head tilted like a Renaissance Madonna, still, serene, looking at the Christ Child – that baby she didn't ask for but here he was – in her arms.

The woman of restricted growth, dressed beautifully, but her face a map of the world she has seen and is seeing; looking beyond the canvas both with a 'What you lookin' at?' gaze and also as if she is surprised that she is here. Surprised that anyone would care about her enough to paint her. Let alone a Master.

There is a little girl beside her, diligent, focused. A Head Girl in embryo.

In the midst of the small group from which the woman of restricted growth stands aside are two girls, solicitous, helpful, relegating their lives and being – the blonde child in the middle, the Princess, sure of her beauty and her power in the world. She knows that she is the fulcrum of this small group, its epicentre – the epicentre of desire.

In the shadow stands Velázquez himself, the Painter.

His failures, his accomplishments, are all visible in the eyes of the world and we are here with him in real time. This is his studio, his work place. He stands before a huge canvas, about to work, or has he paused like all people do before a big work, asking themselves: Is it possible? Can I do it?

In the shadows on the walls of the studio are other paintings, perhaps studies or cartoons of work yet to be made.

In the mirror of his studio ... outside of the canvas – beyond us, the viewers, but controlling everything – are the King and the Queen.

The King and the Queen in the mirror.

They taught me that our innate aggression is the will to

live. It is the irrationality of our species, too, as well as our need to conform, our inborn conservatism, our herd instinct. And also our yearning for transcendence. Our constant looking-up at the stars from what Oscar Wilde called 'the gutter', and the majesty and beauty and poignancy and bravery of that.

They taught me that we – the only species as far as we know – who exist with the knowledge of our own end and yet continue ... do continue because they did. They did that every day of their lives and they did that not in a 'religious' way ... but from an acceptance of life.

When I was a little girl and had installed them in my own private pantheon complete with a padlock, I could sense the high refinement that Mamma and Daddy had within them which must have drawn them to one another. I saw it, too, in the faux Fragonard wallpaper they bought for the basement of the first house we lived in that I can recall.

I could sense their natural delicacy and refinement, a kind of 'Nick and Nora Charles' in their own minds. I was and still am convinced that I interrupted their movie by getting conceived and born.

I tried to apologise by being a good kid but couldn't get a word in edgeways because of their intense dialogue with each other. 'The smallest and the oldest,' Dad used to call me.

They were beautiful dressers; Mom made her own clothes from patterns that she studied assiduously. Nothing overly shiny, nothing cheap or false. 'Cool' is not even close to what they were together. I was a klutz, a spectator. And in awe.

But they had no way in what I call their 'day life' to exercise this beauty and grace on a regular basis.

Mamma was what used to be called a 'housewife' – 5 a.m. to 2 a.m. the next morning. On the job.

Daddy, the fount of my prose.

He was very handsome, very bright and very powerful.

I really didn't begin to know him until a few years before he died. He came to see us in London – he made the trip alone; Mamma is afraid of flying (because she can't control the aircraft) – to commemorate the fiftieth anniversary of D-Day, in which he had a part.

We were walking back to our house – my husband David's house. Daddy, of course, was staying with us.

The night before, David had taken him and two male neighbours out to the local pub.

Daddy told me – in quiet awe – that no one turned to stare at him as he walked in with three young white guys, the way that the black shoppers at his local supermarket back on the South Side of Chicago stared as David followed him with a trolley around the aisles a few years earlier.

He said to me: 'Now when they ask me why you moved over here, I can tell 'em.'

That meant more to me than I could say to him, than I knew how to say. We were, to me at that moment, like two English people, the sort who never express emotion to one another and yet all of the emotion that they have for each other exists in the handling of a teacup, the inflection of the voice, the tilt of the head, the glance of an eye.

I moved a bit closer to him as we walked down Notting Hill Gate back to the house. I wanted to hold his hand because I never had, at least since I was a child.

I had fought this man, in so many ways – not even conscious to me – from as young as I can remember. And here he was, acknowledging my choice of life. I had done the right thing. He had spoken.

Because he was the King, the Man. To me, he made sure that everyone knew that he controlled everything and we were to do what he said. No questions asked. He almost slapped me once when I was about ten and came home crying because some teenage girl gang members had mugged me for Mamma's cigarette money. He expected me to stand up to them. That wasn't possible, they were much bigger than me. But he had stood up to white men at his factory, white men who had wanted to beat his brains out with a baseball bat because he was a union organiser. No child of his was running away from a fight, especially a fight administered by girls obviously so stupid that the only outlet they had was to be in a gang and dress alike and look alike.

He threatened us all with his belt and sometimes used it, too.

I can remember that something in me fought him back. I fought him back. He made me sniff out what I felt was tyranny, especially in males.

Nuts, I know. But that's what Daddy's 'power' created in me.

And at the same time, because he was so beautiful, I yearned to be 'taken away' by some overpowering dude I didn't actually know but somehow I would discover in the prison he made for me.

All I had to do was be quiet, be an object. Somewhere inside me I still don't understand power, or how it can be good.

But I love sheer power when I see it because it is so simple. So clean in a strange way.

Naturally, this attitude has led me into some interesting episodes and narrow escapes involving men in my adult life. Sometimes I didn't escape.

The mystery of my father – his aloofness – was the very embodiment of Professor Robert Farris Thompson of Yale's concept of African American 'cool', that concept of what used to be called 'grace under pressure'.

'Cool.'

The way that some guys in my neighbourhood would cross the street. Even when a speeding car was right up on them, they never broke stride, never corrected what was called the 'pimp' – a kind of half stroll, half dance with one hand in your pocket and one shoulder jutted forwards, and never, ever hurried no matter what the circumstances.

I discovered Farris Thompson's *Flash of the Spirit* – a masterwork that analyses black American art and culture – when I lived in New York in the 1980s.

The guys I knew used to laugh when I raved about Farris Thompson because to them he was 'Jungle Jim', the white guy who used to front a show about the African jungle on TV when we were all children.

I would really get angry because I didn't see what the colour of Farris Thompson's skin had to do with anything. But when things like that happened, Dad would always say to me: 'The information is what matters, not who gives it to you.' And, when folks made disparaging remarks: 'Consider the source.'

And I always do.

Dad gave me the contradiction of the need and pleasure of human relationships combined with a profound necessity for solitude, something he never really had. Except at the end when he died alone in his bed sometime in the night, his face turned towards the window.

He was vastly interested in human beings and wanted to be a presence in the lives of people he encountered on a regular basis, but his sharp intellect saw their shortcomings and would criticise too much.

He often spoke before his great compassion came through – another trait I inherited from him.

And no matter what he said, I knew that when he spoke that way it was a cry to be left both included and alone… alone … to read, to hunt, to tinker, to think and ponder.

He had a beautiful smile which he used often, but not to me. He was too busy trying to keep me alive, trying to prevent me from suffering the kind of racism and the lack of opportunity that he had experienced.

He was a man from the Old School, our father, a patriarch in every sense of that word.

Men did certain things and women did certain things.

Girls cooked and cleaned and boys took out the garbage.

But he never said to us girls that we could not pursue the life of the mind, his daughters as well as his sons. No man was better than us. Not in education anyway.

Even the idea that women were not capable was absurd because – as a rationalist – he saw the human brain as largely composed of equal capabilities and possibilities.

The notion that a woman was incapable of the highest intellectual achievement was a non-starter and he wouldn't hear it even discussed. Even black women could do it. If somebody would just give us a chance. Being black in a white world was his constant realisation.

He knew and I knew the quality of his intellect, its potential. But he had no opportunity to express it, to test it. He studied various trades, read the manuals, passed the tests. But he wanted to talk about *Paradise Lost*, the Rosetta Stone.

I take after him – somewhere I didn't think I had the chance to be fully myself.

Who would allow me to pursue philosophy or to paint or to study mathematics?

No one allowed my father.

Better to work, stay alive, stay out of the way of those

who could crush you, erase you.

He never said this but it was in his voice, in his eyes when he would tell me later on to 'be careful, Bon.' He'd grown up in the Deep South during the Depression. He'd seen and heard of too many people taken away in the night for 'expressing' themselves.

Education was the way out, the way to beat them. And education wasn't just about getting a job, although that was important. No welfare folks for him. He believed purely and simply in learning for its own sake.

'They can take everything from you but what you know.'

But the other side of the scholar was a free-living bon vivant; a man-about-town lived inside of him. He needed to be on his own, to withdraw from time to time. His inability to withdraw, to do that, was not only because he was too busy providing for a wife and seven kids but because he had no model of a black man who had lived the life of the mind and survived.

He needed to be away from us and away from Mamma to see the world that fascinated him.

He'd kept his GI, World War Two, D-Day French, much of which I don't think he could actually repeat in polite company. And when he finally did travel for the fiftieth anniversary, he strode off the plane as sprightly as a teenager.

He was an autodidact supreme, a man who read way above his schooling.

He was devoted to the *Encyclopaedia Britannica*, which he bought monthly from a door-to-door salesman. He bought those books for us and for himself. They made me come to see European history as it unfolded in its pages – Europe itself – as a breath of fresh air, a haven.

The illustrations of the statues in the British Museum were amongst his favourites. He could never have dreamt that I would become Deputy Chair of that museum some day.

But maybe he did. Maybe he saw it in those pages as we talked about Pliny and Euripides and Socrates. Maybe he knew.

Because of those books, and our talks – fleeting but intense – I came to understand that some things are better than others.

Daddy taught me that Tolstoy is better than Tolkien; Michelangelo better than a Hallmark card illustration. This stance has narrowed my range, kept me out of the loop, made me deeply uncool. But I know what is a classic. And that there's no such thing as an 'instant' one.

He read the same articles over and over and showed me how even a piece of writing ripens with age – like the bourbon he liked to drink clandestinely.

When – after he came to visit us in London and David introduced him to single malt Scotch whisky – he finally knew what 'the good thing' was, he took a bottle back to the South Side, to the neighbour next door, who simply stared at it in awe. David explained to him that he was never to mix it with water and Dad understood and never did.

The rest – what he'd had before – was nothing to him by then. It was gone.

For him it wasn't about 'the best' but the true. Great art – great writing, great film – all of these things are very rare, he would tell me. And he said, too: 'You don't have to take substitutes until the good stuff comes along. Just keep with the good stuff. It'll never get tired.'

He may have narrowed my cultural palate. He may have made it impossible for me to enjoy the popular. I run away from it more than I run to it. He wasn't being a snob. 'Life's too short. Go to the top,' he'd say. For me, he was right. The great work never gets tired.

Daddy did not like embellishments. He was very spare and elegant. He got the best that he could afford. Always.

He knew what a thing was worth and what a person was worth, too.

'Consider the source' he'd always say, which gave me the ability to objectively listen to anyone – no matter how prominent or famous they are. I don't kow-tow to fame or erudition because Dad taught me what the bottom line is: the quality of the mind. The mind for him was an instrument free of banality, fear of others; always searching and discarding, honing, pruning, testing.

There was no 'going for the One' with him, no ultimate answer. He implied to me – though he believed in God himself – that the bravest life is the life lived without a belief in a Supreme Being.

To live life for its own sake, not out of fear, or seeking a reward, or even for love secular or divine.

Just for life.

He was self-confident in spite of all he had to go through. And he gave that to me, too.

It's not arrogance. It's solitude. In other words, he taught me to spare my awe.

He taught me to not be afraid of being disliked.

Another one of his lessons that I didn't learn very well.

Mamma, the fount of my fiction.

One of my earliest memories is of Mamma's lamp. The inside of the lily was enamelled a greenish yellow.

When it was lit the colours cast a soft light on anything it touched.

I can only imagine that for Mamma it lessened the

cruelty to her senses that her surroundings must have rendered. The communal kitchen and bathroom – the only thing available to a young, poor, black couple with a new baby in the late 1940s in Chicago, relegated to the 'ghetto', hemmed in by de facto segregation, living the cruel life of 'up North', which didn't even have the kindness of good weather. Just snow and cold and poor wages and the fear of white people who lived, as far as black people were concerned, with impunity.

The shared house and toilet, the communal front room, the communal smells, the communal sounds. The rat holes.

I knew very early on that I would never be as beautiful as Mamma was and still is. I would never have her natural elegance, her natural ability to command a room. She knew that she was cute. 'Light-skinned', she would have been a prize for a black man, and unfortunately 'light skin' is still prized now. It was crazy then and it's crazy now. I never could figure out how black people could complain about the white man when we do the same thing amongst ourselves – division by complexion, the nuttiest sort of demarcation there is.

At about the age of seven I calculated that the time between May and November was not enough for a full-term baby.

I knew this because Mamma had gotten pregnant a number of times after me so I was a kind of expert on gestation.

I asked if I was premature (I knew about this, too, somehow). Mamma, who was always busy, replied that I wasn't, that I was normal and healthy.

Then... Since I was a 'why is the sky blue?' kid from the moment I could talk, she realised that she had made a mistake. But she knew how to handle me.

She wove an elaborate tale about my birth and the birthday cake, which I can't now recall but I knew didn't add up. But since I always wanted to support her completely, even in her attempts to control reality, I allowed it to pass.

Mamma, the fount of my fiction.

I began to weave little stories myself, that became fiction. Inspired by her. As soon as we brought the groceries home – an expedition that I loathed because it was so monotonous and so *sad*, the mommies just looked so bored and sad to me – I hurried to put everything away so that I could draw on the brown paper bags and write stories about the Campbell's Soup kids that I saw on the cans.

I had my little corner at the zinc kitchen and I wrote away. I never 'became' a writer; I was never not a writer. My first play – at about ten – was about the Virgin Mary on the brink of giving birth to the Christ Child. I didn't create some astonished Holy Virgin, staring in disbelief at the wonder of it all. I created a pregnant woman who was trying to do her best in circumstances over which she had no control, and who was pretty frazzled into the bargain. The nuns at school asked me how I knew all this – how I knew to paint that kind of picture of the Blessed Virgin.

It was Mamma, I explained; Mamma was always pregnant and with babies.

Cooking was a trap, a prison (as was typing), as was being a conventional wife and mother – although I longed for these roles.

But Mamma warned me, and she knew. Above all, I wanted to please her. Then maybe she might have some time just for me. Just a little.

Mamma saw usefulness as the mark of a good life and that's true. She was always useful. She didn't like sad sacks or the depressed. She was quite cruel about that – at least in front of me. Her own mother had had a rough time from her husband – Mamma's dad, William, a man so good looking that they called him 'the Black Clark Gable'.

That was Mamma's background yet she worked tirelessly for us and for her brothers and sisters, too, as long as they lived, and for those selected few.

Mamma hid her true inner life, the things that she really believed in, from me, just as she hid her purchases of beautiful shoes and dresses from Daddy, the stuff she managed to scrimp and save for.

Her extremely well-deserved extras, as far as I'm concerned.

She never apologised for the Closet, an Aladdin's cave of gorgeous shoes – her passion – and dresses and coats and hats, all locked away. All hers.

She sewed dutifully on her Singer, but the real stuff was in that Closet. I capitalise that 'C' because it was a place of regeneration, where legends were.

Mamma emerged with the fruits of that treasure trove like a Queen because that's what she is.

That's where she had her dreams. She'd never actually encourage her girls to sew as a way of strutting our stuff.

She didn't have any limits – at least on the surface – and so I learned to live with no barriers when it came to other people and what they needed. I came to feel that I didn't exist unless someone needed me to help or be there or sacrifice myself on their behalf, because Mamma was always there. There when I came home from school every day. Yet, from a very early age, I sensed that she was paying a price and one day the whole thing would explode.

When I set out on my travels at about the age of nineteen, she was worried and a little infuriated because she couldn't turn me into the 'proper girl' that she had raised me to be. But she said to me: 'You can always come back home.'

I never knew what a talisman that was until Alzheimer's set in and she began to stop sending me birthday cards and little notes and we didn't talk on the phone once a month. When she could no longer answer when I gave her a weather report of light snow and cold, and she would reply that this was the weather on the day I was born.

It pleased me when she said out of the blue when I came home one day, years after I had moved away, that she was surprised because it looked like I might survive out there: 'You're doing what I wanted to do. Keep doing it for me.'

Dad worked hard all of his life but the world never accepted his capacity. The world never knew who he was. Like I never knew. I think he suffered for it.

But Mamma knows what the world is, and she tells it like it is, and this is what has kept me alive in the years since I haven't lived under her roof.

Which has been two-thirds of my life.

My parents gave me a great gift.

In Italo Calvino's series of lectures 'Six Memos for the Next Millennium' (The Charles Eliot Norton Lectures 1985–86), which are actually five lectures (he died before he could write the last), one of the essentials for a writer is considered to be 'visibility'.

He quotes Dante's *Purgatorio*: 'Then it rained down into the high fantasy…'

Calvino writes that Dante comes to see that it is better to place the visions that he had directly inside his mind, rather than make them go through his senses, where they would be ordered according to the conventions of society.

Where they could become banal.

Calvino quotes Dante again: 'O imagination who have the power to impose yourself on our faculties and our wills, stealing us away from the outer world and carrying us off into an inner one so that even if a thousand trumpets were to sound … we would not hear them.'

We black people who survived the Long Passage, the brutality and cruelty, the lack of free movement, the stripping away of our names and religion, our culture; the banality of being under the yoke of another, we survived, too, through sheer force of imagination.

My parents, through their sacrifice of themselves to a family life that could not contain and satisfy all of their complexity, gave me security and this security gives me freedom, the freedom to roam, to imagine.

Besides giving me life, this is, to me, their greatest gift.

As well as this knowledge: I knew from an early age that I was, in a sense, the outlaw of my parents' relationship.

But had no words nor consciousness to express it.

I embodied – in a sense – everything they tried to fight, everything they tried to escape from, dancing away nights at the Club De Lisa. And finally falling in love.

The irony of it was that they had escaped, had almost got away with it.

Daddy through war, Mamma by virtue of the fact that her father had died and she needed to go out to work. To be free.

They could have lived that crazy bohemian dream. Paris, as always, was in love with their person as well as spirit. They were young and beautiful. It was possible.

Daddy told me, as we climbed the cliffs at Normandy, away from the beach below, that he never thought that he'd ever be back. I felt that he meant not only as a man, but as a human being, whose child had gone to live somewhere else.

I felt that I owed him that walk up to the cemetery, and then the long look down.

We sat at a café in Honfleur and he talked about the hunting dog he had as a boy and how they looked for possum.

And when I sat on the bed he died in four years later, the one he shared with Mamma for almost four decades, I could see in my mind's eye that he had become a boy again.

That he was just going to take a bit of time off from being our father.

At last.

And then he would come back to me.

And he has.

EIGHT

There are thirteen months between me and my sister Lelia, named after Daddy's mother.

I was born in mid-November 1948, Lelia at the beginning of December 1949, and our brother Ben in late November 1950.

Benny and Lelia are the same age for a few weeks each year.

Three babies in nappies.

I was never able to talk to Mamma alone. I could never learn what she knew except when she reprimanded me. I can't recall either her or Daddy actually spending time with me alone until I was an adult many years later. I tell myself that they were too busy: too many mouths to feed, too many little bodies to keep clean and clothed and protected. I understand that.

And I don't. She showed her life to me through criticising me and I do the same to those I love. Maybe I can correct this before it's too late.

Every child experiences childhood in their own distinct way.

This goes without saying, but often it's not possible to know how a sibling saw childhood until asked.

I was at first shocked, for example, when I discovered that Hemingway had so many brothers and sisters. You never get the sense that he was a human being who had to share his life with six other people around his age.

My focus was on Mamma and Daddy, I needed to understand them, reach them. Brothers and sisters were on the fringes of the drama, although I loved them.

Lelia. Lelia is the opposite of me: outgoing, beautiful, athletic, fearless. With four beautiful kids, even more beautiful grandkids, and a husband who made me cry with envy over their marriage.

Benny is sensitive, a poet, a teacher, a helper of human beings, Mamma's favourite son, and kind. My first full memory is of him getting his hair cut in the basement at Troy Street, sitting in his high chair, his mouth wide open and screaming in fear and rage. I couldn't imagine what was happening to him as Daddy told him to be quiet and sit still. I thought to myself how could he do that with great pieces of hair falling to the floor, hair that twenty years later would have made a magnificent 'fro. Gone, gone, gone, and Benny exploding.

Regina is a genius and a dynamo, a creator for other people with the most devoted circle of friends I have ever seen. And she is very funny, ever since she was a baby.

Of course I was writing, writing all the time, re-ordering, shifting around, changing. I had and still have no idea whether my childhood was actually happy. I didn't see it that way.

It was my Day Self, where I was 'proper', and my 'Night Self' – the parallel life where I could swing through the glen with Robin Hood or be Zorro and sweep down on Little Rock, Arkansas and take down the evil white people stopping black kids like me from going to school.

For a not very athletic child I swung through loads of branches and jumped off lots of buildings in my mind.

So while I was saving the world and dictating to it, too (there's a photo of me at six months old, barely sitting up but with a look on my face as if I'm in deep conversation and trying to make my points as emphatically as I can), my brothers and sisters were having a childhood.

Our apartment had only two bedrooms. Mamma and Daddy had one of them. The rest of us occupied the other bedroom and slept in bunk beds. Our bedroom was located across from the kitchen and Mamma's and Dad's room was across from the living room. It opened on to a passageway separating us from the brownstone next door. There, gangs initiated girls. Every night, I lay awake, no more than eight or nine, listening to gang sex, not understanding what I was hearing. But I could remember male laughing and female pleading. Every night.

I knew more about sex at a young age than I should have and it was bad sex, quite possibly rape, and it has scarred me, I know.

But still there was the building, Troy Street, a brownstone – built in the Gilded Age of the late 1890s – a magical place to me…

Nostalgia.

The word's root, it is said by some scholars, lies in the word 'nostos' – homecoming.

The word 'nostos' occurs many times in *The Iliad*. But it cannot be achieved, you can't win it, without destruction.

In this great epic, the cornerstone of everything we read in the West and know as literature, the destruction, the achievement, is the elimination of a city, a place where people are living their lives, caught up in the consequence of one act of will.

I've always been afraid of that. Being caught up in the

consequences of one person's desire, will, need. Yet, isn't that one of the main engines of the world?

In the poem, 'nostos' cannot be satisfied, cannot be quenched unless a city is destroyed: Troy.

Troy.

The name of the street I lived in as a little girl.

Troy Street. 1310 South Troy. West Side of Chicago. County of Cook. State of Illinois. Midwest of the United States. The United States.

Nostalgia.

The author of *The Iliad* may not have existed at all; the epic could have been a series of oral poems – songs – finally written down under the command of a dictator. Every writer knows about the dictator. Every child, too.

Some scholars say that the name has echoes of an old, old word that means 'reunion' and refers – again speculating – to a formal assembly of competing minstrels.

Memory: an assembly of competing minstrels.

With Troy Street, Mamma finally had a garden. We called it a yard.

It was part of the first home that I can fully recall – a brownstone that Daddy bought with Aunt Bernice and her husband, Uncle Joe, a gargantuan guy from Texas, a gentle giant. But you could sense that underneath was something lethal that had no name.

Uncle Joe and Aunt Bernice had a cleaning business. The funeral home, the cleaners and the church. They say if you can get to own one of those businesses in the black community, you'll never starve.

And my uncle and aunt, compared to us, looked as if they lived in the Taj Mahal.

The last time I saw Troy Street, while making a programme for the BBC, it had become a wreck. It looked like a crack house. The edifice was barely standing, it looked as if it had its sides shaved off and the glass had been replaced many times.

We didn't film it. I don't want to remember it. By then I had been living in London for a long time and I knew about old houses and how they can have ghosts, too.

I was the ghost.

But by the time I was able to form a memory of it – at about three or four, 1954–55 – it was a sturdy Victorian West Side brownstone carved into two large apartments on the same floor with a connecting door and a huge basement. We lived in one apartment. Aunt Bernice and Uncle Joe lived in the other one: the Taj Mahal.

The yard had a fountain, an ornate Victorian one that must have been a symbol of wealth and station in the Chicago of the 1870s. By the time we arrived, eighty years later, descendants of the Great Migration from the South, there wasn't any water. The fountain's bowl had been dry for decades but its faux-Greek statue was still there. Ancient fern trees stood in our yard like sentinels, keeping us from the other kids on the block and also away from our neighbours.

Mamma's aim was to keep us contained. I suspect this was partly because we lived in one of the biggest gang neighbourhoods in all of Chicago: Lawndale, on the West Side, home of the notorious Vice Lords and other black and Puerto Rican gangs.

Unfortunately, we had to leave the yard to go to school.

And so, from about seven years of age, I was routinely mugged for the small amounts of money that Mamma gave me to go to the corner shop and buy her obligatory pack of 'Viceroy' cigarettes. 'Stingy Bill', a white man with a dried-up, pinched face full of the silent anger he must have felt in seeing the community around his family business change. I knew that he was out of place; I could feel the siege within him whenever I came in. He never spoke. Just took my money and gave me the cigarettes. And sometimes, Mamma's little pocket money wound up in the hands of the 'Big Girls' – Italian or Puerto Rican, I couldn't tell. The archetypes that *Grease* – which began in Chicago – is based on: big hair; headscarves tied under the lower lip; tight skirts; bobby socks; tight blouses and sweaters; they smelled like sweat and tobacco and cheap cologne. They had no soundtrack to accompany their demands for Mamma's money as they shoved me against a wall and threatened to beat my brains out.

I wanted to go further down our street, go as far as the Douglas Boulevard, the grand street that seemed like the beginning of the universe to me. But our parents quite rightly held on to us. I learned very early on how to live in – perhaps prefer – a small, confined space.

Whenever I could get away from the chores and duties of an eldest daughter in a traditional family – washing clothes in the big washing machine in the basement, sending everything through the big roller, then hanging the clothes on the line, fastening everything with wooden clothes pins; peeling potatoes and carrots; shelling peas; sorting collard greens; changing nappies and bathing babies and walking them until they stopped crying and feeding them with the bottle after making formula and watching it on the stove to make sure that it didn't boil over; scrubbing the kitchen and bathroom floor and ironing Daddy's blue work shirts and his grey trousers – his uniform for the can factory – and our school uniforms with their white blouses and navy blue serge skirts over and over while listening to the farm report on the radio early in the morning and the soap operas after school – whenever I could get away I would tell stories about a world in the stars. The

Above: My maternal great great grandmother Caledonia at the end of the 19th century.

Right: My great grandmother on my mother's side – Willie Boone – in the early 20th century.

Above left: Great Grandmother Randolph, my grandfather William Randolph's mother. She was Mamma's paternal grandmother and my maternal great grandmother.

Above right: Great Uncle James Randolph, Great Aunt Lillian Randolph and Grandfather William Randolph in the 1930s.

Left: My great grandmother Randolph and her son, my grandfather, William Randolph, in the 1930s.

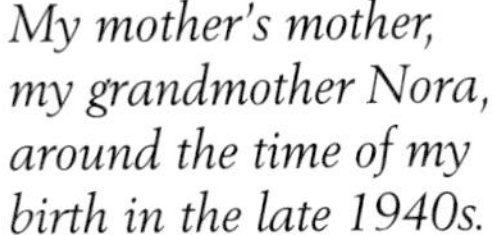

My mother's mother, my grandmother Nora, around the time of my birth in the late 1940s.

Mamma's uncle and my great uncle: James Randolph in the early 1950s.

Seated from left to right are Uncle 'Bubble', a family friend, Mamma, Aunt Ernestine and Uncle 'June'. Dad stands directly behind Mamma. She aptly wears a tiara. A family friend is on Dad's right.

The family gathers on the front porch on the South Side, for Gina and Theron's wedding. Dad, Mamma and Harry are next to Theron; Gina has her hand on my shoulder. Lelia, with the pearls around her neck, is right below Theron. Ben stands at the top left with his hand on Uncle Kaydon's shoulder. Aunt Lillian and Uncle James peer behind Benny, with Aunt Bernice and Aunt Ernestine looking over Mamma's shoulder. Nieces, cousins and nephews a-plenty!

From left to right: Mamma and her two younger sisters, Ernestine and Ida.

Left to right: Mamma, Great Aunt Ida, Great Aunt Donnie, Aunt Ernestine and Gina, my sister, in the 1980s.

From left to right: Mamma, Great Aunt Donnie, Aunt Ernestine and Great Aunt Ida in the late 1980s.

Main: Dad's mother, Mrs Lelia Greer, in the 1950s.

Inset: Dad, a proud and active member of the Steel Workers Union for 40 years.

Top left:
Benny, six months old.

Top right:
Me, six months old.

Above: Benny and Gina at Troy Street in the 1950s, aged five and three respectively.

Right: My certificate of Baptism.

Certificate of Baptism

ST. AGATHA CHURCH
3147 DOUGLAS BOULEVARD
CHICAGO 23, ILL.

This is to Certify

That Bonnie Greer

~~Son~~ Daughter of Ben Greer

and Willie Mae Randolph

born in Chicago, Illinois

on the 16 day of November 1948, was

Baptized

on the 19 day of October 1958

According to the Rite of the Roman Catholic Church

by the Rev. Daniel J. Mallette

Sponsors being Cortez Dixon / Estelle Dixon

as recorded in the Baptismal Register of this Church

Dated March 17, 1960 Vol. 4B Page 1 No. 3

Rev. Daniel J. Mallette asst Pastor

SEAL

Confirmation here – March 6, 1960
Bishop Hillinger

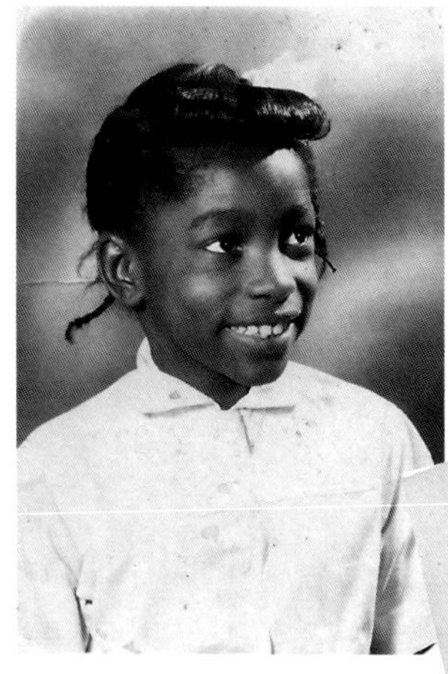

Left: Me, in second grade.

Right: In grade school, in the late 1950s.

Left: My brother Ben in 1969.

stories gathered a little following so that in the hot summer months, after catching fireflies in the yard, dozens of children would sit on our stairs and listen to my tales.

I made them up on the spot, standing before them, a little Bard then, fearless in my ability to weave a tale, to hold an audience. I was escaping with them, flying away with them, taking them away, too, from the constant violence we felt.

Sometimes I wonder now if that violence had been bred in us, part of our DNA.

We were all the children of black children of the Depression, most of them from the Deep South. People who knew terror.

One summer of my childhood – I was too young to know or understand this – a boy from Chicago by the name of Emmett Till had gone to Mississippi to visit relatives and had been found brutally murdered in the Pearl River. His crime: he whistled at some young white girls, a Northern lad who had momentarily forgotten where he was and had been fatally punished for it.

I learned later on in the '60s, when I had become one of that generation who would refuse to turn the other cheek, that Emmett's death had been a turning point for the black people of the North and everywhere, along with Rosa Parks' refusal to give up her bus seat to a white man.

Emmett Till's murder must have hung like a canopy over our street but we were kids, and we were catching fireflies in our yards and dreaming of life beyond the stars.

Alone when I could be, I would stand or sit on the back stairs and gaze at the Greek fountain statue for hours, contemplating its curves and its shape, comparing it in my mind to the illustrations of statues in the British Museum contained in the *Encyclopaedia Britannica*.

I wanted to know more – much more – about the civilisation that could create a statue like this. It was 'the other'.

I saw it all around me.

At the entrance to our yard there was a beautiful, ornate gate, from the same period as the fountain, a very Gilded Age thing at which I loved to gaze. Angels in iron curled around a globe. There were fairies, too, dancing in iron woods.

I learned that the gate had been built in the 1890s in Chicago, a civilised time that I could see as plain as day, being the dreaming child that I was. Our families kept from us the fact that the 1890s was also a lynching time, a pogrom so ferocious that black people had fled the South on whatever they could.

No one had time to plant flowers, to decorate the yard in rose bushes.

So I did it. In my imagination. And so I planted my garden, my wild place.

I planted those flowers thick, a deep carpet of them that I could fall asleep in like Judy Garland's Dorothy did in *The Wizard of Oz*.

In my imaginary bed of flowers, snuggled deep down, I could look up at the sky, block out the screeching cars on the other side of the gate along the crowded street, block out the constant arguments and rancour from Out There – and sometimes from inside our apartment, too.

NINE

To have been an American child growing up in the mid to late 1950s is to be a Dickensian.

It didn't matter what colour you were, or your gender, or financial circumstances. You were brought up in whatever abundance could be had.

Abundance was your birthright.

Those of us who were little kids during this time were the first generation of Americans born and raised to consume.

Consumption was our birthright, our responsibility, our duty.

We came to expect and to want 'goods', 'stuff', what we saw on TV.

The New.

Everything.

We judged one another on our loot; our brands, being first with them, showing them off. We were rich, no matter how poor we were, the richest kids in the world, the richest who had ever lived.

We were programmed to spend and to bring our offspring up to spend, and the amount and display of our money was our true religion.

Money was always the class definer, even if, by colour, you

couldn't drink out of a water fountain if you had money, you could go back to your community and lord it over those who didn't have your education, or skin tone, or whatever.

Or buy your own damn water fountain.

To say that the US is classless is absurd. The Republic reeks of class, class based on money above all.

In America, if you have money or access to it, all of the doors will open. And if they don't open directly for you, you can pay someone to represent you for whom the doors will open. Or buy the doors for yourself.

We '50s kids wanted everything and our parents, by the sweat of their brow and in remembrance of their own Depression-era childhoods and wartime young adulthood, gave us everything.

What must it have cost a man like Dad, who worked at night on an assembly line, with four mouths to feed plus a wife? With three kids sent to a fee-paying school.

The man was making tin cans on an assembly line. At night.

And the ruse: lugging home (and hiding in our aunt and uncle's flat) the boxes and boxes of stuff for our Dickensian Christmas.

He did it because he wanted us to have that safe, glorious 1950s childhood; he didn't want us to not have it. And we were happy. Cookies and milk left out for Santa were consumed by Daddy as he built train sets after we were asleep, and assembled miniature stoves and kitchens. Our stockings hung chock full of oranges and candy, a huge Christmas tree left a beautiful pine smell throughout the apartment. Christmas cookies that Mom made from scratch, complete with sprinkles on the top.

Tinsel; wrapping; a big turkey with all the trimmings.

They gave us the happiest childhood that they could because they needed to, not only for themselves, but because

THAT was childhood in the 1950s. We were spoiled rotten with our paediatricians and baby formula and careful coddling. And Mom was always there, always there. She was the rock and the centre of stability and as much as I complained about her control and her essential conservatism, she gave me an anchor in the world.

She made me unafraid because she was always there.

Always. And in her heart is there still.

We gave money at school for the 'missions in Africa', that 'country' where the people looked suspiciously like us. Benevolence. Benevolence: 'bene' – 'good will'; 'volence' – 'wanting'. Wanting to give good will. Even when you hardly had anything yourself.

That's because poverty was considered to be individual, an inner failure that could be corrected by will, hard work ... and the benevolence of the better off.

But above all, Christmas was used to teach us to be kind. Kindness: one of the highest virtues that could be instilled in a 1950s child.

'Kindness' was an individual thing, too, a state of being with its own choices and goals and reach. Kindness was bestowed. Justice, equality: that was an individual choice.

And kindness began at home. On TV.

When I first saw MGM's classic version of *A Christmas Carol* (it had become a staple on holiday TV in Chicago in the 1970s), it matched the images I had in my mind as a child, the images – and the music of the story, its inner music, the music that conjured it up more than the words did – that had become a part of the parallel life I carried around in my head.

Released in 1938, the film was born in Metro Golden Mayer's golden age, that dream factory amongst many dream factories.

I recall films usually scene by scene, and always from the score or a camera shot. Not words. Film is, for me, the work of a director, and I like to see style and the 'authorship' of film.

A Christmas Carol was one of my 'England' films, one of my 'London' films, and MGM has a lot to answer for.

That glorious black-and-white footage sprinkled through with light to give it that dreamy sheen; a cheery, cocky-matey London bright, clear-eyed – the Metro look – that distinguished MGM from Warner Brothers and Twentieth Century Fox and RKO. Bright, bright, as if everything was filmed in sunlight and you, too, became part of that sunlight.

This is apparent at the end of *A Christmas Carol,* when Scrooge bursts out of his front door and into the street, into the new day, a man of giggles and good cheer who yells out to the young boy outside his door to, 'Go get a goose!' then, catching his coin, the boy runs off in glee. Where before Scrooge was a miserable guy, cowering in the dark of his candlelit room, awaiting another apparition, this new Scrooge was gorgeous, radiant, beautiful.

Because he had become kind. Or rather scared kind. The results were the same.

And at the end, when Tiny Tim looks into the camera, his eyes big with gratitude, and says: 'God Bless us everyone!' surrounded by the bursting-at-the-seams Christmas goose with all the trimmings, and a table groaning with food, I felt it too, I was happy, too.

I was happy as I was meant to be, curled up at the end of the couch, holding a little brother in my arms, feeding him his bottle with one hand and reading with the other.

But at the back of my mind, watching it on TV, listening to it as a child at school, there was always that nagging question that I wanted to ask our teacher, any adult: 'What about the other children? What happened to them?'

I could see that this wonderful story was a tale of individual awakening, individual will, an 'all's right and God is in His heaven' world.

But what happened to those who didn't get help? Who couldn't have benevolence?

What happened to the boy who bought the goose for Scrooge to take to the Cratchit family? What happened to him? Where did he go after the philanthropic eye of the man who was frightened almost to death by his past and future – a guy scared into kindness – moved on to somewhere else and someone else? What about the other children who didn't have a Scrooge in their lives?

This seemed to me to be a flaw in Dickens and somewhere inside me, I started searching for the answer to this, and the search lessened my enjoyment of him. Because the question was there.

Many decades later, still troubled by the genius of Dickens and seeing how so much of popular film and novels has its roots in his view of the world, I discovered that Dickens had been on the wrong side of a question whose roots lie in slavery.

Dickens was one of those Dad had said that I would have been surprised about.

My husband, decades later, gave me an essay on Dickens by Orwell that answered it for me. Dickens was never for the people. He was for order.

'Read with your eyes open. Think with your mind open,' Dad would say, something that he thought black people didn't do enough of and he wasn't afraid to say so to anyone who would listen. As well as telling me to put my book down at the table.

As my sister Lelia says: 'You ate books and inhaled food.'

I was writing, writing all the time, in my head, looking out at the world.

And Lelia and Benny were having a childhood. Here are some of their memories:

> On Saturday mornings the fish truck would come down the alley. The men on the truck would yell, 'Fresh fish, get your fresh fish here!' Another truck would come down the alley during summertime with watermelons. The men on that truck would shout: 'Watermelo, we got watermelo here!' The knife grinder would come down the street, too, on Saturday mornings.
>
> Our family car was a 1952 Pontiac Chieftain two-door sedan. I remember that it was green-coloured and had an Indian head figure on the hood of the car and a sun visor. It wasn't air-conditioned. In 1959 Dad took our entire family to a drive-in in that car to see the movie *Ben Hur*.
>
> Sears & Roebuck department store was on the West Side not far from our house. Sears was a sprawling complex and was spread out across several blocks. Their headquarters was there and they even had a YMCA. I also remember when there were dime stores on the West Side back then.
>
> Daddy didn't too much care for grocery stores. 'Moo and Oink.' Daddy would buy a whole side of beef, had the cow killed, Moo and Oink cut it up into portions and Daddy freezes it for winter. Smart and thrifty, he said it was cheaper than buying pre-packaged meats for a big family.

Mamma got upset with Daddy once when he came home with some friends with bushels full of peaches to teach Mamma how to can peaches? Man... She was pissed! But went along with it.

He went to the fish market and bought chickens with their heads still on and the gizzards in a pouch in the chicken's belly.

And Daddy going hunting early morning and bringing home rabbits? He cooked it himself ... Yummy, I would sit there with Daddy picking through it after he fried it!!

Our first telephone number: CRAWFORD7–5012

There was a small neighbourhood store on Kedzie Avenue where the store owner had two fat cats. We used to call the store 'Mr Cat's Store'. (Actually, I think he was a Mr Katz.) We used to buy notebook paper and penny candy at that store.

And 'Stingy Bill's Grocery Store'. A block of notebook paper in his store cost a nickel back then.

The sawdust on the floors in the meat markets; especially whole catfish with scales. The men in white coats with blood and guts chopping the fish up.

The Cat Lady slicing up her pimp in the alley. She had leopard stretch pants.

The block parties that were held in our big basement. Mamma had a joint birthday party for me with Gina when I turned nine.

I never understood why we had our birthday party together that year.

I remember when Dad took me on my sixth birthday. I wore white pants, a striped sports jacket, black shoes and an Ivy League cap. Dad took me to a studio to get my picture taken. We also went to see a movie called *The Rainmaker* that starred Burt Lancaster.

More from Benny and Lelia:

Also Daddy stopping at the cookie factory on the way home at night to pick up the imperfect crates of banana cookies. I knew Daddy was home because I could smell the bananas.

Don't forget the roller rink in the basement. Seven kids who were told they didn't need friends because we were enough.

The corner candy store on Douglas Boulevard where we bought Jay's potato chips. The shop owner opening the bag, adding hot sauce if you wanted it. And the huge sour pickles with candy canes slid down the middle to balance sour with sweet.

I remember the picnics that we would go to that Dad's job provided and the amusement park rides we played on at those picnics. I remember the Christmas party events that Dad's job held and the gifts of toys they would give.

A girl name Ella Mae and her gang of boys were always trying to beat up you and Lelia.

And I can remember bits, too.

I was eight and we were all dressed in our Easter clothes.

You dressed up on Sundays; even if you played in the streets, you still did it in your Sunday finery. My petticoat was light pink and stiff and I stood on the side as the other girls jumped rope. I was watching them. Inventing them.

Benny:

> I remember that our home address on Troy Street was 1310 South Troy. Our family lived in the first-floor apartment and we had to enter it from the back which faced the backyard. Aunt Bernice and Uncle Joe had the first-floor apartment that faced the street. There were two other tenants in the building but I don't remember them. We had a bird-bath in the backyard with a statue of the Virgin Mary.

Lelia:

> 'We lived the American Dream.'

And there was another American Dream on the other side of us.

In a similar but decidedly unkempt brownstone lived Mildred.

She was my first example of an adventuress, a dark-skinned, wild-haired woman who talked loud. A woman who metaphorically had her hands defiantly on her hips twenty-four hours a day. A woman who laughed loud and talked loud and called out to people from the other end of the street.

Mamma detested her.

Mildred was also considered 'country', the dreaded verdict

rendered on those of us who were perceived to have not quite left the rural South behind. Sitting on the front steps, singing in the street, all of these were 'country'.

I was to learn later, in our new neighbourhood on the South Side, that the fear of 'country' had risen to an art form, precise in its delineations. The community there was a Byzantium of avoidances of any vestiges of the South. The South was a phobia there, even though the Illinois Central railroad, running down to the Southern end of the state, an area as Southern as can be, echoed through the street and in my mind.

Mildred. The perfect name. A James M. Caine heroine. If he could have imagined a black woman like Mildred.

We were going to Catholic school by the time I was aware of her. I would catch Mamma as she ironed a few altar-boy cassocks from time to time in order to reduce our fees, watching her window, watching her window on the other side of the fence.

Mildred had two children our age, Belinda and Jesse.

Jesse was a boy in glasses, a delicate kid who was as much of a bookworm as I was.

He would lean over his porch and stare at the sky like I did, too, and his smile was infectious and large and always present.

Belinda was what used to be called a 'tomboy', but what she actually was, was a replica of her mother, except that Belinda played in the street and rolled around in the dirt.

There was a kind of trench on the other side of the fence that separated our property from her apartment.

Sometimes Jesse and Belinda poured enough water in to turn it into a mini muddy river – real muddy waters, sloshing and splashing the wire fence on to our pavement. Then Mildred would emerge from their dark flat with a bed sheet which she'd shake out – and dozens of cockroaches would start swimming for their lives.

On our side of the fence, I, and sometimes my sister and brother, would join Jesse and Belinda in watching those roaches swim. And if there was too much water, watch them to the death.

Mildred assured us that even if the Russians did drop a bomb on us – a great fear that all of us children held in our heads and our hearts – roaches and rats would survive. Roaches could outlive a nuclear attack, she explained, because they were extraordinary creatures, half insect, half something else.

We were right to be fascinated by them. We could learn something from them, too, about how to survive above the odds.

Somewhere I knew inside me that to tell Mamma Mildred's analogy would have made her explode out of the house and drag us back inside and away from our friends for ever.

But it didn't stop me pondering it. Not at all.

Mildred had a boyfriend who came every other Saturday.

He was always dressed well, but anyone could sense that beneath it all was a man who had known hard times and had worked with his hands and his back.

Sometimes he would serenade her on her back porch on the other side of the trees – those huge ferns that lazily draped like something out of an amateur rendering of a Tennessee Williams play.

I'd stand sometimes on our back porch and listen to the boyfriend.

He drove a shocking pink truck, which he sometimes parked in front of our house. Mamma really hated that.

Along with sitting on the front stairs, chewing gum in the street, and talking loud, that pink truck was typical of 'country'.

But above all, Mildred's boyfriend sang … the blues.

His deep voice had an edge of melancholy and the

Mississippi intonations that my father had. That 'sippi twang and the way that sometimes an 's' would be put on words. I can hear the 's' in my mind, but not the word. Only the sound. Only the sound.

When he sang, I imagined myself walking down a long road, a long road in sunlight and shadow, away from Troy Street. To another world. A world in which I could be as free as Mildred seemed to be. I could see his songs.

But Mildred's boyfriend's worst offence, in the eyes of the 'proper' people of Troy Street, was his name.

'...and what kind of name is – Muddy Waters!!!' Mamma would say. Who calls himself 'Muddy Waters'?

Frankly, I thought it was an odd name, too. 'Muddy Waters.' But listening to Mr Waters – all adults were 'Miss' or 'Mr', we never called any adult by their first name under any circumstances; we barely looked an adult in the eye, it was considered impertinent – made me forget his funny name, his pink truck, the neighbourhood, everything.

Mildred (some of the older kids called her 'Mil'ho', I didn't know why) and Muddy Waters found a niche in my parallel life. I kept faith with them as best as I could. I keep faith with them.

When I hear him sing one of his songs, I can see that pink truck.

And understand how defiant, disruptive and insouciant his shocking pink truck – that colour choice – was for that man from the Delta.

That blues man.

TEN

I don't remember the actual move to our new home.

But with a pregnant woman and six kids – Kevin was born in 1956 and Michael two years later – it must have been epic.

I don't recall saying goodbye to anyone. Because like dinner parties and small talk, I don't like doing that. But I must have.

The house had an upstairs and downstairs.

The downstairs consisted of the front room as you entered in, through to a dining room, a kitchen and, if you turned back on yourself and down a short corridor, the first of three bedrooms – our parents' room, where Daddy died four decades later – and a bathroom. Theirs.

A large basement was underneath it all, only a third of the size of Troy Street. But enough to hold a washer/dryer, and Daddy's working space which he used for various odd jobs and also became his workshop for repairing TVs, his job in addition to the night work at the factory.

Outside was a back garden – not as big as Troy Street, but substantial. Flowers and vegetables could be grown there. Mamma could hang her washing there. We could run and play there.

There was no front gate, but a back one leading to an alley.

The old fruit trees that ran along the back fence and the

one that stood in the garden gave great shade in the boiling heat of the summer and were positively magical in the winter, their branches laden with snow like something on a Christmas card.

Now I can see how lovely and tranquil the yard was.

My sisters and I shared a room, and down the tiny corridor was the other room that the boys shared. In between was a bathroom that we all shared.

Looking back at that floor – with three teens, two little boys and a girl in the middle of the two generations, all at one time crammed in two rooms – it had to have been madness for our parents. It certainly was for me.

I found a space for myself in the corner, a space where I could be alone to read and write and draw and think, where I could read the *Encyclopaedia Britannica*, with my books and drawing paper.

There was a window that overlooked the garden. I would sit there in my tiny space when I could, listening to the whistle from the Illinois Central train whose tracks were just a few streets away.

The Illinois Central. The legend. You can hear it in every blues harmonica, in the urgent guitar and in the voice of anyone who sings the blues and is part of Chicago. The train's north–south route, from the Gulf of Mexico to the Great Lakes, was one of the means of transport during the Great Migration from the South in the 1920s.

I listened to that whistle as it sped past, and dreamed of riding it. Of going far away and into my life.

While Lelia was learning to ride a bike and meet the neighbours and grow active and pretty and Gina was as lively as ever, I was going the other way. Deeper into myself.

I began to carry a piece of paper around with me so that I could write things down: impressions, feelings.

I looked at the men in the magazines. They were always men who wore their jackets and smoked pipes and worked away hours at a time.

I played the music that was then in my head and let the words flow. Couldn't imagine anyone like me, not anyone. And so I didn't see the possibilities. I couldn't see the Image, which was always key for me.

I had to find a place of peace and quiet where my questions would be answered, and if not, I could be left with some kind of peace. It was easy to see that life was much more than the routine that Mamma fitted into.

What was 'coloured', 'Negro'?

I heard it all the time on the news, that spring and summer of 1960.

I couldn't put it all together. I was too young to understand the political ramifications of the sit-ins at lunch counters by students just six years older than me. I couldn't understand why these perfectly dressed and polite people would allow a bottle of catsup to be emptied on their heads or milk thrown in their faces simply because they wanted to eat a sandwich? Why couldn't they eat the sandwich?

But I knew, too, that it was all jumbled up.

The Church was authoritarian, too. I didn't like authority.

But there was a promise at the end of all that 'yes' stuff. There was a promise.

I held on to that for as long as I could. I wanted sanctity. It seemed a good idea at the time.

Our neighbours on either side were nice people – one a very glamorous woman, older than Mamma, who smoked with an elegant cigarette holder and was as tall and thin as a silhouette.

She was neither beautiful nor pretty, but I learned from her what attractive meant.

Unlike Mamma's desperate puffing, five ashtrays scattered around, necessary for a busy mom up at five and falling asleep in her chair by two the next morning, the same thing starting over again in three hours, Mrs Taylor was like an ad in one of Mamma's magazines.

She never appeared rumpled or frazzled – in other words she had no children and was not in the least bit domestic. She had a small, delicate face, with tiny eyes and a pinched nose. Her garden was 'arranged', 'done', as opposed to ours, which depended on when Mamma could plant some seedlings or Daddy could.

Our backyard was for playing and Mrs Taylor's was for *being.*

She'd sit in her lounge chair in the summer, sipping something brown and strongly alcoholic and smoke and smoke. Her voice had that scratching sound that some smokers have, and her laughter was ready.

I liked to think that she had been everywhere, but I also suspect that our street was the length and breadth of her world, too. But there was a bit of danger about her.

I don't know what she did or didn't do in the world once upon a time. I have no idea. Nor of her husband, a timid man, rumoured to be her second, who never spoke. Nice man, but you got nothing out of him. I made him into a spy in my mind.

On the other side was a family like ours – the Franklins – the children contemporary to us, their father a steel-mill worker and mother a housewife like Mom. Just normal, good people.

I'm pretty sure that like me my sister Lelia and my brother Ben didn't want to move from Troy Street.

Gina was too young to have a choice and the latest additions were too young also.

But I sensed that Mamma was pregnant once again, so

a move had to be made. We all couldn't live in that two-bedroom place any more with the youngest sleeping with our parents like I had done.

The South Side – its very name had the sound of an Elysian Fields full of effete kids raised to be Little Lord and Lady Fauntleroys.

It sounded to me, through the assistance of my synaesthesia, like the Fragonard universe on the basement wallpaper at Troy Street – a part of the city that had people with the equivalent of powdered wigs, snuff and carriages.

What did South Side kids know about negotiating gangs; the sound of gunfire as a regular ritual; junk men in wagons and their street cries and the horses dropping manure; the street cars with their cables; the candy store and the big churches, filled to the brim on Sundays; the all-day preaching?

Sometimes Daddy would take us, I guess to keep in touch with his roots, and ours, and then afterwards the big suppers in the church hall and running around and playing all day in our Sunday clothes.

What did South Side children know about the blues that rang from every house and teens singing doo-wop on every stoop?

And anyway, we had friends and we didn't want to leave them. No kid wants to do that. We knew that we were under the control, at the mercy, of adults. If they so wished, there would be no way that we would be allowed to come back and see our friends again.

I cried my eyes out. Not that I had any deep friendships. Much too much of a bookworm and Mamma's helper-in-chief. Lelia, the outgoing, beautiful one, had the friends. Benny, too. No, for me it was about change, upheaval. The New. I was scared.

Besides, there were things on my mind and what with the

move I wouldn't have time to sit in my place in the corner of the couch and contemplate them.

I was trying to work out what heaven was. Hell seemed cut and dried: you did evil and you went down below to eternal fire. Pretty straightforward to me.

It was heaven I was having a problem with.

To me, Mamma and Daddy seemed tyrannical.

I know that they loved me. But they never hugged me nor kissed me. They never really answered any of my questions like, 'How does the sun set?' or, 'Why did God make the Jews if they couldn't go to heaven? Why did he do that? Didn't the catechism say: "God made me to show forth his goodness and to be with him in the next world"? So, why would God make people who can't do that or women who can't be on the altar? And why are people different colours ...'

I never stopped talking or asking questions, my little glasses firmly on my face, like a shield.

But what I really didn't like was the fact that they were always telling me to do things for no reason that I could see. I didn't dare ask 'why' – not out loud. I was much too timid and also I wanted them to smile at me, appreciate the docility and calm that I provided within our turbulent household full of little kids.

Or so I thought.

I expressed my feelings while helping Mamma peel potatoes, but my feelings were hardly of any consequence to her. Keeping all of us alive and thriving, our Dad happy and, somewhere in all of that, holding on to her own sense of self-worth, had to be her priorities.

But there were important things on my mind. I was grappling with a spiritual crisis. I wanted to be a nun, but didn't know how to tell Mamma.

I found myself reading the catalogue of the order of nuns that taught at St Agatha's on the West Side. Their headquarters or motherhouse was in someplace called Dubuque, Iowa.

I can't recall how I got this book, but I had it.

I stared for hours at the pictures of the postulants and novices wrapped in peace and quiet and ritual.

I projected myself amongst them.

A life of prayer and service and peace and quiet and regularity: matins and Mass.

I hid the catalogue and my thoughts on the subject of nunhood.

When the time came, I knew that the Blessed Virgin would guide me to stand up to Mamma. Tell her what *I* wanted.

Who *I* was.

No one on the South Side would understand.

The street, like all the rest surrounding us, had been emptied by 'white flight'. And then we, aspiring black people, filled it up again with great pride. But we weren't left alone. In the early days, white boys from further out in the southern part of the city or from the southern suburbs,would sometimes ride in groups down our quiet streets like something out of a Wild West movie.

That didn't last long, though.

Daddy, like all of the men on the street, and the women, too – in fact like most of America – believed in what is informally known as the 'Second Amendment remedy'. This 'solution' is seen as having the ability to deal with any transgression or perceived transgression. In other words he was armed and would not hesitate.

He and the other fathers on the street would gather in their backyards on New Year's Eve and there would be a chorus of gunshots, each coordinated one after the other.

When he lay dying, he kept a gun under his pillow. For a while, after he died, we still hadn't found all of his guns. I think that they've all been accounted for now.

I wanted to take advantage of living in a new place to begin to live a life of piety as best I could. Even though I didn't know what that meant for an eleven-and-a-half-year-old.

But I had a range of saints to inspire me.

The saint we were told a lot about at St Agatha's was not Agatha herself, but St Maria Goretti. I suppose that was because she had been a young girl, mortally wounded while fighting off a would-be rapist. She fit the times, the age I was growing up in, the age that had invented the 'teenager'.

Goretti, about twelve years old, was on the brink of it.

So she was good to go with as far as my – now former – grade school, surrounded by gang territory, was concerned. But she wasn't for me. I couldn't use her as a conduit, a means to funnel and refine my growing identity. There was no one. And I was in a new place and had to find my own way again.

We were not yet enrolled in the local Catholic school because we had moved mid-year, so it was off to the state school. There was a freak snow that early spring.

We were told by the kids of our next-door neighbours, who we were getting to know, that the best way to run home after school – because we would have to run home – was through the tracks left in the snow by the lorries on their way to the interstate highway and on to Indiana. After school was the time that white boys – 'peckerwoods', 'crackers' and 'honkies', the older people called them – from the neighbourhoods further south would ride through the streets whooping and screaming and throwing rocks at us.

We were, after all, integrating 'their' school. Although it wasn't put to us that way. We were just going to school.

But at three o'clock, when that bell rang and we got our coats, we began to run home.

And if it snowed, we were inside those lorry tracks, slipping and sliding all of the way home. Frankly, if they had wanted to get us they could have. You can't run very fast in deep snow.

No, I don't think that they wanted us. I suspect that they enjoyed the archetypal image of black folks running away in terror.

But I prayed for them. How could they adhere to the same faith that I did – the thugs were Polish and Irish and therefore 99 per cent sure to be RC – and treat us that way? I didn't interpret the faith to say that it was OK to be a racist. What they were about didn't make sense to me.

I could hear Daddy asking the same thing and ending with: 'It don't make sense!'

I had to endure. I couldn't enter a convent until I was eighteen – a lifetime away. I somehow got to see *The Nun's Story*, Audrey Hepburn's big film, and it made me want to enter the convent more than ever.

In the film, when Audrey, as a newly dressed novice, returns to her hospital ward and one of the patients gives her a bouquet and says, 'You make a beautiful nun,' I wanted to scream at the screen: 'Yes, she does! And so will I!'

But how could I tell Mamma about my vocation?

When I finally found the courage, a few weeks after we'd moved into the new house, I told her. And she burst into laughter.

She'd never laughed at me before. Her mockery was a huge shock.

I stood back as she laughed and laughed. I couldn't believe that she was doing that. That this was her response to my … my vocation!

Of course now I know that Mamma might have laughed out of the sheer horror of the thought of me in a cloister. And she laughed, too, as a means of dissuading me, of turning me back. And because I was a very serious and probably quite pompous child, who knew nothing about climbing out of my shell and joining the human race.

She called me 'the little old lady' because I didn't dance. I was too busy reading or thinking or writing. Now she was laughing at me, too.

Mamma was about to have what turned out to be her last baby and her seventh child, adding to the baby/child population on the street.

You could almost hear the theme tunes of various American sitcoms ringing from the trees. There was the school run; the late morning hum of washing machines; lunch and afternoon soap operas; kids home and cookies and milk; homework and dinner; some TV and to bed.

Since Daddy worked nights at the can factory, we never actually saw him except at the weekends because he slept during the day. The Routine.

Suddenly my life was about to open up.

But I had to wait.

Mamma was about to go to the hospital.

I was old enough to take care of everyone – Lelia and me – but Daddy got in a kind of minder who must have cost him a great deal of money.

I don't remember much about her other than that she was kind and neat and brought a different presence into the house.

I thought maybe I could talk to her about being a nun. There was something ascetic in her bearing. But I didn't need anyone else now.

That summer of 1960, we were finally liberated from the racist state school. Daddy had found a Catholic school further south. We would have to ride a school bus, but it would be worth it.

The order of nuns who taught at the school were called the Oblate Sisters of Providence, out of Baltimore, Maryland.

They were black.

Elizabeth Mary Lange, said to have been a refugee from Santiago in Cuba and possibly of Haitian origin, began the order with three other black women and a Sulpician priest at Baltimore in 1829.

A year before that, she had founded a school for black refugee children. Mother Lange started the nation's first Catholic school for African American refugee children a year before founding the Oblates, the first religious order for American women of African descent.

She did this while Maryland was still a slave-holding state. She did this thirty-five years before the Emancipation Proclamation.

I don't know if Daddy chose the school – Holy Name of Mary – because it was run by black women, but that couldn't have hurt. Daddy, a self-described 'race man' – black people first – must have been delighted.

Right away I realised how coddled we had been back at St Agatha's.

By that I mean that the nuns there were quite gentle, firm, but softly spoken.

They made sure that we saw and venerated the statue of St Martin de Porres, the little sixteenth-century Latin American monk of African descent that was the only black statue I would see in church for years, until priests and nuns of the 'liberation theology' bent in the 1970s decided that it might be a good idea to make Christ and the Virgin Mary ethnically closer to people from Palestine rather than from Scandinavia or northern Italy.

Where St Agatha's was bustling, as a school with little kids in it would be, HNM was like the *Bounty* and Sister Marcellina, head teacher, was Captain Bligh. Except that Marcellina was not about to be cast adrift.

She was tall and dark-skinned and looked like a Nigerian sculpture. She moved like a lioness, her every step bristling with suppressed violence.

She wore a habit with a white wimple and a rosary and crucifix at the side of her gown – the normal kit for pre-Vatican II religious. She could look right through you, so you dare not lie. An invitation to her office was an invitation to doom because usually one or more parents would be there and that was that.

No excuses were accepted for lack of homework, untidiness in any way, and any hint of defiance. She taught her lessons by rote, and waiting for the school bus after class, I could see some hapless boy (it was always a boy) writing something one hundred times on the chalk board, his sleeves rolled up, tie off, and looking utterly miserable. Not only did he have a punishment, he had also missed the bus, which meant that a parent had to come, which meant a butt-kicking, sometimes in front of Marcellina herself. Without an ounce of compassion, she would sit in her chair, behind her desk, as a kid got thrashed by dad for any number of – to me, anyway – minor offences.

An utter and complete tyrant, her face only melted at Mass, a ritual she clearly loved.

I once caught her looking at the elevated Host, her face soft and warm. I could imagine her as a girl, a young postulant, waiting for God, believing in her vocation. Then she was pretty, beautiful even.

When Mass was over, she would stand at the church door,

her hands folded in her sleeves in that nun-like gesture of submission and modesty that I rather liked, and wait for us to leave.

Then she would swirl around in her shiny black brogues and genuflect as gracefully as a dancer. I suppose, if I really think about it, she was magnificent.

Sister Carmela was my teacher.

She was tall, too, but built like a tank. Her robes swirled around her like a river, and those robes were always flowing as she moved up and down the aisles like an Exocet, checking to see if we were working properly. The boys, of course, were always the focus of her ire, and we'd jump out of our concentration when she'd violently slap the back of some poor guy's head, probably for staring into space.

Every day after playground, we'd return to find some boy bent over a chair at the front of the classroom, getting the dust beaten off his corduroy uniform trousers by Carmela's yardstick.

There were times when I honestly wondered what boys had done to make her so angry, but I had enough to keep myself on the straight and narrow.

She called us 'borderline Negroes', a reference to a kind of split personality that, I assume, she perceived in her native Baltimore. 'Borderline' for the Mason–Dixon Line.

No doubt about it. Our nuns were black women and we were black kids. They loved us, no doubt about it.

Therefore they brooked no interference from us. None whatsoever. Our parents approved 110 per cent.

I changed into a quiet girl, with an inner life that burned with such ferocity that I had no words to express it.

ELEVEN

I must have been about eleven or twelve when I saw Mamma and Dad in an embrace.

I had never seen this before, and rarely saw it again.

It was one of those moments that you catch out of the corner of your eye. You blink. It's over.

But in that moment, maybe a fleeting second, it all came together. My ordering. My system.

It is a system compromising music and images. Not politics or categories. Music.

In that summer of my parents' embrace – a rare thing because they maintained a parental propriety in front of their children at all times – the airwaves were filled with a standard called 'There Is No Greater Love'.

It must have been 1960 or perhaps 1961.

And when that brief embrace was over and Mamma and Dad stepped back from one another, smiling at each other, I heard it.

Their own 'There Is No Greater Love'.

First, Mamma's version.

It was Dinah Washington's two-minutes-and-seventeen seconds' masterpiece from the 1954 album simply entitled: *Dinah Jams*.

It is ambitious, confident, ground-breaking and recorded in front of a live audience. Dinah had some of the gods of jazz playing with her: Max Roach, Clifford Brown, Harold Land, Richie Powell, Maynard Ferguson and Clark Terry.

No wonder she was called 'the Queen', a title that also, by the way, appropriately describes Mamma.

Dinah takes the ballad and swings it in a matter-of-fact way, not caring who knows what she's got to say. Like Mamma, too.

On the album cover her face is right up to the mic, right up to it.

There are those purists who accuse 'the Queen' of selling out, of bad taste (she used strings!).

But her greatest offence was to be herself.

She simply, just plain REFUSED.

If the Queen wanted to sing country or blues or gospel or ballads and mix them all up into one, she did so.

'Ain't nobody's business if I do,' she sang.

Dinah used the term 'salty' a great deal to describe something almost indescribable: a manner, a kind of edgy defiance.

Her voice is high, like a siren going off, her diction is clipped and precise and underneath it all is the blues: Chicago blues; West Side blues.

Like my Mamma.

Dinah once said when asked about her politics: 'I am who I am and I know what I know. I'm a Democrat plain and simple, always have been. I'd never vote for a Republican because in my opinion they don't have what it takes to run any kind of private or public office. That's all.'

That's Mamma, too. Straight – no chaser.

And Dad.

Dad's version is the magnificent, jazz-changer that is Ahmad Jamal's 1958 *At the Pershing: But Not for Me*, recorded in Chicago in early January 1958, when I had just turned nine years old.

Dad played it over and over at home. It was the background music to his thinking.

It always offered something new, something fresh, something surprising.

The very definition of a classic.

'Ahmad Jamal,' in the words of the critic and musicologist Stanley Crouch, '…is a true innovator of the jazz tradition. His unique musical style … resulted in a unique and new sound … Through the use of space and changes of rhythm and tempo Jamal invented a group sound that had all the surprise and dynamic variation of an imaginatively ordered big band. Jamal explored the textures of riffs, timbres and phrases rather than the quantity or speed of notes…'

Sparseness, precision. That was my Dad. Those words meant everything to him.

Ahmad Jamal said once: 'I … heard Ben Webster playing his heart out on a ballad. All of a sudden he stopped. I asked him, "Why did you stop, Ben?" He said, "I forgot the lyrics."'

Daddy was a word man, too.

And his name was 'Ben'.

After their embrace, my parents walked together to the backyard, not talking, just walking.

As they stood close together, I could hear in my mind Miles Davis's version of 'There Is No Greater Love', made with his first great quintet, which, as it happened, was recorded on my seventh birthday – 16 November 1955.

The album's title: simply *Miles*.

Welter-weight boxer-turned-pianist of genius and influence, Red Garland, is featured on it. His piano evokes a jazz club in the 1950s – a black jazz club. Garland's piano style is insouciant, seemingly effortless, in the manner of 'blues people': the people Langston Hughes loved, and Zora Neale Hurston loved, and culinary master and poet Vertmae Smart-Grosvenor, among others.

They dedicated their lives to setting down the talk and the beauty of folks like my parents, set down who they were in words and recordings.

They kept them alive in truth and purity and beauty.

Miles, the Master. His version of 'There Is No Greater Love' is slow, full of his muted trumpet.

Always that sound, that sound as if he were strolling on an urban street, looking through his mind's eye at the entire history of the African in the West with its melancholy, its longing, and the irony of it.

The Workin', Steamin' and the Cookin' of it.

The resistance to Fate of it.

The recording ends with Miles restating the theme.

And aiming for hope.

Because I was a black child growing up in a country whose foundations denied my existence, I couldn't come to know the unmediated world.

Or rather, I have come to know it late and it is a world ordered by music … by colour, a world in which words are the end of the process.

They are the emissaries to the world out there. But they cannot convey the sound of that world.

I remember through the senses – and above all sound and music, with its ability to conjure up particular landscapes, people, stories and feelings.

The stories continue to unfold in the realm of the senses.

And never end.

TWELVE

I devoured the nightly news, especially the CBS evening news broadcast with Walter Cronkite. He was known by the simple title 'The Most Trusted Man in America', and he was.

He had broadcast from London during the Blitz, and while that meant nothing to me and my generation of baby-boomers, it meant something to Daddy and Mamma so I paid attention to him and hung on his every word. As did the nation.

1960 was the first time that I paid attention to politics.

The first President I can recall was the rather cosy, grey and avuncular Dwight D. Eisenhower and his staid, pearl-wearing wife Mamie.

He was on television quite a bit in relation to the Civil Rights marches in the South, but I didn't know what that meant.

Daddy certainly talked back to him a lot if the president happened to be on TV at the weekends, when Daddy was at home with us for a full day and night. I finally looked him up.

I just couldn't imagine him as Supreme Allied Commander in the Second World War; that absolutely did not match the man I saw on screen. I did not understand the complex manoeuvres he was accomplishing in order to uphold the Constitution in relation to the civil rights of black people in the South.

It was Eisenhower who federalised the state troops – normally under the command of the governor of the state – and ordered them to escort black students to school.

It was Eisenhower who had warned the South that they were violating the law – its spirit and letter. It was Eisenhower, in his final address, who warned the American people about the growing alliance between big business and the military.

Richard Nixon had been his Vice President, and was as grey and as dull as Eisenhower and there was something else, something inside that only a child – unmediated by adulthood – can sense: something too-eager-to-please, something sweaty-upper-lip; there was something inside driving him that being President of the United States only started to address.

I didn't want him.

Running against him was a man who looked like Ken, Barbie's boyfriend.

I was on the cusp of outgrowing my paper dolls, outgrowing the daily cutting-out of clothes and putting them on my array of paper deities, then along came Jackie to fuel the addiction even more.

There was a little girls' book out about her: *Jacqueline, It Rhymes with Queen* – Jack and Jackie.

Mamma started doing her hair like Jackie's. That soft, floating helmet. How could Nixon and his wife Pat compete with that? Kennedy looked like a new day, he looked like he could talk to all the people, especially the young. He had a little girl called Caroline. In short, what was not to like?

Cronkite interviewed both candidates, but Kennedy looked so much more interesting, so much more vital, so much more about the future. We all saw the debates on TV, too, in which JFK stood out while Nixon looked like a man of shadows. A stone loser.

Our house was going with 'Kennedy! Kennedy! Kennedy!' as the chirpy campaign song said. He was very tied up with Chicago, too, but most people had no idea about the dark side of that – the possible Mob connections; corrupt union officials, 'buying' votes.

I found time to spread all of my paper dolls out in my tiny space in the corner. I shooed my sisters away and there, made my world. I had some Jackie Kennedy things that I added to my collection.

I projected myself into the world of these smart Park Avenue matrons, not knowing who they were or what they meant. I made up stories about their adventures – meeting royalty, taking trips, falling in love with their Dream Come True.

I would stay awake at night, after the kids had gone to sleep, and tiptoe downstairs to sit in the temporary quiet. Mamma would still be awake, working or trying to take a bit of rest before her day began all over again.

What would a new President mean? Would it mean that we would have more freedoms?

Could I go to the South someday, maybe even go to school and not have to worry about hostile crowds and vicious Alsatian dogs and water hoses turned on me?

On the back of one of Mamma's brown shopping bags, the ones that she saved and kept in a cabinet under the sink, I wrote a story about a little girl, like me, who one day wakes up and she is invisible.

No one in the street sees her; no one sees the colour of her skin. She could walk around, this girl, walk into shops and try on clothes and go to school without anyone paying any attention to her.

My world was black and, in a sense, hermetically sealed, but I knew that one day I would leave it.

Maybe Jack and Jackie would help me. Help my mother and father and my brothers and sisters and aunts and uncles and our whole little black-aspirational street.

When JFK was elected, we all jumped up and down.

I can still see him, still hear him say, brimming with confidence: 'So now my wife and I prepare for a new administration and a new baby.'

'O tempora! O mores!'

THIRTEEN

Since we grew up in the shadow of the Bomb, another threat from Russia – a place we were taught to see as Godless and evil – was nothing new for any of us.

When our nuns told us that there were missiles in Cuba and that we might be attacked, we prepared our usual 'duck and cover' and knew that nothing really was going to happen.

But I was having problems sleeping.

I lay awake listening to the train in the distance, wondering if it contained black people escaping from the South or their dead bodies. I tried to imagine what an atom-bomb attack would be like and oblivion.

I tried to keep my soul in a state of grace – the image being this great white circle that we were supposed to always keep good and pure and available for God. But what I couldn't understand and no one could explain to me was why God allowed this, why would he make the earth and everyone on it fight? It made no sense to me.

I tried to do my homework, tried to help around the house, but I found myself feeling more and more under the control of things that I could not stop.

I'm sure that I wasn't the only adolescent who felt that way, and not the only child, either.

I think that this has shaped us, made us who and what we are, my generation.

I think sometimes that we live in a half-world and although we are old now, there is still the sense of the uncertainty and tremulousness of life, that it can be cut short in an instant.

One night in late October, Sister Marcellina got on board our school bus, asked us to make the sign of the Cross and say a little prayer because we might not be coming back to school the next day.

Mamma was doing her usual things around the house, completely oblivious to it all. The music going on around me had a strange, discordant sound. I wanted to set it down but I was never taught to play an instrument. There was no money for lessons, so I hummed it to myself to get it out of my head. Ironed our uniform blouses and my brother's shirts, one ear on the television.

When I became an adult, I decided, I was going to stop all of this, stop the control and the madness. Be free. As soon as I could.

The Crisis passed but it seemed to me that no one apologised for it, no one came to us – the children – and apologised for the world that they were making.

I held this inside of me – a kind of anger – and I still have it. No permission is ever asked.

One afternoon the following year, at my high school – an all girls' school where there were hardly any black girls and I felt the fear that was growing inside of me become stronger – we were called out of lunch to assembly.

This was highly unusual.

The principal told us in a matter-of-fact way that the President had been shot.

We were told to go home.

I walked home in the rain. People were crying in the streets.

I was just fifteen years old and the world had come to an end.

I watched the funeral, asking myself the same question one of the black girls at school had whispered to me in the locker room: are we going back into slavery?

Daddy was silent and I knew that meant he was very upset.

Mamma was crying.

Our little cousin drummed the funeral march on our living-room table every time he came over until he was a teenager. I could hear it echoing over and over.

It was the drumbeat of my life. Until Dr King was murdered.

And then the drumming stopped.

But:

I think of Nabokov, the Nabokov of *Speak Memory*.

The supreme synaesthete, the master of this parallel life of sound and colour, moving through the world as something on the outside. But on the inside, the place where no one else touches and cannot control, where he was and where he lived, and from which he made his work. His 'sough and sigh of a thousand trees'.

He knew this. He honoured this that was him.

I have had to learn to honour that which was mine.

PART TWO

SONGBOOK

1964–1978

Girlhood is a state of being formed, not in its own time, but in the future. Years after it has ended. Girlhood is unknown when you actually are a girl. Then, you are simply in your life.

It is only when you look back, when you weave together, that 'girlhood', as young womanhood, comes into being, shapes itself.

It comes back to me in song, in music.

A kind of soundtrack in the movie-dark of remembrance.

THE GLORY RIVER

ONE

There are some singers – from a synaesthetic point of view – who sound like the cities they come from – and/or sing about.

Charles Aznavour sounds like Paris.

You can imagine its grey skies the *gris* of them mixed with blue in the low sky, and the rooftops. Tony Bennett is San Francisco, not just the picture postcard of it, but the view of the Pacific from the Golden Gate at a particular time in the morning when it seems that nothing has ever touched this particular ocean, and it is possible to see its tranquillity and calm and eternity.

When I first heard Laura Nyro sing, accidentally in one of the many places I crashed as a student, I saw New York City.

I could see it in Henry James, too, and sense it in everything that Baldwin wrote; he, who had that knack, that gift – like Hemingway – of always not writing about what he was actually writing about (in Hemingway's case, the War, always the War). Baldwin was always fleeing New York, always looking for that boat down at the Battery or on the West Side that would carry him away, that would give him that glimpse of New York that he yearned for – the skyline in retreat from him as he sailed away from the shore.

Nyro's New York was love and awe and her own attempts

to make it beautiful, weave it into the mind of the listener to her music. Which she accomplished with me. I was to discover how she was able to do that only very recently.

But what I did know when I first heard her voice was that I knew her and I believed that she knew me. If only I could find her.

The search for The Person/The Place/He/She who Understands Me. A coda in my life.

Unlike my sister, Lelia, who I think always knew.

As far as I could tell, Lelia always had a great time. While I agonised over finding my 'True Love' and thought I saw him in every man I met, Lelia dated and flirted, and men adored her. She found her True Love in her early twenties and has been married to him now for over forty years.

She was named after Dad's mother, Lelia, and she gave Mamma's mother's name to her own first child, Kelly Nora.

In a photo of me on Mamma's hip, like a South Side of Chicago *Madonna and Child*, it is possible to see Mamma's gently rounded belly and me looking pretty annoyed. I think I knew that a usurper was on the way.

As little girls we were dressed alike for a long time, and wore, on Sundays, the stiff white petticoats underneath our dresses that were the fashion in the mid-'50s, along with hats called boaters tied underneath our chins. Little anklets with lace tops on them and patent leather shoes that buttoned out at the instep, all matching, were what most people saw us in when we came out from behind the gate in Troy Street.

Regina was born just after I had turned four, and I was well on my way to being a little girl then, so it is Lelia who is my connection, the sister I really know. In a way.

Lelia saw Mamma as the happy Household Goddess, working away in the kitchen, full of pleasure and happiness. She recreated this to such an extent in her own home that her two daughters have become culinary stars on the Food Network.

This is what I saw: Mamma up at 4:30 a.m. to begin breakfast for us; combing hair; checking that we were all clean; making our lunches; then, while we were at school, washing clothes, cleaning house; waking up Dad for the night shift at the can factory, after having prepared a three-course lunch for him, making a packed dinner, and ironing his blue workshirt; then taking a break to pick at something to eat; next having milk and cookies for us when we came home from school; getting the evening meal ready; ironing and washing for the next day, and that's just for her husband and older kids. On top of all that she had two toddlers and a newborn in the house.

Of course, we were damned lucky that we had a father who worked himself night and day so that Mamma could go to these consumer emporiums to feed us. But it bored me rigid and it bored her, too. I knew it and she knew that I knew it.

But for Lelia, it was the Magical World of Mamma. And she became, when it was her turn, very good at it.

As for me, being the eldest girl in a traditional family, I became Mamma's helper at about seven.

I saw Motherhood, red in tooth and claw, at an early age. I saw no romance about babies. Then, with babies, there were no discussions, no books.

Sometimes I expressed this opinion out loud. Needless to say it was not appreciated.

What Mamma gave me, instead of the beauty of it all, was the image of an exhausted 1950s housewife, the upholder of the American Home –'Why the Boys Went to War'.

I swear she looked at me one day and said: 'Don't. Ever. Do. This.'

And I never did.

TWO

There were devils. Everyday devils that I was taught to fight. Devils that were me.

I remember as a teen looking at the rather twee film version of *The Diary of Anne Frank* because, like every young girl then, I was interested in this girl who became Hitler's most well-known single victim.

There is a moment when the voice-over of Anne says something like, 'And then something happened to her,' and the 20th Century Fox orchestra becomes suddenly flowery and arching and longing as the actor who plays Anne gazes up at the clouds.

Clearly that 'something' was her period.

Every girl knew THAT.

I first began to menstruate between eight and nine. This, I think, created an artificial shyness and reclusiveness. Mamma hid me. Because she wanted to hide IT – the normal response of a proper 1950s mother, maybe even now. I was a gregarious, loud, curious child.

But after my period began, I was shut down. I don't think I've ever fully recovered from it.

This was the child I was before: I was walking and talking and telling everyone the state of the world. Aunt Bernice would help Mamma out by taking me to the shops with her. I was, after all, the eldest child of her dear brother.

Once she took me on a bus – I was between three and four – and a man complimented her on her 'little girl'. Aunt Bernice tells it like it is, so she said that I wasn't her little girl. I looked a lot like my father then and therefore a great deal like her, so the man – I suppose he thought that she was hiding me – rolled his eyes in a kind of 'yeah, sure' gesture. Aunt Bernice says that I set him straight, some little pipsqueak with a big mouth dressed in a baby bonnet. The man was taken aback not only by my voice, but how deep it was. I used to be mistaken for a little boy on the telephone, so I had to set that straight, too. That caller never rang again.

I didn't like my Aunt Bernice's husband, Uncle Joe. I was jealous of the time that he spent with her, I suppose, and anyway, little girls don't like grown men in general.

I was once sitting in their apartment, a florid affair that might have been put together by Rachmaninoff if he'd been an interior designer: lots of deep red and big picture lamps put in the front window – a tradition that implied wealth and civilisation not only to neighbours but passers-by, and lots of noisy plastic on everything to thwart us Greer kids and keep their world tidy.

I turned around abruptly from switching on their massive TV to catch my aunt and uncle cuddling. I was outraged by his usurpation of my auntie, his audacity to do it around me. I glowered at him, I am told. He quickly unwrapped his wife and sat apart from her with a cheesy grin on his face.

I turned back to the soap that was revealing itself onscreen. BUT – I saw them out of the corner of my eye. They were at it again.

My auntie loves telling this story. I quickly turned around to face my uncle, my little hands behind my back. I walked up to him with a smile on my face. Then I pulled my hands out, covered in saliva, and rubbed them in his face. I did it to see what would happen. That's all. I was the embodiment of Emily Dickinson's, 'Not knowing when the dawn will come I open every door...'

At the age of nine, as I lay on the table at the office of Dr Kaplan, our paediatrician, I overheard him say to Mamma, 'Does she know what's going to happen?'

That night Mamma took me to the bathroom, locked the door, pulled out a box of Kotex, explained what was going to occur, showed me the little porcelain bowl where I would wash my underwear and then hid it away.

My bleeding had to be kept secret from my siblings, especially my father and brothers.

I couldn't run or play any more. Mamma told me to be careful. I was afraid to stand up because it seemed to me that I was nothing but blood and secrets.

I told my dolls and I told my saints, but what could they do about it?

My breasts were developing, too, and they were sore, so I was afraid to play because I could get hit in the chest.

I carried my extra sanitary pad in a bag with my books, but I could never actually take care of myself properly. I was at that age when some girls were bleeding and some were not, and you certainly weren't meant to let anyone know. I looked in the eyes of the handful of other girls who hung around the corners of the playground – were they bleeding, too? I could only pray that I didn't embarrass myself when I stood up to recite.

The fear of blood – my blood – made me very tense. I started developing headaches and biting my nails even more.

I couldn't talk to anyone about it, and I was also frightened. Mamma told me that I had to be 'careful' now, and that I definitely had to stay away from boys.

I didn't actually like boys, so that wasn't a problem, but what if they liked me? What if they came to get me, snatched me into some kind of alley and made me do the things that I had heard the girls do when I lay awake listening in my bedroom on the West Side?

These fears, together with the perception – from the nightly news – that we lived in a dangerous and turbulent world, worsened both my eczema and nail-biting.

So I prayed harder at Mass, imagining the Paradise that awaited me if I stayed good, didn't allow anyone to see the blood; then I could be sure in the belief that the world I sought was truly *saecula saeculorum* – 'world without end'.

But sometimes I had accidents at school and there would be menstrual blood on my uniform. I had to stand and recite and I knew that my classmates were talking about me and that the nun was embarrassed for me.

I was starting to smell, so I used deodorant under my arms like Mamma showed me – to keep the odour away. I was allergic to it and scratched all of the time.

I bit my nails to the quick from the sheer tension of trying to contain the explosion that was my young womanhood at such an age.

Mamma, I know, was frightened, too.

I had breasts and little girls like me were snatched into the alleyways that snaked through the neighbourhood and raped. I could hear it happening at night outside my window. I knew.

So Mamma hid me as best she could, and in time, I took over from her and hid myself.

Like most little girls, I was naturally modest. But my own natural inclination, my own modesty, was irrelevant in the face of one overwhelming fact: I was a black girl growing up in a country in which my black female body was a commodity, a breeding ground, a site of relief and release, a playground, anything and everything but my own. My mother and other black mothers hid their daughters away, strapped them down before they went out in public, kept them small and modest and quiet and invisible.

I had no idea to what lengths Mamma and other black mothers went to keep us – their daughters – safe. And I have been grateful all of my life.

I was brought up to be 'proper' for my own sake.

To keep me alive.

At around this time, I realised that I had a slight curve in my lower back: scoliosis (I only discovered the name for it a few years ago). I wore glasses because I had one eye far-sighted and one near-sighted.

It seemed that my body was ganging up on me.

And every war needs armoury.

Besides the 'training bra' for my rapidly growing breasts, my little behind was put into a girdle at thirteen. Because that's what you did.

'Proper kit'.

The girdle was also essential so that you wouldn't wiggle when you walked, which, as young girls, we were told was a provocation. There was no further explanation, but as a Catholic girl, I was taught that the female body was and is always an occasion for sin.

My life was spent, from little girlhood to mid-adolescence, in a navy-blue serge skirt, pleated and shiny from over-ironing; a white blouse cut like a man's shirt, whose collar (I only had two, which I rotated) I scrubbed obsessively to clean away the dirt line from my neck and hair, something I can't stand to see to this day. Me: matching jacket, white socks, plain shoes.

I suppose that the uniform was meant to smash the individuality and femininity – the real Devil – that we were meant to suppress.

But at home we had our dollies: my blonde, brown-haired, blue-eyed dolls, and the one black one that Dad insisted we have. The Alien Doll.

And Barbie.

Barbie was the type of woman that I – that all of us – was meant to be.

This type of woman was exemplified in her tiny body, the little 'stories' that illustrated each outfit that Barbie wore. They quite simply said, 'Little girl, this is what you are supposed to be': 'Barbie wears a new red swimsuit with red open-toed shoes and simple pearl earrings …' Barbie on a summer night in her 'Movie Date' dress: crisp blue and white- striped cotton with a white organza overlay … the overlaid gathered skirt, fitted sun top plus matching bow and simple white open-toed shoes … 'Garden Party': a pink rosebud and polka dot-sprinkled white cotton summer dress with white broderie anglaise-layered front detail, topped with a pink satin bow at the waist…with white tricot gloves and white open-toed shoes … Sorority Meeting outfit: 'a lovely crisp cotton' dress topped with a knitted wool jerkin edged with cream wool blanket stitching, brown open-toed shoes … and not to forget Barbie's own underwear: 'pleated tricot panties, bra, slip, matching girdle in her hand, open-toed shoes with pompoms on the front, and a hand-held mirror…'

All of this … and then the weekly ritual of pain.

I told my husband shortly after we married that he was about to enter one of the most arcane, elaborate and emotionally fraught spheres: the deeply psychological world of black women's hair.

It was (and in some instances is still) like this: every black household smelled like fried hair and some sort of pomade as mothers up and down the land took the hot iron to straighten out their daughters' hair, usually in time for Sunday service or Mass.

Mamma stood at the stove, heated the hot comb and did my hair, and, because she was so busy all of the time, burned me sometimes.

I didn't have the lovely hair that Lelia had, or the fine, blondish fuzz that my little sister Gina had inherited from Mamma, and which had given Gina the nickname 'Chicken Little'.

My hair was thick, coarse, nappy, shortish and needed to be 'tamed'.

Like every little black girl with hair like mine, I had my battle scars on the scalp, or somewhere on the head.

Later, when I was older, I was sent to the hairdresser's – that true palace of black female pain and redemption – where the real torture began.

I was sent there for what was called a 'permanent', i.e., for my hair to be 'permanently' straightened – until it grew out and back to its natural state, to be conquered once more.

I can still feel the pain of it all, something that both men and women endured. Look at the photos of early soul and blues singers and musicians.

The ritual of pain consisted of, first, the chemical that straightened the hair, which was lavishly dolloped on. Its base was lye, so the scalp was thrown instantly into pain.

You learned to endure it.

Then, after the chemical was applied, you had to sit and wait for it to do its job.

Which was to make your hair straight as an arrow.

Years later, the process became much more gentle, much more refined, but this new way hadn't come by the time – at about twenty – that I decided never to straighten my hair again. (One of the first black millionaires, Madame Walker, made her fortune on hair-straightening products.)

After a certain amount of time, the hair is rinsed and washed – small bits of the scalp having been eaten away– and then the real work can begin: the battle to make the hair bounce and shine and blow in the wind!

I knew, even when I was a kid, that none of this made sense. How could anything that hurt so much be sensible?

But the other option couldn't be imagined on my street.

In a recent survey, it was found that a demographic of black working-class women born in the 1980s and 1990s tended to be shorter than their mothers born in the 1960s.

The next generation is usually bigger, stronger, as nutrition is improved, living conditions are better. But not lately. Somehow and for some reason, things seem to be going in reverse for poor and working-class black people.

In the richest nation in the world.

I think about the devils, all of the devils.

They are still there.

Even now.

THREE

It took me until I was almost twenty-one to realise that I was culturally deprived.

More than once, I had been at a Civil Rights march, or an anti-war demo, on an anti-poverty drive, and I didn't properly know ONE GOSPEL SONG!

I once stood next to a Harvard professor whose ancestors had come over on the *Mayflower*. He knew and sang robustly the words to 'Follow the Drinkin' Gourd'.

'Precious Lord'? I could only mouth the words, sometimes getting caught out if I was suddenly asked to sing a verse. I couldn't. I knew nothing.

People would quote from the Bible in the midst of a rabble-rousing speech against war, and I could only nod.

Because I had never read the Bible. I'd read bits of it, as required, but I hadn't – and still haven't – actually read it through.

Because I was raised Roman Catholic.

The priests read the Bible for you. And explained what it meant, too.

Our parents decided very early on to send me, Lelia and our little brother Benny to Catholic school. This was because the local state school, in the notorious Lawndale area on the

West Side of Chicago, was no place that we should be.

The local school, Lawson, was a potential gang centre and it was bad enough having to worry about muggings in the street without fearing them at school, too.

So, somehow, Daddy found the money for our tuition, our uniforms, our books, and food for our lunches, complete with Mickey Mouse Club metal lunch-boxes. Like everyone else.

I was set back a year because the school felt that, since I had started out in state school – called 'public school' in the States – my education had by definition been inadequate. No one tested my reading, my writing, my verbal ability. I had been reading – adult books – since I was four.

It was a great blow to have to stay back, and to re-read the children's books I had always found boring and never finished because I had found the first one given to me intrusive. Those kiddie tomes were too didactic and interfered with the world and the sound in my own mind. Adult books had bigger spaces, wider terrains.

'See Spot run. Go Spot, Go…' Well, it just wasn't quite up to the mark.

I had no one to talk to about this, no one that I could explain my point of view to. I had to sit there and watch and listen to people who had power over me, decide my fate and my destination. When I joined Lelia in class (she was in her correct year), I was crying with rage inside. The Church came in the nick of time. It gave me somewhere to pour my heart out. To receive solace in a topsy-turvy, dominating world.

Since Catholic school is designed to educate children in the Catholic ethos (I see Christianity as the faith, various branches and practices of it as a kind of ethos), it was cheaper to go there if you were baptised. Besides, all of the girls in class were preparing for their First Holy Communion, complete with white dresses, white petticoats, white shoes and frilly white socks, a white rosary and a white missal, all topped by a beautiful white veil. A tiny wedding dress, in other words. I wasn't going to miss out on that!

Besides, the Catholic Church suited me.

I loved High Mass, the tall candles, the robes, the incense, the organ, the Irish tenor up in the choir loft who sang Bach and Beethoven and Mozart and Gregorian chants. The Church gave me my first listen of European classical music.

Our parish church, St Agatha's, had been built by Italian immigrants. It was opulent, rococo, full of bleeding and weeping statues; an ornate Madonna; Christ pierced through and through; icons trimmed in gold; side altars jammed with various saints with mountains of candles burning night and night and day. There was a long, winding aisle leading to an altar that only God could have created: huge, marble-encrusted, banked with flowers, and when the priest turned to show the monstrance at High Mass, it shot out gold rays from the light of the candle and the ornate lamps swinging from the ceiling.

I do not know how that church, or the rectory or any place else connected with it, did not get robbed on a daily basis. Everywhere else in the neighbourhood did. But not the church. At least not in the late 1950s.

This was so much better than the Baptist churches, which were storefronts – full of great food … but their services were all day. You had to listen to a preacher 'get happy'; people fainting; masses of Good Shepherd hand fans waving; and above all it lasted for hours. And hours. Whereas at Mass, one hour: done.

It must have taken a great deal for Mamma and Dad to leave that culture, their expression of faith, to get baptised for the sake of our tuition fees. Although Dad was buried in the Church and Mamma wants to be, I think it's because it's much less of a bother.

No day-long sermons.

In preparation for our First Holy Communion, we had to study and know by heart 'The Baltimore Catechism'.

This manual, based on a catechism devised by St Robert Bellarmine – the Jesuit who forced Galileo to recant, under pain of death at the stake, the fact that the earth revolved around the sun – was Americanised and was the standard from about 1885 to the late 1960s.

We were studying a work based on a man who had written to one heliocentrist:

> …the Council (of Trent) prohibits interpreting Scripture against the common consensus of the Holy Fathers; and if your Paternity wants to read not only the Holy Fathers, but also the modern commentaries on Genesis, the Psalms, Ecclesiastes and Joshua, you will find all agreeing in the literal interpretation that the sun is in heaven and turns around the earth with great speed, and that the earth is very far from heaven and sits motionless in the centre of the world.

This was the man whose manual our manual was based on. And we had to know it by heart.

The first two questions a Catholic child was taught then were:

'Who made you?'

Answer: 'God made me.'

'Why did God make you?'

Answer: 'God made me to show forth his goodness and to be with Him in heaven.'

If you couldn't recite and answer key questions – by rote

– there was no baptism for you.

But I had two problems with this. If God is perfect how could He make some people less than perfect, like black people who were being hurt in the South, and Jews, who we prayed for every Sunday after Mass 'because they had not yet come to accept that the Messiah had come'; and, above all, why did God make women and then not let them be priests, or be Pope?

My second problem was: if God was showing forth His goodness, why was there suffering? Why was I scared at night by the sounds from the gangs outside my window? Why did everybody make us scared of the Russians and the Bomb? Why did the Bomb exist, if God was good?

When I raised my hand and asked these things in class, I was told, at first with compassion, and as time went on and I persisted, with growing irritation: 'Bonnie, it's a mystery!'

Not good enough. In confession, I told Father that if God didn't want me to figure all this out, He wouldn't have given me this mind, right? For instance, the Blessed Trinity, one-God-in-three: easy. The same God in different states – like water: in one it can be solid; another vapour; another liquid. It was still water, wasn't it?

I soon realised that to persist got me nowhere. I must have been insufferable and I must have felt that, too, because gradually I stopped asking and began to ACCEPT.

Besides, I didn't want anything to jeopardise my chance to wear that dress and walk down that aisle. But also, the truth is that I did believe.

My baptismal certificate listing Mom and Dad, two sponsors (the Dixons) and signed by the new young parish priest – a year younger than Mamma and who remains our family priest over half a century later – is dated 'October 19th, 1958'. I suspect the whole family was baptised that day. He came to bless our house when we moved, and buried Dad thirty-eight years later.

He's one of the few white men Dad had any time for.

I can see the photo of me at First Communion, gazing up at the ceiling of the church, trying to penetrate it with my prayers, a little black girl in a miniature wedding dress in a dangerous world, just BELIEVING.

Believing that I could keep my soul white and not spotted and certainly not BLACK (a state of grace made the soul – always drawn round like a disc – white as snow). The spotted disc was purgatory, where you went after death to get cleaned up before going to heaven.

And a coloured-in, black (as night) soul ... well, in the immortal words of the Munchkins as they sang 'Ding! Dong! The Witch is Dead' to Dorothy in *The Wizard of Oz*, the perennial Easter movie that every American kid in the late 1950s flocked around the ubiquitous TV to watch – with a black soul you'd go 'down where the goblins go: below, below, below!'

In brief, a black soul got you below, and that couldn't be tolerated, so I tried my best in word, thought and deed to keep my soul white. Or at least more white than black.

And then there was the fire. Shortly after my tenth birthday, a fire broke out in an old wooden school, Our Lady of the Angels. Ninety-two children and three nuns died. The nuns were the same Order as the nuns who taught us. Some of them cried in the corridor as the news came through, just before we were set to go home for the day.

Chicago pioneered the concept of 'Eyewitness News', news on the spot, news that moved with events, something common today.

Then it was unusual because most news was read from a desk in a studio in a very stately manner. The news of the fire was told minute by minute and we could see, at home, the children being carried downstairs on the backs of the shocked firemen; the screaming moms and dads being held back from the building that had gone up like a tinder box; the Mayor, his face contorted in grief; Mamma holding all of us close as she cried along with all of the adults onscreen.

The funeral Mass was white, which meant that the Church had decided that these little children had gone to heaven. It was beautiful.

A year later, one of our classmates was hit by a car and killed. He was laid out in his Holy Communion suit, his face exactly the same as it had been in life, his hands around a rosary.

And as was the custom, we filed one by one past his open coffin, to gaze on the face of a saint. Because he had a white funeral, too.

Then would there be a statue for him? Because the only black saint in Church was Martin de Porres. His warm, chocolate-coloured face in a benign smile, he looked down on us from his perch in the sacristy as if to say: 'Be good little black boys and girls, and you, too, will be up here!'

'But only one black person is in heaven?' I asked Dad. He didn't reply. Guess it was a mystery.

I loved my holy cards, and my saints; the ritual, and the music. Above all, the music.

I first heard Mozart's Requiem at a Mass. And when, years later, I stood in St Peter's Square, looking at Michelangelo's saints, like gossiping, judging denizens of some Roman salon instead of sacred entities, I loved the heart-held, sensuous, direct nature of Holy Mother Church.

But one day, later on, after I'd moved to New York, I walked into an early morning Mass on the feast of the Holy Name of Mary.

There was a sprinkling of women there, heads bowed, praying. I joined them.

The young priest walked up to the pulpit to give the sermon.

It was about how Mary had come to overcome the Snake that was the Devil, and to vanquish Eve, the inherent evil in women.

I don't think that his words came out quite right, and that he meant what he was saying. But as I looked around at the handful of congregants, mostly women, mostly older women, women who maintained the church itself, kept it clean, etc., I got very angry.

In the middle of his sermon, I stood up and walked out.

I've gone back to Mass since, but now not any more.

I respect the Church and the good people in it, and the good of Christianity.

But I no longer believe in God, so it's hypocritical for me to be there.

I'm not someone who thinks that atheists are grown-ups and deists are children or mentally and emotionally and intellectually deficient.

Atheists who believe that – who promulgate that – forget a very important thing about human nature: we are transcendent creatures. We look UP. We believe. It is crucial for us, and is one of the definers of our humanity.

To laugh at this is not to understand at all how people function. How we stay alive, and co-operate and hope.

I suspect that if I'm wrong about all of this, and there is a God waiting to judge me, he'll know how he made me and will get it. And I'll take my medicine.

But at ten years old, I actually had two gods, like every little American girl: the other one's name was Shirley Temple.

FOUR

I told our priest that I wanted to be an altar boy, then a priest and finally Pope.

He replied that girls couldn't be altar boys, nor priests, nor popes.

When I asked why, he said: 'Because there were no women at the Last Supper.'

That didn't seem to me to be – even if it could be verified – a good enough answer. I thought: 'I'm a child. You should help me explore.'

But, of course, I kept this to myself.

Instead I transferred my need to worship and adore – like millions of other little American girls (and not a few boys) – to 'Curly Top': Shirley Temple.

In the mid to late 1950s, when it was understood that TV was creating a new demographic, that we children of the Baby Boomer Generation could actually influence our parents' wallets – plus what they saw on the Big Black Box that had become the new family fireside, therefore bringing in those advertising dollars for TV channels – networks raced through film catalogues to find kiddie stars from yesteryear.

And there was never, and there never has been, a bigger child star than Shirley Temple.

It is impossible to state her ubiquity, her total impact on every aspect of the life of a little girl growing up in the USA.

She was the flipside of a terror we lived under – so everyday to us that we really didn't notice it – but nonetheless a terror that haunted our dreams at night: Total Annihilation.

There was a bad country out there called Russia and this bad country wanted to kill us. The way that they would kill us was by dropping a huge nuclear bomb on us, obliterating everything in a second.

We would not have time to do anything about it, and hopefully our mighty Air Force, under the cover called SAC (Strategic Air Command), would take revenge.

The stories I was reading in Dad's *Reader's Digest* – 'On the Beach', for example, about Australia being the last refuge on earth before everyone died of nuclear fallout – terrified me.

But at night, after I did my homework, there was Shirley – first, a cute little blonde who could dance anyone off the screen; and then grown-up Shirley, the same age as Mamma, her blonde curls now black, who presented a programme called *Shirley Temple's Storybook*.

The grown-up Shirley would appear at the beginning, the same twinkly expression, the same smiling eyes, extending her arms to all of us as she sang in a soothing voice:

> Come away, little man.
> Dream as long as you can.
> May all your dreams come true.
> Dreams are made for children.
> And for children all dreams really do come true.

Her recent death would have affected any woman old enough to own and adore a Shirley Temple doll. My sister and I each had one, a little goddess that we dressed and undressed, bathed, talked to, and listened to, too.

When I drew self-portraits in school, they were always of Shirley. No one said anything, nor pointed out that this wasn't what I looked like. But Shirley was what I looked like inside. Maybe they thought that I would outgrow her, outgrow my obsession. But it was also because Shirley danced, she danced down stairs, up the street, down the aisles of planes, and I longed to dance. In addition to the music in my head, I was dancing there.

But Mamma only ever took me to one ballet class at the community centre near us – and never took me back. She was afraid of my crossing the great boulevard that divided us from the centre, and also, she was afraid of the gangs. She loved to dance, too, and was always a great dancer – she met Dad while out dancing and I was told that her mother met her father while out dancing – but our area was too dangerous.

In our first home on the West Side we were not allowed beyond our gate – except to go to school and to the store once in a while – so I would gather together the neighbourhood children and tell them stories about a world beyond the stars.

They would sit on the steps and listen to me improvise a civilisation that we all longed to see: 'Candyland'. I called it that, no doubt inspired by Shirley.

I knew that little girls like me were integrating schools, being escorted by policemen and federal troops through howling mobs, some filled with little white kids no older than I was.

Dad – a Mississippian born and raised in the bad old days of segregation – would sit us kids in front of the TV to watch the evening news. He wanted us to know what the South was, what being 'Negro' was about, what we might have to face in the fullness of time.

But even as I watched this, in my head was Shirley Temple, dressed like a fairy queen, her twinkly wand, her delicate dress, her whispering voice ringing in the smoky ether, beckoning us to forget the 'crackers' down South – as Daddy would call the white people.

Forget them and 'come away'.

I knew why Dad hated the South. I could hear it and see it.

For example, Governor Orville Faubus, the governor of Arkansas and arch-segregationist, conjured up in my mind's eye flames and coal being shovelled in to feed them. Faubus, voted one of the 'Ten Men in the World Most Admired by Americans' in 1958, was literally the Devil to me.

The mayhem and rancour, the sheer cruelty of grown people trying to stop little kids from going to school, all of it could be ameliorated by my beloved Shirley singing in the way that I imagined a piece of gossamer sang:

> You're a queen, you're a king
> When your heart's young as spring
> Oh how bright the world can seem!
> Dreams are made for children
> And we're children as long as we can dream!

It was Shirley Temple's world that interested me, just as my Shirley Temple doll did, not the black baby doll our father had bought us. Shirley opened up a pathway into another world. The black baby doll – as cute as she was – didn't allow me to dream.

I felt a deep compassion for the little girl on TV who looked like me and who was trying to integrate a school.

I knew, too, even at a very young age, that I'd have to find not just an empathy with her as a suffering human being subjected to a gross injustice. But that I would have to find a sympathy with her, too. I would have to 'be' her.

She, in time, would become a 'me' – one of the 'me's that I would have to cultivate in order to survive. I already knew that, thanks to Dad.

I learned, in a sense, about being a black girl from Shirley. I learned what wasn't open to me, what wasn't available to me. She was a more reliable, more precise guide to who I was in the land of my birth than anyone.

I held my little curly-haired blonde dolly to my face with its relentless porcelain smile and dimples. She had replaced my other blonde dolly, the one that I had at three and had to throw away because my little baby brother Benny ate her hair.

I didn't care that Shirley had white skin or blonde hair. It was that Shirley and dozens of Shirleys were all around me – were free.

Then, soon after my eighth birthday – a magical year in which I began to see that there were two sides to everything and everyone, that there might be a kind shadow that ran along what was clear and open and visible – CBS premiered *Eloise* with a young blonde actress, too: Evelyn Rudie.

Eloise was a little blonde, but she was a tearaway.

She lived at the Waldorf Hotel in New York, the poshest hotel in Manhattan in the 1950s.

Years later I read somewhere that *Eloise* was loosely based on the life of Liza Minnelli, who lived at the Waldorf at the time with her mother, Judy Garland.

Eloise was the opposite of Shirley, a girl who set out to right the world, all from the vantage point of a ten-year-old. She knew everybody and, above all, everyone allowed her to talk, to speak, to be. I became obsessed with her, too.

I read in the morning paper one day that the actress Evelyn Rudie had travelled to the White House to try and meet the First Lady, Mamie Eisenhower. She wanted her help in getting another acting job because *Eloise* would never have a long life.

I think it was because she was a little girl who spoke her mind and was outspoken with it. Not very Barbie Doll.

Whenever she told an adult that they were wrong, or that they were playing her because she was a little kid and therefore incompetent, she'd tell them off. The nuns at school used her as a cautionary tale. I loved her.

I'd lie on the floor at home and draw myself as a princess, blonde ringlets and all. I would put myself inside of Mamma's beautiful women's magazines.

These slender, tall, small-nosed, white-skinned women with their serene smiles and perfect houses, kids and husbands, seemed to me the essence of life.

All presided over by Shirley's twinkly wand and gossamer dress.

My Depression-era mother, poorest of the poor because of the colour of her skin, made our lives as perfect as she could. My sister and I had the toy stove; the recipes to cook miniature dishes on it; the baking pans and the aprons; the cooking glove; the pots and the pans and the dishes.

Mamma must have imagined giving these toys, this preparation, to her own daughters when she lived in a tiny bedsit during the war, sending money from her job at the parachute factory to Grandma, and dreaming of someday being able to be at home, over a stove, cooking in peace and quiet and stability.

This is the difference, I learnt later, between being a feminist and what Alice Walker called a 'womanist'. For some women, staying at home, being with their children, cooking, cleaning and sewing for them and not for anyone else's children, is the victory.

And giving your little girl any doll she wanted.

This, too, was a time of profound loneliness and isolation for me. I was quiet and obedient and reclusive on the outside. But inside I was searching and raging.

We moved to the South Side, to a house with a garden and a driveway and a garage.

There, I met my two best friends, the Snow White and Rose Red of my existence who, in their contrast, started me on my life.

FIVE

When I first saw them, Diane was walking down the street on our side and Felicia was across the street at her house, standing in the doorway. And there was a moment when an axis was created in my mind and they both moved through it, and their music emerged – something that always happens when someone or someplace is about to become significant.

I heard their music.

I knew that these two girls – even though I didn't know them, I didn't even know if they knew one another – were going to be my friends.

More than that.

Diane lived down the street from us. She was nine months younger than me and three months older than my sister, Lelia. She had a little brother about Benny's age, Freddie, who played piano and wore glasses like Benny did.

Felicia lived across the street. She was a few months younger than me. She had a sister Benny's age, Maria, and a brother, Curtis Jr, Gina's age.

Diane was medium height, brown-skinned, rather plain and wore glasses all of the time, unlike me who wore them part of the time. We both suffered from tension headaches.

She had eczema very badly, which she scratched to the point that it had discoloured the skin on the back of her hands. I had eczema, too, small patches on my neck that I clawed until my skin was dark, and we both bit our nails ferociously to the point that they would sometimes bleed. She was asthmatic, too, and used an inhaler.

Diane was an intellectual, inquisitive, and got excellent marks at school.

She was shy and her shoulders were raised slightly, which made her look perpetually anxious. She laughed a lot at stuff I didn't understand, but I could see what she was laughing at anyway, even if I didn't always get it.

She had no sisters, no one that she had to share her room with. Her home was identical to ours except that hers was quiet and peaceful in contrast to our continuous noise and bustle and drama.

Our joint imperfections, coupled with her beautiful mind; her quiet and steady demeanour with its hint of a person who looked at the stars in wonder; the precise way that she used words; the fact that she was an avid reader and we could discuss books: all of that endeared her to me totally and completely.

Plus she had big plans. She was going to leave the United States as soon as she graduated from college. Diane was going to live in The World.

I told her about my, by this time boring to me, plans to go to Iowa and enter the convent as soon as I turned eighteen. I thought she'd laugh like Mamma had. But she completely sympathised. She was going to Africa and to Paris.

She helped move me away from taking the veil. Her life sounded much more interesting.

Felicia was the exact opposite of us.

She was tall and slender with a magnificent body that

every man – young and old – noticed. She was built like an African Venus de Milo – if Venus de Milo had had big breasts, long legs and a round high butt.

Felicia had a completely natural hip-swaying walk that caused all of the cute boys, and some creepy old guys, too, to come out of the woodwork. I'd see them coming back to her house to talk, getting no further than the front porch and the screen door in the summer, and the peephole in the heavy house door in the winter.

Her mother chased all of those males away like so many roosters – and rats. Felicia didn't have an intellectual bone in her body, but she was curious and she had a sharp mind. It was just that school bored her.

She preferred the 'School of Life' and she always said what was on her mind. She was the one who told me one day, point-blank, that Mamma wasn't especially welcoming to her. I was shocked. I never saw that. But it turned out that Mamma didn't care for my girlfriends, or any women outside her immediate family in those days.

The intellect in Felicia's family belonged to her younger sister, Maria, another statuesque beauty. Maria got the grades. Their little brother, Larry Jr, and their father, Larry Sr, made up the family.

Diane and Felicia shared my taste for the music of Little Anthony and the Imperials and the voice of Dionne Warwick singing 'Anyone Who Had a Heart', all of it full of that teenage quest for Eternal Love.

We devoured *Ebony* magazine together, with its stories of black celebs and its annual 'Fashion Fair' fashion show and the pages and pages full of French haute couture – all on black models who looked like our mothers and aunts (glorified), and us, too, in our dreams.

We were too young to understand the significance, the

utter audacity, of a Chicago black woman going to the great Parisian fashion houses asking them to lend her their clothes.

We read *Photoplay* together in Felicia's backyard, gossiping and poring over the paparazzi shots of movie stars, especially those of Elizabeth Taylor and Richard Burton ('Liz and Dick') pursuing their love affair, the scandal of the age.

Felicia went on to marry a man named John, a friendly, quiet, but troubled giant who, in the end, she had to leave. She took their son with her, Johnnie, the love of her life.

Her sister, Maria, Diane and I all spoiled him. He was a happy, loving little boy.

I'm grateful that his life began that way.

Diane went to university and did not marry. And I went to university and did not marry for a very long time.

We three had the same tastes in music.

Anything by Marvin Gaye and Tammy Terrell was perfect. We danced in Felicia's basement to 'Ain't No Mountain High Enough' because the lyrics of that song were true. It was about us.

We cut each other's hair short like Twiggy, and our mothers screamed.

We bought Mary Quant eyelashes and dreamed we were in Carnaby Street, three black girls, for a moment, in another place.

And we loved Shirley Bassey. We loved the fact that she was black, the colour of people in our family, our mothers! We'd never seen or heard anything like her.

It was completely astonishing to us that a black woman could sing the word 'finger' and make it sound like 'fingah'. The amazing refinement of that. And yet there was something in Miss Bassey that no one could contain. And we knew it. Because it was in us, too, waiting to be free.

We talked about her as often as we could: What could her

life be like in 'Swinging London'? Was James Bond himself her man? What dragons did Shirley Bassey slay?

All of the black women we saw on television seemed somehow to be strapped down, laced up, straightened out, and Shirley was OUT THERE yelling the truth:

'His heart is cold! He loves only gold!'

One day, we made a plan: when we got to this demi-paradise, this London, she would be the first person we'd look up.

One thing was for sure: we'd do this together; we'd never part. Not ever.

Decades later I was in the same space as Dame Shirley.

We were part of a gathering come to see and celebrate the re-opening of a room in Windsor Castle after its restoration following a fire.

Dame Shirley was holding court by the buffet table while the Queen was swallowed up somewhere, who knows? Dame Shirley was the only monarch I saw that day.

I was alone.

But Diane and Felicia were with me in spirit, and I raised a glass to my friends.

We'd made it.

SIX

Children are conservative beings.

They don't like change, a breakdown in routine and order. Even if it's for the good, a child suffers in change.

From the time that we moved to the South Side and for several years after that, I was struggling.

I didn't know it, didn't understand it, but there was something wrong around me, and inside, too.

Mamma and Dad had a new baby in the summer of 1960 – their last – Penny, a lovely little girl. But with the new house and the new neighbourhood, getting adjusted to a new school and the strain I felt that Mamma and Daddy were under just to maintain this new life, I retreated further inside myself.

My nail-biting and headaches got worse.

Mamma tried to stop me from biting my nails by showing me all the lovely nail polish she had on her make-up shelf in the bathroom, but that didn't help me, even though I wanted to have pretty nails. I started taking aspirin tablets and developed an addiction to them, a mild one that I still have.

I lost myself in Dad's encyclopaedias, in the fiction published in *Reader's Digest* and in the women's stuff in Mom's magazines.

When I wasn't doing chores or helping with my little

brothers and sister, I would find a corner and write down what I had read from the work of others, trying to fashion it into my own voice.

I wrote a novel out in longhand on lined paper and sent it to Random House. To New York City. That's what all the tortured male writers with patches on their sleeves and adulterous wives did in the fiction I was reading in those *Reader's Digest* editions: Herman Wouk, for example. I got a note back from an editor who said that she liked it very much, but it had to be typed.

I like to think that the editor was Toni Morrison, but that's the fabulist in me.

I was in love not only with writing the novel, but with the pages, the piles of paper, the whole Hemingway/Faulkner thing of paper and a typewriter. And while Mamma put me off cigarettes – she never looked as if they were a pleasure, just a desperate respite (and I am eternally grateful for her being the reason that I've never touched a cigarette) – I loved all of the rest: the Writer. And he was always a man. At the time I didn't know that women wrote novels. Just poems or maybe songs and lullabies. But not big works, not epic chronicles of the human spirit.

The books I read and which formed me were always tales about men struggling to find their voices amidst the corporate greed and angst of America, men who held big promise but fell because of some flaw in their soul.

Their lives were a million miles from mine, but maybe that's why fiction exists, maybe that is why it's needed; and as I changed a baby, or fed a toddler, I'd have one of these books in my other hand, trying to imagine, trying to imagine.

Somehow, and I don't know how, I got hold of a copy of James Baldwin's *Another Country*. I read it under the covers by flashlight, and hid it during the day on a shelf behind a row of family photos.

I read *The Spy Who Came in from the Cold* over and over, its sheer bleakness an antidote to the James Bond films – which I loved like everyone else, but le Carré was different, and I knew, somewhere inside of myself, he was telling the truth.

There were Mafia trials on TV, and they competed with the Civil Rights movement as the news that occupied my head, took over my thoughts when I wasn't at school.

Chicago was a big gangster town and everyone knew it. One of my favourite programmes as a little kid at the end of the 1950s was *The Untouchables*, about a squad of special FBI agents who tracked down Capone. In fact we all played *The Untouchables* in the basement and the big garden we had outside our apartment in the brownstone on the West Side.

But now, in the 1960s, something evil was emerging. There was something called the 'Cosa Nostra' that really ran America, that was a part of all of us. The 'Cosa Nostra' were on Wall Street, not just in the street. Even 'the White Boy' – Dad's pejorative term for white people – was under the iron fist of 'Our Thing'. And they were Out There, too, and added to the sense of doom, of entrapment, that I was starting to feel.

It was the isosceles right triangle that saved me, that gave me life.

My fascination with the number three, which manifested itself in my interest in the Holy Trinity, found a home in the triangle. I loved them. I loved drawing them and imagining how they existed, what they comprised, how to create them: was there a formula for them. Where else did they exist in nature, in architecture?

I also intuited the Fibonacci sequence when, in a biology class, I noticed how rabbits procreated, their sequence: 1,1,2,3,5,8…

Triangles and this number sequence were like breathing fresh air (they still are) and I was desperate to learn about them because it was a place where I could simply be. Where I could roam and play.

But the nuns at my school told me gently that I was just to learn what was in my maths books – and that I'd better take up typing instead and pay attention in my Latin and Spanish classes.

So I made one of my typical shoot-myself-in-the-foot decisions: I learned neither Spanish nor to type properly. It was my rebellion.

And I put the triangles and the numbers away.

Until, one afternoon, four decades later, while working on my second novel, I watched a television programme about Andrew Wiles, the man who solved the great maths problem: the Riemann hypothesis concerning prime numbers.

I just had the programme on as background, and suddenly I looked up at the board that Andrew Wiles was working on. I realised that I knew what he was doing. I didn't know in the academic sense – I had had no training, no exposure – but I understood what he was looking for. I understood what he meant and felt when he said that this problem had been an obsession since he was twelve, and that he had married and had children, not only out of love, but because they gave him a life, kept his feet on the ground, kept him away from the board and the problem.

I understood when he cried as he accidentally found the solution in a pile of equations on his desk. I was crying, too, crying for his success, crying for my loss, for that little girl who had been stopped, and who knew it was happening at the time and could do nothing about it.

At this point in my life, there were no women visible to me, no black women visible to me who were doing what I wanted to do – whatever that was exactly – and I knew that it would take a great deal of courage and stamina to make myself into what I wanted to be without these examples, without these models.

I was determined to try.

I loved Mamma with all my heart, but I didn't want to be her.

She knew that, too. Because I told her once during one of our blazing rows.

That must have added to her stress, and her worry about me.

She couldn't see any other life for me or her daughters except something secure, with a husband. Because that's what she chose. And she was coming to a crisis point about that decision.

I knew it. I felt it.

It added to my turmoil.

I was taking sides.

Choosing Mamma was to be my first feminist act.

SEVEN

My sense of doom, of heaviness, added to what I felt and sensed in Mamma.

I can't imagine how we all lived in that small house.

It was the summer of '65, when I was sixteen and a half and about to leave my all-girls school for a mixed one.

Mamma was only thirty-eight that summer, Daddy just forty-one.

She was the principal carer of two teenage daughters, a teenage son, a daughter on the verge of adolescence, two little boys, and a little girl.

After she got through my, Lelia's and Ben's adolescence, she had to get through four more.

She was beginning to crack.

She was beginning to have that rebellion that Grace Metalious wrote about in *Peyton Place*, that perfect 1950s enclave, that perfect American environment that hid so much.

Mamma kept the house neat and clean and pristine.

She decorated the house in American Colonial, a homage in polished wood to George Washington, Valley Forge and Betsey Ross. It was probably the fashion of the time, and looked much better than the grander, more Napoleon III style of much of the rest of the street: big, dark furniture, heavy rugs, drapes with ornate hangings and heavy lamps, the grandest in the front window as a kind of display of wealth and class and opulence.

All of the houses on our street, all post-war housing, homes 'fit for heroes', homes for 'the boys', every one of them housing a dream – first a white one, then a black one, but the same dream – the American Dream, that poisoned chalice and Holy Grail at once.

I didn't help Mamma.

Her marriage was the same age as me – I was born six months after she and Dad married – so it was in its teens and turbulent.

She had to get out, go out with her girlfriends, have a drink and a conversation with adults because she was still a woman, still a person, not a mommy machine who washed and cooked and swept, and tended to everyone.

She didn't hate us, but she hated IT – her condition, her choice.

I started to feel that it was all my fault. If she had not become pregnant with me, then she would have been free.

I became obsessed with the films noirs being shown on TV – *Double Indemnity, Sorry, Wrong Number, The Killers, The Woman in the Window, The Lady from Shanghai, The Third Man* – because I wanted to put Mamma there, put her in a bedsit, alone, wondering what to do, what choice should she make?

Did she lie awake, trying to decide if she would have me or not, and did her worrying shrink me, make me smaller than her, smaller than my mother, the opposite of what a next generation should be?

It was impossible to comfort her, to comfort myself.

I tried to show my solidarity, my being with her, on her side, by sitting up at night while she was gone, in order to watch the kids, be there if any of them started coughing or crying, but also I wanted to be a bulwark in case she came home too late to change and jump in bed before Daddy got back from the nightshift.

He must have known that she'd been out, had a drink or two. She brought in the scent of other people and other places.

I started to see him as a tyrant, as someone without feelings because I never saw them talk, just sit down and talk.

Just routine and work and work and work.

And I didn't help. I was warped in my own world, scared to death of going to a new school, a school with boys. I wasn't pretty; I wasn't scintillating. I was nothing but a reader of books, and a doodler of numbers. I couldn't even ride a bike or drive a car, neither of them held any interest for me. But who could I tell that to?

I was nothing like Lelia or Felicia. I didn't have the courage to work as hard as Diane was working to get a scholarship to university and go away, far away.

I was caught in the headlights of my own existence, full of angst and confusion and infantile need.

I was a nightmare for Mamma.

We fought all of the time, every day. I needed to breathe, and I knew that she needed to. I knew that she needed to break away, but she was Mamma, my mother, so I had to nail her down, be one of her jailers, too.

I despised her housewife role, her wife role, with its cooked meal with meat for Daddy every afternoon before he left for his shift, and the way she'd stay up half the night ironing for us all.

I willed her to run away, but I needed her more than I ever did.

I swore to God that I would never end up this way, trapped in a house with children and routine. Routine.

I wrote a short story about a woman who discovers that her unmarried mother had tried to abort her. It takes place in the 1940s, during the post-war recession.

The soundtrack was bebop: Charlie Parker, Miles Davis, Max Roach.

No women sang. How could any woman sing to this?

I was the daughter of a woman whose mother had suffered at the hands of her husband. Mamma had seen the supremacy of men, how their absence, their carelessness, could destroy.

Her own father had died in his mid-thirties, a failed artist, a man who did not quite live up to his responsibilities, beautiful, feckless, cruel. A Billie Holiday lament in flesh and blood.

One night, on Troy Street, soon after Grandma Nora died, I came into the kitchen to find Mamma standing in the gloom. She said, as if no one was there, that she had just seen Grandmamma. Her mother had just passed through.

I look now at that moment, at the two of us standing in the dark, and I try to think back and back and back, back to the plantation and the slave ship and the distant shore before that. I think about the abuse and the cruelties and the indignities and who knows how much of that lies within the genetic pool, time bombs ready to explode who knows where and how.

Mamma and I were the descendants of generations of women who had stood in fear, powerless, our reflexes turned in on ourselves and our own.

And there was Mamma, working harder than anyone deserved to be, and in the midst of it trying to hold on to her personhood, sewing party clothes for parties she had no time to go to, clubbing clothes for clubs she couldn't visit, all based on the housewife-friendly McCall patterns that she would outline and cut out patiently and sew and hang in The Closet to look at from time to time.

When we had a truce, Mamma and I would sometimes sit down and watch the vintage movies that we both loved – *Top Hat* especially, because of the routine with Astaire like an angel, dancing out of time, the male dancers behind him trying to keep up, to understand what he was doing.

Mamma and I both loved to dance, and we'd watch him, laughing with delight.

Of course these movies weren't vintage to her.

They were her movies, the chronicle and the spur of her time.

She was a free young girl again when she watched them.

She was in the presence of her Bette Davis and Olivia de Havilland and Joan Crawford and Greer Garson and Ginger Rogers and Carole Lombard.

She was back again working at the parachute factory, eating Chinese food because it was cheap; dancing at Club de Lisa in her fake fur chubby – and her pretty dresses with the orchid pinned to her shoulder.

My love of vintage film, of British and European film, came from her. I learned these from sitting with her.

Sitting with her, too, I learned the difference between loneliness and solitude.

Mamma didn't allow anyone to visit us at home, and I've taken that from her.

Her home was a refuge, private, not open to outsiders. I feel the same. I know that I'll have cast off the last vestige of my childhood/girlhood when I can open that door to others.

None of my friends visited. She wouldn't allow it. And I didn't visit anyone else. I was too frightened to go to other people's homes.

But sometimes, when I stopped being afraid, I visited Diane's house – identical to ours, but quiet and cavernous and dark.

Not in a gloomy way, but in a kind of monastic way. Her father was from the same part of Mississippi as Dad and her quiet, gracious mom was a nurse who worked all hours.

Felicia's mom was gregarious and friendly, outgoing, always open, always welcoming. I wanted to be there, not at our house.

Once, in one of our screaming matches, I yelled at Mamma as she looked at herself in the mirror that I was glad that I didn't look like her, glad that I didn't have light skin.

My growing black consciousness, no doubt.

My insult must have been all the more painful because Mamma's family, when she was a child, had been divided between the 'dark' ones who took after her mother and the 'light' ones who took after her father.

This wasn't within her immediate family but, she told me once, on her paternal side, the Randolphs.

Mamma took after some of them, her hair was ash blonde when she was a child, and this, along with her light skin, got her invited up 'to the hill' for tea. They must have been appalled at Grandpa's choice of wife, little, dark-skinned, quick-witted.

Mamma's complexion would have made her a prize then.

Even now.

The pressure of the caste system of light skin was much greater in the state high school – Harlan High, a posh school, rapidly being integrated by the black middle class and upper working class who were buying up all the homes in the midst of the area's 'white flight' – than the Academy that Lelia and I left at the end of our sophomore year so that Daddy could provide a private education for his other children.

The boys there were known to prize light-skinned girls (although Lelia did pretty well).

The girls considered pretty had long hair and light eyes.

The school even had a yearbook category called 'the prettiest eyes': for those with hazel, green and blue eyes.

There was a kind of blue-vein society: when you turned your wrist over and the veins were visible, you were considered light-skinned enough to join.

This kind of thing was destabilising and demoralising for any young girl. And this was within the black community, a psychotic state of being that grew out of the condition of having been a commodity, a thing. Like a racehorse or a painting.

The strongest, the prettiest … things.

Light-skinned girls were protected and sheltered by their mothers and fathers, and often picked up after class, even seniors who would have been seventeen and eighteen years old.

They were precious jewels.

I was beginning to be very worried about Diane – one day I noticed that her hand, the part that was usually dark from eczema, was lighter. I thought, at first, that it meant that her condition was getting better.

No, she explained, she was using a 'lightening cream', something that she had seen in one of the black magazines. The magazine advertised it as a way of 'getting rid of spots and blemishes'.

There was always a 'before' picture, a disgruntled woman with blotches on her face, and then the 'after' photo: light-skinned and happy.

This practice still exists in Africa, in India. Madness.

Diane was using bleaching cream. Other girls at school were using it too.

Gradually she stopped.

By then, she was aiming for Africa, the Sahel and the Peace Corps.

I was losing even more of my confidence and had become

a compliant little mouse-girl: fretting over my hair and lipstick, trying to look good on my way to school and in class.

I was a little brown-skinned girl who had to go to the hairdresser's every week and get lye on my scalp so that my hair would be straight. I had skinny legs, wore glasses, and loved Shakespeare and the life of the mind.

I had an English teacher, Mrs Kroll, who knew that I was a writer and encouraged me.

I wrote poems. The one published in the yearbook was about the Zapruder footage of the assassination of JFK, and something about sitting in a tree and looking at the sky – a bit eighth-rate Blake.

I decided that, to have a social life, I would have to become a Conversationalist. Cultivate the art of Conversation.

I would learn to TALK, learn to debate.

It didn't matter that my interior life was musical, that words came from music, that I could not assemble my inner world into words, that words could not describe what I saw and felt.

I learned to be articulate.

I had always been a chatterbox, but now I would learn to speak in public in a public way. Even though I struggled and still do to find the words.

They are never quite there. Never.

No one knew how I had wound up with Carl T. Miller, a light-skinned boy with green eyes and who drove a Mustang, the car everyone wanted.

He was also a star basketball player and a member of student government.

His parents lived on Pill Hill, the elite district where black doctors and other professionals lived in a kind of splendid isolation.

At the Academy, in our all-female environment, we were much more raucous about boys.

Something called 'pettipants' was the fashion, pantaloons with frilly lace that we wore under our dull uniforms. Any male, even the poor old head priest, got a full display, our legs coyly open as he tried to read from the catechism.

We didn't do it on purpose; it was simply the presence of a man.

Girls came on to you in the showers and kissed you, and there was a wild kind of freedom, but around boys this died.

I was shy and dainty at Harlan and overwhelmed that Carl was with me.

Mamma was making me a wonderful blue gown for the prom and I would be going with him.

One evening, after we finished our usual session in his Mustang, he asked me to sit with him on the park grass. He had a blanket on the back seat. He took it out, pulled out a condom and said that he wanted to have sex with me.

I was a virgin, and somewhere I saw that black soul of mortal sin looming in the background. But I liked him, maybe loved him, and so we 'did it'. It was painful and boring, but it was done. Under the stars. Which I stared at the whole time.

Then, of course, he didn't call me again. I saw him in the corridors. He was polite but distant, and suddenly, I saw him again with his old girlfriend – a childhood friend actually, one of the 'Pill Hill set'.

He explained to me that his parents were insisting that he take her to the prom and that he couldn't do anything about it.

I had counted on him to be my date and now I had none.

I wasn't going to go with my brother.

I didn't want to think that I was the 'dark-skinned' girl he used for sex, while his 'light-skinned' true love he was saving for marriage and a family.

They were snooty, an exclusive, NAACP people (National Association for the Advancement of Certain People), I was told, and Carl had a kind of 'intended', Patricia, just as light as he was, whose dad was also a doctor … I thought that I was in love with him and that he loved me.

I'd listen in my little corner at home to endless Dionne Warwick records and Little Anthony and the Imperials and dream of a life with Carl.

I told Diane and Felicia. Felicia told me that Carl was using me because he wouldn't dare have sex with Patricia before marriage.

She was right.

I think that Mamma would have told me this, if I had shared my life with her.

She would have told me to beware of him; her own shrewdness, her laser precision in judging people would have saved me.

I cried my eyes out.

Diane and Felicia consoled me. But I had also been humiliated, too, at school.

This was my first public humiliation.

It wouldn't be my last.

This was around the time that I first heard Laura Nyro. And I knew that she knew something about being broken.

I was voted 'Best Conversationalist' in my graduation year, and the male winner offered to take me to the prom. We had a great time, and I didn't see him again until I bumped into him five years later at a gay bar where he was up on the stage miming to a Diana Ross record.

I'd always known that there was something I liked about him.

But in the midst of all of this, Diane and Felicia and I were still living in our own Technicolor, candy-bright world, our own Swinging London. We loved Yardley cosmetics; even The Beatles, who it was OK to like in the black community by then.

We especially liked the Beatles' wives and girlfriends, particularly Patti Boyd. There was something about her, something that kept her outside of it all, something that said: 'I don't give a damn.'

When I mentioned this to Patti decades later, she said to me: 'Well spotted.'

In spite of it all, Felicia, Diane and I were still girls, still close.

But we knew, too, that something was coming to an end.

Diane was going away to university. I was going to university, too, but staying in Chicago.

I knew that I would be leaving home as soon as I could.

Felicia was going to get a job and have a husband and kids and a big house.

And she said that we would never part.

Never.

EIGHT

'The dream of the two young brothers...'

When I first heard these lyrics in Laura Nyro's song 'Save the Country', I thought that it might refer to the Kennedy brothers, assassinated between my fifteenth and twentieth birthdays – the teenage years of my entire, massive generation.

Or 'the two young brothers', Malcolm X and Martin Luther King, assassinated in the same timeframe.

Or the two boys from across the street who, along with their sister, had their car driven over a cliff on a Mississippi back road. Their death drove their mother mad.

Or were they 'the two young brothers' killed by a street gang, or by the police, or in Vietnam? Were we all 'the two young brothers', drowning in the urban poverty, the racism, the sheer tension of being in our big, devouring, grinding country, an invented nation necessary because 'all men are created equal'?

The song, as the album it's on, *New York Tendaberry*, is built entirely around Nyro's voice and acoustic piano. This powerful marriage of voice and piano is true of Nina Simone, too, who I was beginning to listen to at the end of the 1960s.

But Laura was my age, and seemed to capture all of the turmoil and tenderness of that. Her voice, bruised and broken and yearning, was a lifeline for me. That voice was the voice of a woman coming into being, coming of age on her own terms. Whatever the terms happened to be.

I didn't read *The Female Eunuch* when it was first published. I was wary then of the trendy and popular. I've grown to see that the popular isn't always bad. Mainstream equates to 'not good' is something I learnt from Dad. I've come to lose that notion.

I also thought that *Eunuch* wasn't the book for the descendant of women who had been in bondage.

Instead I read and re-read *The Golden Notebook,* a novel about a different kind of bondage. It is the only book that I've ever technically stolen. I never returned it to the university library.

But it was Nella Larsen's novel, *Passing,* which made me think on a deeper level about what being a woman meant, even more than *Mrs Dalloway* or *Madame Bovary* had.

I read it slowly, over and over, especially the beginning, which is full of of the inner life of a black woman, free of the sentimentality, the metaphorical blues harmonica or the 'blue note' that accompanied anyone or anything black on screen.

The novel chronicles an inner life, one that ran alongside and beneath the outer life of its black heroine, hiding herself in the world by 'passing' for white.

I was passing, too.

I was dancing at a topless bar on the North Side, part of the never-ending drive to pay for my university fees.

I took *Passing* with me to read in the tiny dressing-room between shows, one hand turning the page and the other hand moving back and forth across my nipples to make sure that the eyelash glue that held the pasties on was stuck tight.

Because once you were out there, dancing in front of the businessmen who came to the little club every night, standing close to the lip of the stage, staring up at you as if they were in a house of worship, you couldn't check on the glue.

You had to keep your mind blank. Not on the customers. Or on the sob stories backstage that many of the women brought in along with their joints, cocaine, booze, comfort food, and pictures of their kids.

You had to block all of that out, too, eventually, or become too involved.

So I read.

And I wrote on the sheet of blank paper that I always carried with me. Because everything was for the writing.

I did this until one day when I stopped.

When I couldn't see the purpose of somebody like me – a black girl – writing about herself and what she felt and what she knew.

And even then, reading and writing between my dances, I wasn't sure about fiction.

The first novel that I ever read written by a woman was *To Kill a Mockingbird*, at the Academy, because everyone was reading it.

I decided that I couldn't say those things, I had no 'authority' for fiction, so I turned to journalism, which I considered to be lesser. And facts were safe. You couldn't expose yourself in facts.

And even though my English teacher, Mrs Kroll, encouraged me to write fiction, I decided to work on the yearbook at Harlan.

I was unaware that I had been born and raised in a city with a great history of journalism. I didn't know there was a 'Chicago School' of writing: clean, direct, fearless writing.

I didn't know about Sinclair Lewis and the other muckrakers who had exposed the poverty and corruption of this mighty metropolis on the prairie.

I worked hard on the yearbook and the school newspaper, creating a style, as Emile Zola had written, 'forged in the heat of deadlines' that was as sharp and clean as I could make it.

And my writing gave me a place, some visibility in a busy, competitive school.

I was developing a mask in order to survive, hoping that there was a place that I could escape to, where my real self could come through.

While reading those books that came through Dad's *Reader's Digest*, I first came upon the idea of Paris as that place.

I couldn't know that I wanted to join a long line of black American exiles, escapees, like my idol James Baldwin who had left for Paris in November 1948. The month that I was born.

I needed a new emotional link, a safe shore that I could flee to.

Because Diane and Felicia were leaving me.

Diane was away at Oberlin.

Felicia got a job as a secretary downtown. Sometimes she went with me to the University of Chicago to spend time with our friend Tom, and also, for a time, she shared my fascination with the white male members of the freshman intake. They were exotic to us. An adventure.

Just as the builder who built the driveway next door to us was to me, when I was fourteen. He was very blond and it was summer and he wore no shirt. I watched his skin grow brown over the month he was there, breaking concrete and listening to country and western music on his transistor radio.

Felicia and I were intrigued by him, and I put him in that world where my white male imaginary friend – I called him David – lived. Not for his white skin. But because he was different. 'The Other.' I wrote stories about them both.

Just as I wrote about the people in the cars that drove southwards at rush hour every day on the main street near ours, Halstead Street.

I would stand on the corner there and watch them rush past on their way to the Interstate to Indiana and beyond.

I just stood there, sometimes writing stories as I watched.

I can't imagine what those drivers must have thought of me.

I was lucky. No one bothered me.

The off-campus life at the University of Chicago during the gap year before I entered DePaul was like living in a foreign land.

It was an oasis, a kind of fort, surrounded by a teeming black community, much of it on edge at the end of the 1960s.

Felicia's interest in white boys was temporary, and she soon left me to live in that university world on my own.

I left the topless club and found a job as a file clerk in a law office on LaSalle Street in Chicago's equivalent of the City of London.

The firm of lawyers I worked in turned out to be full of sexual predators, not unusual at the end of the '60s and early '70s.

You could easily find yourself in a lift with a man who suddenly would pin you against the wall; or a man who might follow you into the ladies' toilet; or one who would run his hand up your skirt as you bent over to get a file.

Men on LaSalle Street at lunchtime used it like a meat market, grading women as we passed; handing out their cards to girls they fancied, an invitation to visit their offices after work.

And it was not uncommon for a boss to make it clear that unless you agreed to his sexual demands, you wouldn't be advanced. And you could be fired.

We black girls were afforded none of the courtesies or niceties, or preludes or pretexts. It was utterly terrifying to go to work every day.

There were no laws to prevent this. There was absolutely nothing that could be done. Taking a businessman or a lawyer to court was simply not possible. Not only would it have cost a fortune; there was no law to protect you.

All women, black, white, Asian, Latina – all of us were trapped.

I put up with my boss's hands; the attempts of his associate to put his tongue down my throat, his hand down my blouse; his invitation to orgies out of town in the suburbs; his hotel room key when he worked late; his casual interrogation about my sex life and the sex lives of my friends; the extra money on offer if I did what they both wanted: because I needed a job.

I was planning to move away from home as well as go to university. The student loan that was available to me from the federal government wouldn't be enough.

Diane decided to take a year off and go to France.

She wanted to learn French and she wanted to learn how to ride a moped, too. University, and France, were giving her an enormous amount of confidence, so much so that she had stopped using her inhaler.

She wanted me to come to France to see her before she went to francophone Africa for the Peace Corps. I had to have money for that, too.

Felicia soon made new friends, other friends at work.

She went out to have a drink with them after work; she went out clubbing with them on weekends.

Her concern was with her new circle and, suddenly, I realised that we were drifting apart.

I was starting to get involved in a complex relationship with an older man at the University of Chicago, and wanting desperately to be on my own, to leave Mamma and Daddy. I was lonely for her and for Diane.

Maria, Felicia's younger sister, and I had become friends, and she made up for the loss of Felicia in a small way.

But there was no one to replace them.

I sat my university entrance exams and got into DePaul to read history.

I made new friends, found new people.

My sister Lelia, after a glorious and enviable whirlwind of boys, including one with whom she shared an ultra-fashionable apartment on the posh side of town, met a US Air Force man, a recent Vietnam veteran, a beautiful and kind and quiet man.

It was a bit shocking to me that Lelia, after living a high life compared to me, suddenly and abruptly settled down to a suburban domestic life with a thoughtful, serious man.

As always with Lelia, I was deeply envious.

And Felicia, who had finally left the vexatious radical who called himself Captain Shamazz and who caused me a great deal of personal trouble, had married a man by the name of John whom she met in a nightclub. She quickly had a beautiful little boy who she named John Kenya. She was rapidly becoming a stay-at-home mom.

I was going the opposite way.

For a while, I'd run away to the apartment of a woman I'd met at the University of Chicago, a feminist who offered me a bed because she knew that I needed to escape, needed to be away from home and the family and all that was closing in on me there.

I didn't tell Mamma or Dad where I was. I discovered later that the woman had been calling Mamma to give her regular updates on me. She was a mother, too. And I was, underneath it all, still the good Catholic girl.

I'd given her Mamma and Dad's number at home.

I couldn't sleep, not only because I was sleeping on couches, but because I was trying to figure it all out.

Figure it all out as best I could.

I wanted to 'build the Dream with love', but just couldn't find a way to do it.

NINE

For a time I read W.H. Auden. He spoke to me, said what I felt. And something like: 'Poetry never solved anything.'

I knew that this was true.

I was moving away from writing plays and short stories and bits of novels and poems for the high school paper.

There was the war and the Civil Rights movement, and anti-poverty, and I wanted to study something more concrete, more useful. Everyone around me was thinking about the law because it was the law that was getting us our freedom.

Gradually I began to turn away from art.

Fiction seemed to me to be lies, inadequate for the world that was unfolding and revealing itself, a world of international and national violence, and the demand for change from minorities, from women, from young people.

To me, nothing 'made up' could address this, no matter how profound.

The TV set that had brought us *The Mickey Mouse Club* and *Shirley Temple's Storybook* and those icons of the American family like *Father Knows Best* and *Make Room for Daddy* was now bringing us the Vietnam War, and the urban riots, and politicians who were clueless and arrogant with it.

I was beginning to think, like many in my generation, that the things we had been taught by our teachers, by our parents, were simply not true.

Not true that black people were docile, happy-clappy, slow, stupid creatures content with their lot and afraid of ghosts.

We revolted during slavery; fought alongside the abolitionist John Brown in his battle against slavery; were soldiers in the Civil War before we became citizens; fought in the Spanish Civil War, the First and Second World Wars, and Korea. Some had purchased their families away from 'their masters'; some had 'stolen' themselves, as Frederick Douglass described his escape from enslavement.

Not true that women weren't interested in science or mathematics. There was Sophie Germain, Rosalind Franklin, just to name two.

Not true that the indigenous people of the US were savages; that Custer's Last Stand was an heroic fight to the finish, all over in fifteen minutes. Not true that Japanese Americans were traitors during World War Two. The 442nd, composed mainly of Americans of Japanese descent, were the most decorated infantry in the history of the US Army. They gave American English the phrase 'Go for broke' – risk it all.

We were like Dustin Hoffman at the end of *The Graduate*, running out of that stuffy church with the person we loved and hopping on a bus out of town and to our destiny. Made by us.

We young had to stop the lies, the wars, the poverty, the racism and sexism, the stupid, complacent music that we pranced around to in our kiddie dancing classes.

Only revolution could make this happen.

I met a woman in a street downtown one day who walked up to me, gave me some yellow silk cloth and said, 'Oshun', the name of the Yoruba goddess of beauty.

Not that I was especially beautiful, she told me when I

met her in her South Side shop. 'It's just,' she explained to me, 'you needed some beauty. You looked down.'

She taught me to make an altar to Oshun wherever I was. A corner was good enough. Gold, yellow cloth; beautiful, feminine, clothes. Oshun was the deity, along with the rest of the Yoruba pantheon, she told me, who had saved us – not Jesus Christ.

I began to wear gold-flecked eye make-up; a scarf flecked in gold was always around my neck.

I saw black women who curled and dyed their hair blonde not as misguided, but as Oshun's priestesses, out and about doing her work.

I was angry with men and she explained to me that the 'brothers and others' were genetically weaker, that all humans were first born female. She explained to me that I had to stop being on my back and take charge of my life, respect myself, follow Oshun.

I learned about her namesake, Yaa Assantewa, who took on the British; and the women who fomented the Morant Bay rebellion in Jamaica in 1865, which divided British public opinion and changed the nation.

I cultivated within myself a plain-talking woman – partly based on Mamma and my aunties – who took no nonsense, who held her head up high as she moved through the world.

I honoured the blues queens, introduced to me by listening intently to Janis Joplin, sitting down and really hearing what *Pearl* was doing. She was honouring Bessie Smith and Victoria Spivey and Ma Rainey, and this knowledge came to me not from Oshun but from one of my crash-pads on campus.

I could see in my mind's eye the great 'blues trains' winding their way through the South in the 1920s, doing a joyous, raucous thing that came out of the Depression, not making the mournful, full-of-solace blues created by men.

Theirs was a woman's blues, pearl-drenched, full of shiny dresses and big feather fans and lots of gold: Oshun.

Dr Assentewa loved her people, but never had a good word to say about them.

To her, we were always 'a dollar short and a day late'. Too many of us were looking for the quick fix, the thing that would bring praises and fame and sex and money and the blessings of God on high.

It would all end in us selling everything for nothing, and she said once that even our voices, our music, would no longer belong to us. We would be out of style, even in our native land.

She loved Africa but distrusted Africans, particularly those in America. She told me once that a white girl she knew from university had taken her Kenyan boyfriend back to Alabama and everyone crowded around him. They loved him. But if she had taken back there a guy whose ancestors had picked cotton in bondage...

But, she would rail, we weren't paying attention.

Her words were echoed in a letter to me written forty years later:

> ...We have dummied-down our music to the completely asinine level. Easily copied, IMPROVED, and marketed by others. Have you seen K-pop? Korean pop? Biggest selling shit in the world. They have mastered the format! We have lost our musical talents, i.e., properly trained musicians who can play instruments & read music & compose complex, challenging shit! We went for the money & lost everything. If you are not going forward, you are going backwards. Simple physics.

Assantewa said something like this over four decades ago.

But I left her and the sacred pantheon. I had to move on.

I was on a pilgrimage to a shrine I could not name.

I knew that Mamma was suffering, anxious, worried about me. But I had to keep moving, keep going.

I ran into a high-school friend, on furlough from Vietnam, on his way to Canada.

He was a different boy, the way – I imagine – that war makes you different.

He always seemed as if he was listening to something far away. He had been a really bright guy, obsessed with the First World War in school.

He told me that 'Nam was like that: you were always listening, always waiting for the Big One – the thing that you wouldn't hear or see coming – waiting for the guy next to you to be blown away; your ears become strong and alert, listening, listening.

The Klan was there, too, and also something called 'the tripping bush' – a haven where everyone could go and get high because you needed to.

This war, he said to me, was a black man's war – the language and music, all of it, was from the brothers.

When I saw Marvin Gaye's photo on the cover of his album *What's Going On?* and heard the music, I thought of my friend at war, and what he said, and wondered what his life in Toronto was like, and if he would ever return to the land of his birth.

Maybe being eighteen is old enough to know about war. It has always been that way in human history. But I felt that I had been a baby for too long, too self–involved.

I kept moving, kept sleeping on other people's couches, eating other people's food; BEING THERE at the foot and at the tables and in the beds of those who could give me a direction. Create me.

Because I couldn't build the dream any more.

But maybe I could save the country.

I marched in the anti-war demos, yelling to the President: 'Pull out LBJ! Like your daddy should have done!' I had a T-shirt inscribed with Muhammed Ali's reply when asked why he refused to go to Vietnam: 'No Viet Cong ever called me a nigger.'

LBJ decided not to run again, and the nation elected Richard Nixon, a classic Cold War warrior who JFK had defeated eight years earlier and who looked and seemed like dusk walking – if dusk could walk.

The end of the world was nigh.

My university history professor said to us, one day in class, something that I have never forgotten: that one day Richard Nixon will disgrace the United States and himself. It was inevitable. He played us a speech that Nixon made in the 1950s – the 'cloth coat speech', in which Nixon, in an almost lachrymose fashion, explained to the nation that he was an ordinary guy, a poor man.

But not like the poor guys who were the subject of Franz Fanon's *The Wretched of the Earth,* and I became more and more interested in the community work of the Black Panther Party and their analysis of things.

This book, along with the films of Truffaut and Godard and Renais and Malle and the poetry of Rimbaud and *Madame Bovary,* made me want to learn and understand French as best I could.

'The Wretched of the Earth' were the people with whom I belonged.

I came home on Sundays with my new shorn hair, and I could see that I upset Dad. I didn't look like any girl he understood. But Mamma took it in her stride. I think that she was just relieved to know that I was safe and well.

Somewhere.

Lelia married and I was her maid of honour.

I got out of my jeans and combat jacket, my 'African' garb, and dressed properly like Mamma in a boater. I wore a mini-dress and heels and tried to smile.

I was happy for her. Her new husband, Harry, was a wonderful man.

My complicated life would never present me with an opportunity like this, never allow me to stand in a white dress and veil. That part of me that was 'proper', that still lingered, wanted to walk down an aisle, hold a bouquet, move to the suburbs.

I couldn't deny it.

This had to be a harbinger: A woman came up to the make-up counter that I worked in at Marshall Fields, then Chicago's premier luxury store, a bit like the Harrods of its day.

The day usually began with taking inventory of the stock: Estée Lauder had quite a few lines and everything had to be counted in, and then attractively arranged.

We wore a kind of smock, to make us look as if we were 'scientific'.

The manager, Virginia, was old-school – a head teacher type with a steel grey bun of hair at her nape and no make-up.

I think that people came to her because she had an air of authority; she sort of bullied you into making a purchase.

She barked orders to us younger women and watched us carefully at the till.

We had a quota to fill daily and there was a small bonus at the end. I couldn't afford to buy any of the products myself, but was allowed to use them in order to demonstrate them to potential customers.

Most of the women brought pages from fashion magazines

or movie magazines and wanted to look like the stars and models they had seen. Virginia was quite rigorous about this: we were never to lead the women who came to the counter to believe that they could look like the pictures they carried in their handbags. Yet that was the purpose of the whole thing.

Middle-aged and older women clutched photos of teenagers, instructing us to sell them the products that would make them look like what was actually a sixteen-year-old in lipstick, eye make-up and foundation.

But the cosmetics business, like fashion, is about fantasy, and behind that counter I was part of it.

The woman smiled and said that she'd like to try a foundation.

She was black with a light brown complexion and Lauder was just beginning to sell foundation bases for darker complexions.

As I talked to her, I kept thinking that I knew her, that she looked familiar.

I sold her a lot of stuff. She paid, thanked me and then she said: 'Bless you.'

And squeezed my hand. Which was weird.

About five minutes later, Virginia called me to the telephone.

I don't know who was on the other end. I just heard the message: Diane was dead. She had died in Africa.

I stood against the counter, trying not to cry. I was at work.

Virginia told me to pull myself together; I had customers. And I did. But I couldn't see anything. Over the next few days, I pieced together what had happened. Diane was working in the Sahel, in a remote village. This was during a drought and there were huge sandstorms coming off the Sahara.

She was caught in it, and had an asthma attack. She had stopped using her inhaler and she was in a small village where the people had nothing.

She died calling her mother's name.

We couldn't open the coffin because of a kind of ruling from the State Department that if a citizen died abroad – that meaning Africa, and Asia – the coffin couldn't be opened. Fear of a plague blighting the Land of the Free.

So we just had to believe the Peace Corps.

Her parents were devastated, but so grief-stricken that they refused to know the circumstances of her death.

I would go there for tea whenever I was on the block, but I stopped.

I could see that they were maintaining their connection with Diane through me.

They lived for me to come by, and then the pictures would come out, the memories.

I just couldn't take it any more. I couldn't mourn with myself and with them.

I loved her parents and little brother, and I just hoped that they understood and forgave me.

A year later, sleeping on someone's couch somewhere, I found out that Felicia had gone out to a nightclub and not returned.

She never returned.

The police conducted a cursory investigation and maybe the file is still open, but after four decades, I doubt it. Neither of them had clout; no connections, no powerful friends nor fame.

And so they were gone.

Gone.

For a long time I found myself staring into space – just suddenly, out of the blue, I'd stop doing what I was doing and stare.

Sometimes I would see us dancing to Motown, or sitting

on Diane's front porch leafing through the Sears catalogue, imagining the clothes on ourselves.

We all liked Bobby Darin's 'Somewhere', that lovely, breezy song about being 'beyond the sea somewhere'.

We were all going to travel someday and that song was our propeller, as was that doo-wop/pop classic by Little Anthony and the Imperials, 'I Think I'm Going Out of My Head'.

I went to a psychic for a while who told me that Felicia was beside a body of water and waiting to be rescued. There were rumours that Felicia's purse had been found in some guy's apartment along with the handbags of other women. A serial killer, although no one would have defined it like that in those days.

I lay awake at night trying to imagine where she was, trying to communicate with her in my mind, convinced that our connection would somehow transcend whatever and wherever she was.

At one point, Mamma thought that she had run away, but Mamma never thought much of Felicia. I knew that she would never have deserted her son. She loved him more than her own life and would never leave him.

Neither Oshun nor Jesus was of assistance to me now.

One Saturday night I came home, intending to spend the night and have Sunday meal before returning to what my brother Ben would call, in awe, 'The North Side'.

I let myself in.

Mamma, as usual, had fallen asleep in front of the TV.

On it was Laurence Olivier, leaning over the ramparts at Elsinore, intoning 'To Be or Not to Be.'

Like everybody, I think, Shakespeare I considered impenetrable, and intolerable.

My English teacher at Harlan loved him and would read a sonnet or a scene to us once a week, a great opportunity to take a snooze or read a movie magazine between the covers of a school book.

But that night, while Mamma slept, I sat on the floor and listened to Olivier … and to Shakespeare.

And when he said:

> To grunt and sweat under a weary life,
> But that the dread of something after death,
> The undiscover'd country from whose bourn
> No traveller returns, puzzles the will,
> And makes us rather bear those ills we have
> Than fly to others that we know not of?

I've been devoted to Shakespeare ever since.

When I woke up the next morning, I realised that the woman I had helped at the counter was a nun from my high school. She had leapt the convent.

She had leapt over the wall, as they used to say.

I was scared. All kinds of things scared me for a while.

Life was very fragile, ephemeral, random and brief.

I'm still scared that way … not of death … but of how fleeting it all is.

I'm not sure that I've ever made friends with women like that again.

I'm not sure. Something closed down.

There was the film, *The Sterile Cuckoo*, with Liza Minelli, who turns in a fine performance as a university student who falls in love and goes off the deep end. The man she loves sends her away in the end, and the last shot is of her on a bus, looking at him fade in the distance, and you think, What will happen to her? What will happen to her?

I was house-sitting one week, the house of a painter and

his wife – friends. In exchange for some light housekeeping while they were away, I had the chance to stay in a place of my own – the first time in my life.

It was high up and overlooked the lake. The window curved with the shape of the lake.

Their record collection was nothing but women: Laura Nyro's *New York Tendaberry* with 'Save the Country'; Janis Joplin's *Pearl*; Mahalia Jackson's 'In the Upper Room'; Nina Simone; Diana Ross; Dusty Springfield; Aretha Franklin; Abbie Lincoln; Leontyne Price; Miriam Makeba; Carole King; Joni Mitchell; Tina Turner; Shirley Bassey.

There was a reproduction of one of Georgia O'Keeffe's 'Lily' paintings on the wall, shimmering in the half-light from the lakefront.

I poured myself a glass of their awful red wine, which immediately gave me a migraine, but I didn't care.

I sat in the middle of all of these women, their voices and their stories, and let them wash over me. I went wading in 'The Glory River'.

But it was Laura Nyro, above all, and once again, who gave me some kind of road ahead.

She sounded as if she were making up the lyrics, the music, the songs, right then and there. Her voice sounded like the never-ending quest to find meaning, to connect the dots, and then breathe.

I felt as if I knew her.

And so, while writing this, and listening again to 'Save the Country' and other music of the late Laura Nyro, I found this note about how she composed a song and an album that seemed to emanate from her as easily and as effortlessly as breath.

From Wikipedia:

> 'Nyro painstakingly guided co-producer and engineer Roy Halee using colour metaphors. She could not understand musical notation, and used other analogies to communicate…'

I must have sensed this, must have known.

FREDDIE'S DEAD

ONE

When the lyrics to 'Freddie's Dead' were sung by Curtis Mayfield on his 1972 soundtrack album for the film *Superfly*, one of the first reactions from critics was this: how did Mayfield manage to put so much sheer emotion, such political focus, into what had been a less than six-minute instrumental illustrating the death of a junkie/pusher?

The Maestro was able to do this because that's not what he was singing about.

Martin Luther King was assassinated on the balcony of the Lorraine Motel in Memphis, Tennessee, at approximately 6:01 p.m. on 4 April 1968. There was a thunderstorm.

The FBI agents who were meant to protect him were housed in the fire station right across from the motel. Somehow these sharp-shooting, twenty-four-hour surveillance guys, the big, bad FBI, missed this particular bullet.

Chicago is in the same time zone as Memphis, and at 6 p.m. I had just come home from work. I think then I was sorting through subscriptions for *Time* magazine.

I was not on a gap year in the sense that you take a year off to do something else before university.

I had to earn money to pay for my university fees.

Once again – just like in first grade – I was a year behind

my age group and classmates. They had started class in September. This was April and I had still not begun university.

I had to earn more money. There was no scholarship or rich parents for me.

The thing that I really wanted to do on that evening was see *2001: A Space Odyssey*, set to open the following week.

The film was shot using 70-mm, six-track stereophonic sound and was being promoted as a 'Cinerama' presentation with reserved seating. Nobody knew what this meant, but all of us from the office were going to go. No mistake about that.

I was going out to have a meal with a guy from a rival high school. That wasn't the reason I was doing it. He also worked in subscription sorting. Plus he looked a little like Marvin Gaye, whose looks I really liked.

I was putting on some make-up in the upstairs bathroom and listening to my transistor radio to, I think, Otis Redding singing 'Sitting on the Dock of the Bay', which you couldn't get away from then.

And then the song stopped and the news came through that Martin Luther King had been shot in Memphis and it looked fatal. My first thought was, 'This is it.'

Since 1965 and Selma, a lot of us young people had gone off Dr King.

'Selma' was a series of marches in Selma, Alabama, from 7 March to 25 March 1965. The purpose was to increase black voter registration and to protest the death of two Civil Rights workers.

Selma is the county seat and the major town of Dallas County, Alabama.

In 1961, 57 per cent of the population there was black, but fewer then 1 per cent were registered to vote – prevented by a draconian poll test, and just plain violence.

The Student Non-Violent Coordinating Committee

(SNCC), the student wing of the Civil Rights movement, came in to try and desegregate the place, something that would be difficult, to say the least, with a governor like George Wallace who, once in the doorway of the State House, announced: 'Segregation now. Segregation forever!'

In 1965, a year after LBJ signed the Civil Rights Act, a black man, Jimmie Lee Jackson, was shot while protecting his mother after they were both chased down by Alabama State Trooper James Bonard Fowler. It took over forty years for Fowler to be brought to justice.

Sheriff Jim Clark, to battle back the forces that were beginning to assemble against Alabama's segregation laws, deputised all 'white males' for an assault on less than 650 people who wanted to march. The march was televised and the assault against its non-violent participants outraged the nation.

A few days later, Dr King himself led 2,500 people across the Edmund Pettus Bridge.

Earlier he had sought an injunction against being stopped, but the judge instead prohibited them from marching. MLK marched across the bridge, then turned around as the judge had ordered and came back.

This was a game-changer.

The younger people in the movement, the students in SNCC, all of us young people, had had enough of non-violence.

It was clear to us that turning the other cheek, sitting down and taking it, wasn't going to work. Maybe it never worked.

The violence and mayhem and hatred of Alabama had been met with prayers, gospel songs and exhortations for peace. We youth were having none of it.

Stokely Carmichael, a young member of SNCC, started

using the term 'Black Power' in his speeches and that made sense to most of us. We had grown up looking at kids being chased down by dogs; stories of lynchings; trying to eat at lunch counters and having food dumped on your head; preachers and teachers marching arm-in-arm singing and praying; white people saying how wonderful and good black people were.

And what I could hear all of the time: the oleaginous sound of the harmonica and the blues note behind everything said about black people, and everything said by black people, anytime we were in the media.

As far as my generation were concerned, we were done.

I hadn't thought about Dr King for a long time. He had begun to make links between Vietnam and what was going on in America, and he had gone to Memphis to support a garbage strike.

But on that April evening, as I sat on the rim of the tub, stunned, listening to the crying and wailing in the house and on the street, I just saw hell. I saw everything exploding, everything falling down.

And it did.

The black community began to rend its own clothes, tear out its own hair.

It was then that I began to understand what the word 'ghetto' meant and how it ate into everything and you couldn't really escape it.

Only find a place to put it in your mind and your life.

TWO

I was the daughter of a 'race man'. That's what Dad called himself.

He had no reason to like or trust white people. He had been born and come of age in racial segregation. He told me once that at a shop he had seen a jar of pickled entrails on the counter, proudly displayed by the white lady who owned the shop.

It would be safe to say that they had once belonged to a black man. This was common practice after a man was hung in the woods by the Klan – the entrails, ears, etc., taken as souvenirs, as were photos.

The murderers and their little kids often posed in the pictures, too.

There is one famous atrocity picture, circulated secretly well into the 1970s, of a black woman hanging from a bridge.

These pictures and postcards were, at times, openly displayed in places that black people frequented. Just to let them know.

The poll test in Dad's county could be in Mandarin Chinese if the officials wished, and there was no rule of law if you were black.

The Thirteenth, Fourteenth and Fifteenth Amendments guaranteed black freedom, citizenship, and the right to vote.

But the Supreme Court allowed each state to interpret the Amendments, and the Civil Rights movement set out to erase that and bring everyone under the protection of the Constitution, a battle still going on today.

White people, as far as Dad was concerned, had no interest in giving black people anything, but he did not hate them. He was too intelligent to lump people together. Like most black people, he could transcend what he saw on TV, and imposed himself there.

He loved *Bonanza*, the story of a cattle baron named Ben and his three sons. Dad was named Ben and he had three sons, too, and when I once brought up playfully that 'Ben Cartwright' was white and probably would have killed Dad if he showed up at 'the Ponderosa', Dad looked at me like I was crazy. Of course 'Ben Cartwright' wouldn't harm him, and he was right.

Bonanza was created in the age of the Civil Rights movement, just as Martin Luther King's 'March on Washington' had been fashioned for television, with its movie stars upfront and its lack of controversy.

In addition to the *Encyclopaedia Britannica*, Dad also read the works of historian Lerone Bennett and the doyen of black history, John Hope Franklin.

But slowly, through reading these authors, I was beginning to see Western civilisation, then, as a series of thefts and lies.

Aunt Bernice took me to see *Cleopatra* with Elizabeth Taylor as a treat for helping her at her cleaners once, and although I thoroughly enjoyed it, I wondered then why a white woman played her.

When I asked my history prof. the same question a few years later, during one of our Black Student Union teach-ins at university, he explained to me that her family was actually Macedonian. But no one knows who her mother was, this last pharaoh, and if she had been born in America with that mixed parentage, she would have been classified in one of the sixteen categories created for people with 'African blood'.

Dad would agree with me and encouraged my thinking, buoyed by the appearances of Malcolm X on a local talk show presented by a phenomenon, a columnist called Irving Kupcinet, known as 'Kup' or by the name he preferred: 'Mr Chicago'.

Kup was so powerful in the days when news people had few ethics, that he had what were known as 'flacks' – people with information – hired as his taxi drivers so that they could pitch to him. Every night he and his wife held court at all the big nightspots: Chez Paree, the London House, the Black Orchid, Club Alabam and the town's prime spot, Booth One at the Pump Room in the Ambassador East Hotel.

Kup would have his people hanging out at the airports to catch the stars as they changed planes on their way to the East Coast or the West Coast; press agents would load so many gifts at the loader area of the paper he worked for that it embarrassed some. Those were the days when a columnist of his power paid for nothing. So to be on his show was a mark of your arrival, and Malcolm X was on a few times.

It was a huge event: Malcolm striding on with books and notebooks under his arm, sitting back calmly on the couch, ready to turn the white man's words against him.

Dad loved it because Malcolm always got the better of anybody who opposed him.

And 'Kup' would sit back and watch him with a strangely avuncular smile, even when, in those days, Malcolm called white people 'devils' on late night TV. 'Kup' seemed to approve of him because Malcolm X made headlines. He was a star.

Dad didn't agree with Malcolm nor the Nation of Islam, but he liked their self-help angle. Dad would probably have been a Republican if it hadn't been for Roosevelt and the Democratic Party and the New Deal.

The Republicans lost black people like Dad by embracing the South after it left the Democratic Party in response to the signing of the Civil Rights Act in 1964.

And there was Vietnam.

Black guys in my high school – a rather middle-class, largely black school that Lelia and I were sent to in our third year – were beginning to worry about not getting into university. Because not having a university place made you 1A: eligible for the draft.

It was a fact that black men were being drafted in disproportionate relation to their numbers in the population, and Martin Luther King was beginning to address this. His argument was astute, correct and subtle, but we young ones saw it as another example of his being out of it.

Our school was torn between the prom and owning a red Mustang, the must-have car; between 'styling and profiling' and trying to figure out what we were going to do.

Our older brothers and sisters had gone on marches; sat in at lunch counters; sung freedom songs; looked nice and neat and presentable all the time everywhere.

We were growing our hair, letting it go.

I wanted to stop going to the hairdresser for the weekly straightening torture, but Mamma and Daddy, too, would have had a fit. It was not 'proper' to let your hair 'revert', but this was becoming a cause for me.

As I sat listening to the news on that April evening – I think that there were thunderstorms in Chicago, too – I decided that I would never listen to MLK's voice again, never look at a programme about him, never read anything about him again.

I had not been aware of it, but he had been my father, too. He had shaped me as much as my own dad had. All of the years of watching him on TV as a child, seeing him appear at every important occasion, listening to him for guidance, beaming with pride as he accepted the Nobel Peace Prize. And remembering, always remembering his speech that hot summer's day in 1963, months before the murder of JFK, his voice like music ringing over the Washington Mall: 'Free at last! Free at last! Thank God Almighty, I'm free at last.'

Now he was the beginning of my ghosts.

The black areas of Chicago and a dozen other cities burst into flames as black people went on the rampage, our grief and rage, our sense that nothing would ever change, turning in on ourselves because a ghetto is like a concentration camp with invisible walls and guards.

You're trained not to go anywhere else, even though you might want to escape.

For a time, our voices all sounded the same – even though we hadn't been born in the South – because we weren't exposed to other voices. We lived closed-in, in the ghetto.

Dad was exasperated by black people, they made him angry because they did not seem, to him, to have any kind of analyses, any means of looking beyond pleasure and pain.

The few white kids at high school didn't come during the days of conflagration.

That spring of '68 – like 1968 everywhere – was a time of the kind of turmoil that creates you. I'm a *'soixante-huitarde'* in every way.

And except for having to do it for the odd broadcast, I have never listened to Martin Luther King's voice again; nor looked at his face; nor read his words.

He's been locked away now for close to half a century, a part of my youth.

A part that I can never get back.

THREE

It was, I think, 1964 when we all thought that something good was in the air, in spite of the fact that the President had been assassinated and there was a real fear, for a while, that things would roll back. Become bad again.

No one knew at the time that JFK had opposed the March on Washington the year before.

No one knew that the sound system had been in the control of the Washington D.C. police just in case there was trouble, or that if inflammatory words were spoken the whole thing could have been shut down.

No one knew that conservative forces within the movement had prevented James Baldwin and Bayard Rustin – the man who had actually come up with the idea for the March on Washington – from speaking because they were gay. Rustin, especially, was an out homosexual.

Homophobia in the black community would have caused them to be more ostracised than Strom Thurmond – an unreconstructed segregationist Southern senator and racist (who turned out, of course, to have had a secret black daughter, a fact discovered after his death) – would have been had he stepped up to the podium spewing hate.

That would have been dealt with. A gay black man was

beyond acceptance, no matter if he was a great writer – like Baldwin – or the father of the Civil Rights movement – like Rustin.

And as the baby who became Michelle Obama was being nursed by her mother, not far from where we lived, Lyndon B. Johnson's signing of the Civil Rights Act later in the year would allow me and others of my generation from poor and working-class black families to go to school, to university, to begin to participate in the American Dream.

Which was always alive and well in our street.

Every summer there was a 'block party', a chance for the adults on the street to dress up in fancy dress and dance and drink in someone's backyard.

This was to be my last year at Longwood Academy, then Lelia and I would be transferring to the local high school … and the world of boys. Lelia took this in her stride, as she did everything, but I was filled with anxiety.

I felt safe in our all-girls school. Even though I refused to take typing (a huge mistake) because I didn't want to be a secretary (I figured if I couldn't type, I couldn't be hired), I didn't feel any pressure to look pretty. I wanted to be pretty.

Felicia and I would sit on the front steps of my house and look through the Sears catalogue, selecting our imaginary wardrobes, always imagining ourselves sophisticated and urbane. But I felt that I was doing that for me, not for a boy.

Now, with the move to the local high school, which Felicia was already attending, things would change.

The theme for the block party the previous year had been 'Africa'.

I still stare in disbelief at the photos from that party, all of the adults dressed as how they imagined Africa to be.

Above: My parents (the couple on the left) with family and friends in the early 1960s.

Below: My grade-school class on the West Side.

My graduation from high school in June 1967.

My university graduation. Standing in the street on the South Side in 1974.

My university graduation in 1974.

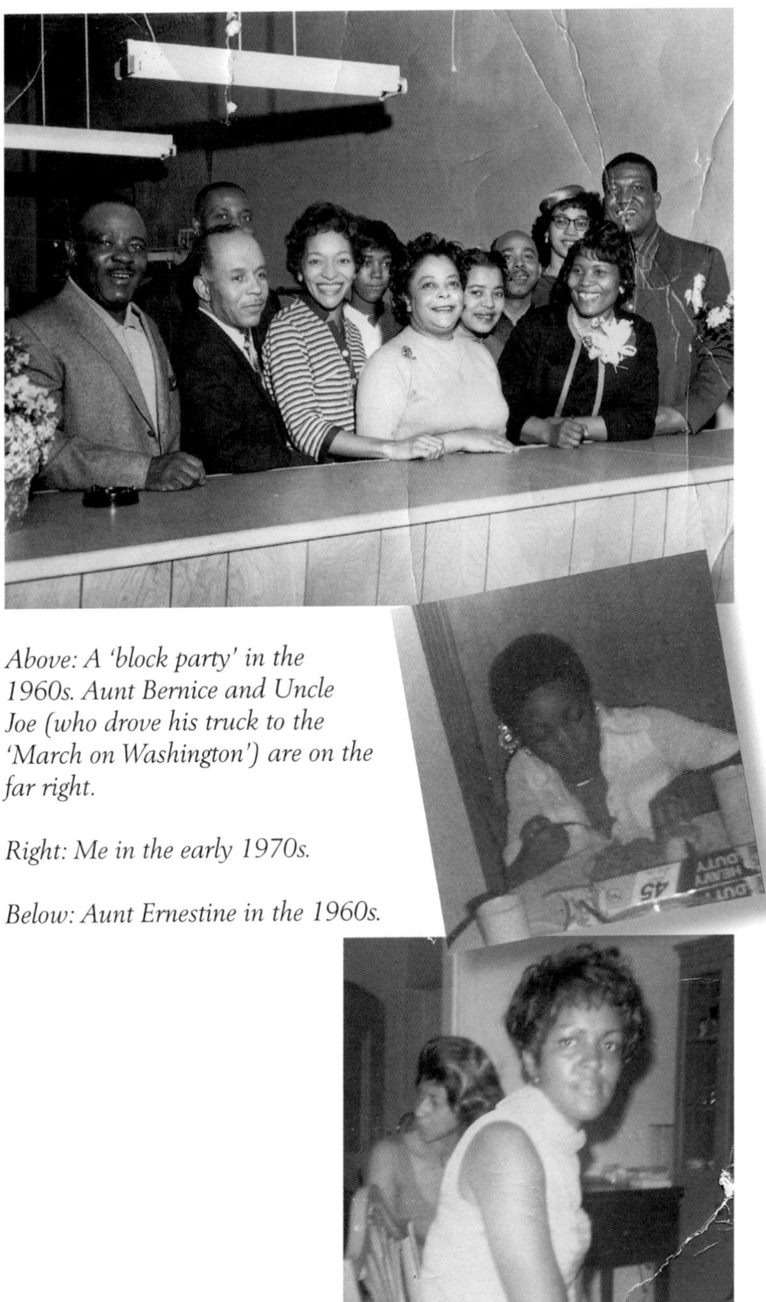

Above: A 'block party' in the 1960s. Aunt Bernice and Uncle Joe (who drove his truck to the 'March on Washington') are on the far right.

Right: Me in the early 1970s.

Below: Aunt Ernestine in the 1960s.

Party time in the 1960s. Back row, left to right: Dad, Aunt Ernestine, her husband, Uncle 'June', and Aunt Ida and her husband.; Front row, left to right: Mamma, her brother, Uncle Kaydon and his wife, and Uncle 'Bubble' (William).

June 1967. 'Best conversationalist' in my high-school graduation year, with my male counterpart.

At DePaul University in the early 1970s.

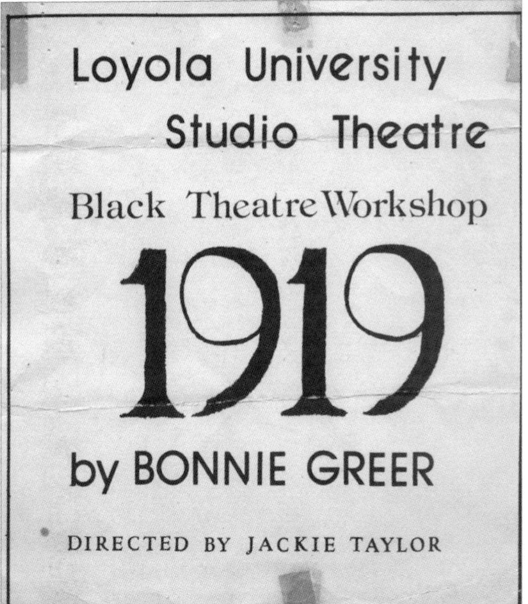

Loyola University
Studio Theatre
Black Theatre Workshop
1919
by BONNIE GREER
DIRECTED BY JACKIE TAYLOR

My first professional production, December 1977.

The action takes place between July 27-28, 1919.

ACT I

SCENE 1: The bedroom of Annise Harris
SCENE 2: The kitchen of Louvenia Harris' house
SCENE 3: Wabash YMCA, late Sunday night

INTERMISSION

ACT II

SCENE 1: The kitchen of Louvenia Harris, late Monday morning
SCENE 2: The kitchen of Louvenia Harris, Monday evening

Cast in order of appearance:

ANNISE HARRIS............PATRICIA PATTON
CLARENCE WILLIAMS.........ERNEST PERRY
EMMETT JOHNSON.........STEVEN WILLIAMS
LOUVENIA HARRIS...........JACKIE TAYLOR

AUTHOR'S NOTE

On the balmy Sunday afternoon of July 27, 1919, Eugene Williams and three of his friends took their homemade raft out onto Lake Michigan. As the black youths' raft drifted lazily toward the all-white 29th Street beach, they were unaware of the altercations that had taken place there earlier in the day. A small group of blacks had attempted to use the beach, claiming that the beaches belonged to all the citizens of Chicago. Suddenly, as the raft approached the shore, it was greeted with a shower of rocks from the angry whites. The boys managed to swim back to the black beach a few blocks north. All but Eugene. His body was pulled from the water an hour later. By the following Sunday, August 3, 23 blacks and 15 whites were dead, over 250 people injured, millions of dollars in property destroyed or damaged and thousands homeless. Of all the race riots and labor violence during the "red summer," Chicago's riot was the most hideous. "1919" is not directly concerned with that riot, but rather with the complex forces shaping a people who were largely the product of a rural, feudal society. It is about four people caught up in the traumatic summer of 1919.

BONNIE GREER is a Chicago based freelance writer. She has written on subjects ranging from Chinese history to punk rock. She is currently writing another play, a screenplay and a novel. *1919* is Ms. Greer's first play. The author wishes to express her thanks to C.B.E., its staff, and the production staff of *1919*, and her deepest love and gratitude to the director and cast for allowing a dream to come true.

Programme notes from '1919'.

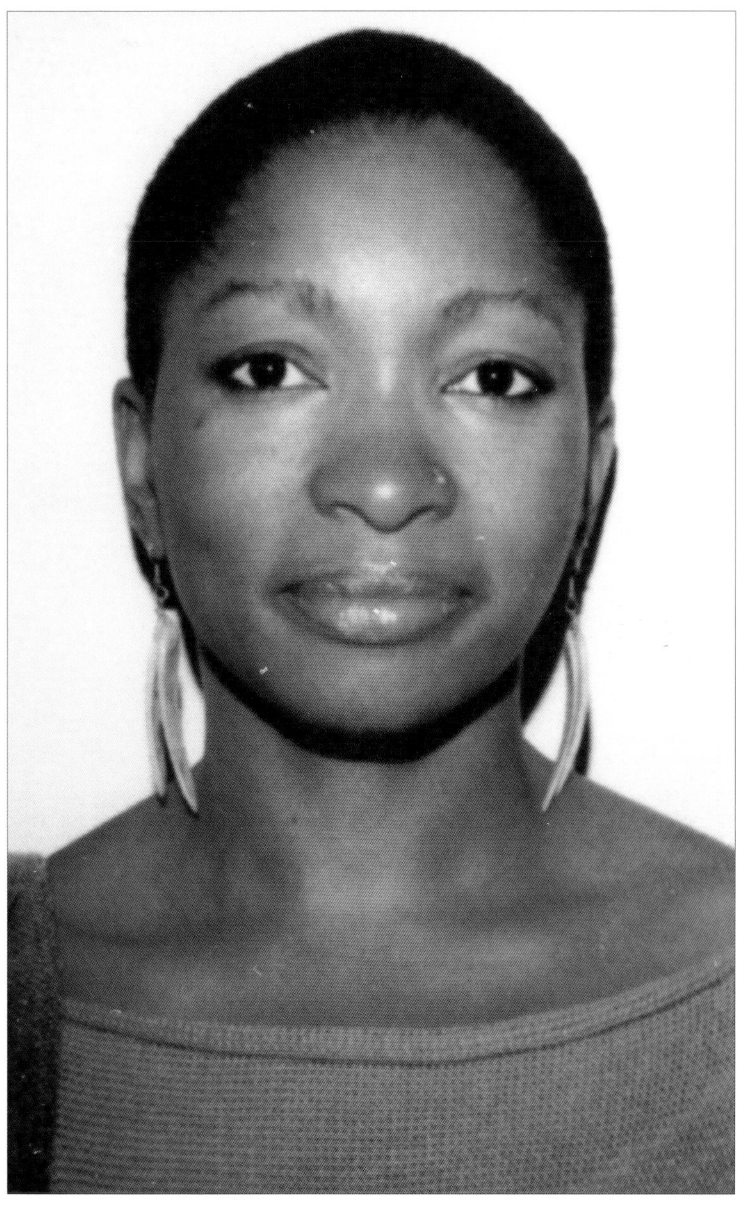

Me in New York City, in the mid-1980s.

Me and Lelia dancing at Gina and Theron's wedding in the 1980s.

Mamma had on a lovely long gown and Dad was in a dashiki, but there were some wild outfits and lots of royalty.

It was as though Africa was a place ... a mythical land from which we had all been stolen off our thrones and dumped here to live in misery. Everyone on the street was glorious and, as usual, we kids watched it all from the windows.

But the theme of the block party that summer was the 'Mississippi Summer'.

Three Civil Rights workers – a black man, James Chaney from Meridian, Mississippi; and two white men, Andrew Goodman and Mickey Schwerner from New York City – set out on 21 June to investigate the bombing of a church.

Mississippi was in rebellion against the federal government and saw what was termed 'the nigger/communist' invasion of the South as something that had to be resisted at all costs.

Everyone knew that Mississippi – or 'Mississippi Goddamn', as Nina Simone referred to it – was the worst state in the Union to be black. Most of the adults on the block had either been born or had family there. Mississippi was the bad, ugly place.

The news for most of June and July was filled with the search for these workers who had simply disappeared off the face of the earth.

Dad and most of the adults on the street believed that if just James Chaney had gone missing, there would have been no search at all. There was cynicism in the air as well as anxiety. Black people disappeared in Mississippi and no one cared.

But this was different. Mississippi had turned into a raving lunatic.

Now those lost men began to haunt my dreams. I saw them tied up in a cave with no food and water, surrounded by men in white sheets. I saw them floating down the Pearl

River, as Emmett Till, a decade before, had.

Prayers were offered for their safe return in all of the churches. But Dad, who knew Mississippi like the back of his hand, said: 'Those boys are dead.'

The FBI stepped in then because the news media picked it up and made it into a *cause célèbre*. They named the investigation and operation to locate them 'Mississippi Burning' (MIBURN). There was almost a sense of relief when their bodies were found nearly two months later.

They had been killed by the local Klan, with the collusion of the authorities. Chaney was killed last, after he'd been beaten.

They became folk heroes, songs were written about them.

The walk to Longwood Academy, which was through a white neighbourhood, began to fill me with terror. What if Dad's hated 'White Boys' drove past and shot me? Or kidnapped me and buried my body?

The story of the three Civil Rights workers added another dimension of instability, and created a sense that I had to leave the US someday.

Later that summer, before the block party whose theme was a Hawaiian luau, we found out that the Robinson children, directly across from us in a house identical to ours, were driving to Mississippi to visit their grandmother.

I remember Mrs Robinson, a tall, slender, ascetic-looking woman with a nervous disposition who was terribly strict about her three kids: a boy two years older than me, a girl Gina's age, and a little boy who wore glasses.

I can't remember their names any more. Just their driving off with a wave, their mother standing in the doorway looking anxious.

A few days later, we heard Mrs Robinson screaming and running out of the house crying to the Lord. No one was quite sure, but it was said that the Klan had forced the kids' car off the road and over a cliff.

Mrs Robinson began to drink and then, eventually, she went mad.

The block party didn't happen that year and they never happened again.

The grown-ups, our parents, were Southern people. They quietly tended to things that needed to be done: cooking, washing, praying with and sitting with the Robinsons in the early days of their mourning.

Then they just as quietly returned to their lives because they all had that tragedy somewhere, if not in the immediate family but way back. Way back.

This Mississippi heritage was mine, too, and it was some of what made me, even if I wasn't aware of it. We were all part of it.

Even if we lived up North in lovely houses with manicured lawns and two-car garages and had garden parties in which we could pretend – for an afternoon – to be someone, something else.

FOUR

I have the ability (thanks to my synaesthesia) to remember a song or a piece of music that strikes me. I can remember where I was, what I was doing, sometimes the year, time of year and time.

I can remember getting something out of the fridge, the light over the sink the only light on in the kitchen, when I first heard Bob Dylan's voice.

I had not heard his antecedents, his elders, sing – Woody Guthrie in particular – so I didn't realise how much Dylan owed him. Dylan's voice was like a razor, it sliced through the air and seemed to come around the corner from the TV in the sitting room and into the kitchen.

Since he didn't appear on *The Ed Sullivan Show*, the nation's number one entertainment show, because he didn't want to drop a song that he wanted to sing, I don't know how I heard him. All I know is that I stood and listened.

The same thing happened one afternoon while I was washing dishes and listening to my favourite DJ, Herb Kent 'the Cool Gent'. DJs like Herb Kent invented and named rap: the art of talking over a record.

You never heard a record straight through on the Cool Gent's programme. The record was in the background, a backdrop to Herb's re-telling of some story or observation he wanted to make about the world. The Cool Gent would analyse the condition of the black community over a Sam Cooke record, or a song by Mary Wells. I suspect that this art form existed long before Herb Kent, and without a doubt it existed long before the Sugar Hill Gang released their classic 'Rapper's Delight' in 1979, another piece of music that I can recall where I was when I first heard it.

Suddenly, this guitar twang came on, and I stopped what I was doing. This wasn't black.

I was brought up on gospel, jazz, soul and doo-wop, and the Cool Gent was the principal DJ on the city's only black radio station: WVON – 'The Voice of the Negro'.

But this twang was not black. Nor was the Cool Gent rapping. He was playing a song called 'Paperback Writer' by the Beatles.

To this day I don't know why he made this revolution one weekday afternoon. It might have been because the Beatles were becoming a phenomenon in America (we didn't know that they would never tour together after 1966), and maybe Herb just wanted to make sure that he was on the crest of that wave.

In 1966, black radio was not a melange of sounds; black people were largely unused to hearing anything other than what was called until about the 1950s 'race music' – that is, black people singing black stuff. But here were the Beatles singing about something I had never heard of: a paperback writer.

I couldn't get the melody out of my head, a major 'ear worm' in a time of great tunes.

I twanged that guitar in my head every time I walked down the street, as I sat in class.

I twanged the guitar to my little cousin who lived with

my Aunt Ernestine, his mom and Mamma's baby sister, whenever we visited them in one of the most notorious housing estates in a city full of notorious housing estates: the Henry Horner Homes, named after a bachelor governor of Illinois who worked for social reform.

The Homes were sixteen high-rise buildings that looked like prisons with their tiny windows. In all, here were over fifteen hundred units. The interior walls were naked concrete; you could scratch yourself on them if you brushed up against them.

My auntie and her family lived at the top, so the playground below was like a tiny speck. It was treacherous down there because that was where the gangs lurked, principally the almighty Blackstone Rangers.

The lifts and stairwells were centres of criminal activity from petty theft to rape and murder. The residents made as much of a community as they could, but there was no privacy, no protection.

The buildings were vermin-infested, with rumours that a new species of rat lurked in the darkness of the basements, where no one dared venture. It was a warehouse, a place to store people away and forget them.

It was as different from where we lived as night and day.

My little cousin held music in his head, too. He would beat out the rhythm of the drum from JFK's funeral procession over and over on the window as we ate Auntie's food beneath her picture of the Jesus with eyes that seemed to follow you around the room.

When I repeated that Beatles guitar riff, he adopted it and made it his own.

I mentioned the song to Sharon, one of the girls in our neighbourhood, and she said: 'They need to do their thing in their own community.'

This was the beginning of a creeping militancy amongst us, a beginning to make a demarcation, to move away from the Dr King consensus. And if mild-mannered Sharon felt that way…

The Cool Gent never explained why he played the Beatles that afternoon. I'm not sure that he played them again.

We made our every-other-Sunday visit to our West Side cousins, sometimes walking across the concrete playground to the Boys Club where my Uncle June – Aunt Ernestine's husband – volunteered and was the guiding light.

He had been a sailor in the war, a chef who spent his time down below where he was routinely insulted by the white sailors. This left him with an indelible dislike of white people, and sometimes I would hear the odd derogatory word about them from a normally mild-mannered and good-natured man. Looking at where they lived, and what they had to endure, it was a wonder that he kept his good nature.

Auntie and Uncle June kept as beautiful and tidy and as safe a home as they could, a home where the Beatles had no part at all.

I was nearing the end of my compulsory education, and I was trying to see life for me as a black girl. A black woman. A black old woman.

The Nation of Islam, the Black Muslims and the Black Hebrews were gaining prominence. They were organised, modest, and there was something in their not being Christians, not being believers in 'massa's religion', that was beginning to appeal to us young people. Even at my high school, which was a basketball and party school, there was a sense of 'blackness' as a condition apart, as a re-ordering not only of the social order but of history itself.

We wanted to be the first generation to take back the piece of time stolen from our ancestors when *they* were stolen. People were changing their names.

I even considered, briefly, the name 'Abena'– Fante for 'woman born on Tuesday'.

But Mamma and Daddy would have both laughed at me and run me out of the house if I asked them to call me something else. I waited almost twenty years to do it.

That day, twenty years later, on a cold day in Fort Greene, Brooklyn, I took a bag of food and placed it at the crossroads, a junction where the Yoruba trickster god and shape-changer Elegba resides. With the new name that I had thought about as a young girl, I went about my day.

It didn't make my life any better.

I watched Felicia out of my bedroom window. She was a beautiful young woman and seemed to be growing attached to a weird guy who wore white flowing robes, a military jacket over it, and a turban. He told me point-blank, without an ounce of humour in his eyes, that he was here to create a black world and everybody on the street, including me, was going to be a part of it.

Mamma laughed whenever she saw him walk down the street with his faux-military air, a look of disdain on his face. I don't think that Daddy paid any attention to him. He was too busy with his second job: repairing TVs.

This guy didn't like me. I think he sensed that I was trouble, a bad influence on Felicia, someone she should never know, never be involved with.

For her sake, to keep her friendship, to avoid losing her, I tried to listen to his theories about the evil of white people, their natural inhumanity. But it was too ridiculous, too implausible, his entire notion of history, of life.

I watched Felicia get sucked into his orbit, his friendships and philosophy.

To assert my credentials as other than a 'bourgeois', I would tell him about visiting my cousins and I would lie and say that I once lived with them in the projects and endured what they endured. This was all so that I did not lose my friend.

Diane had gone to Oberlin, the great college that had been an abolitionist stronghold in the previous century, and she was changing, moving away from me, too.

When Felicia and I began going to the University of Chicago for our visit with our high-school friend, he thoroughly disapproved not only because our friend was white and male, but because it was the University of Chicago, an 'evil, imperialist' centre for war.

I knew that I was in a battle for my friend, and that I was losing.

All through our final year and a half in high school, I knew that I was losing. I was losing not only to a man she was obviously in love with, but to a philosophy, a point of view.

Mamma said that she was heading for a harem.

Two years later, when I was quite active in the Black Student Union at my university, DePaul, I was confident that I had found an equilibrium, a way to 'do this thing', what one of the leaders of the BSU referred to when he talked about 'blackness'.

I was addressing a group one day in the room that the university allotted to us, when Captain Shamazz – that was what he called himself – strode in and posted a handwritten sign on my desk, then turned to my group and dared them to remove it.

It was a denunciation of me in the same style that the French denounced women they called 'collabos' after the Second World War, women who had slept with the enemy. He also put in his sign that I loved the Beatles, which was probably, for him, the ultimate sign of treachery.

There was nothing that I could do. I didn't want him to hit me or anyone else; he was a big guy.

He prowled the room, looking at us coddled undergrads, the potential and pathetic vanguard of the revolution.

He took over my group that day and used me as an example of the evil 'out there in the white world'.

This was my first year at university and I was still living at home. There was no one that I could tell about that day. It was as if he had shaved my head, like the French Resistance had done to women, and left me naked and bleeding in the street.

I went back to a novel that I used to read under the covers at home: *Another Country* by James Baldwin.

Like many of the novels I'd grown to love, I don't know how I discovered this one.

It certainly wasn't in Dad's *Reader's Digest*.

It gave me New York City, above all, a city that I was beginning to see as a mecca for me. A place to breathe.

But it was also about love and transcendence and the possibility of a love that might never die.

I was nineteen. I believed.

Those first six months at university – grappling with the loss of Felicia; the anti-war scene at the anti-war U of C with that labyrinth of relationships; what I was beginning to feel for Carlyle, which, he being black, was that he might save me; and knowing that I had to leave home for good – I found solace in Baldwin's novel.

He disdained what Captain Shamazz stood for because it was a sham.

Baldwin presents his late 1950s Greenwich Village melange of black people and white hipsters as a place where America met its lies. The black nationalism that Captain Shamazz preached, and that I was wrestling with somewhere inside of me, was another part of the American conundrum, and was in fact as American as apple pie.

Shamazz's vision of blackness was built on an idea of American abundance. Just painted black.

'Rufus', the jazz musician and martyr in the book, becomes the man who asks the ultimate question and pays the ultimate price: 'I reserve the right,' Baldwin, through Rufus, seems to be saying, 'to make myself, create myself.'

And above all, Baldwin refused to internalise racism and turn it in on himself, or, because of it, to fashion a new cult in which the wounded becomes the one who wounds.

I understood all of the characters in his book: Rufus, the central character, dead by his own hand but actually killed by a racist society; Ida, his sister, a jazz singer with a white mentor/lover, who is incapable of loving the man who really loves her because she cannot get past the prison of herself.

By the time I was re-reading *Another Country*, the girl who had been astounded by the Beatles was gone.

In her place was an entity looking at the panorama of what was beginning to be called 'the black world'.

My parents, who had endured much more than I ever would at the hands of white people, watched me bemused as I grew out my hair and stopped dressing like a female. Instead I looked like a little soldier in my tiny army jacket and perpetual jeans.

I wasn't their 'proper girl' any more.

James Baldwin saved me that year, my first full year at university.

One of the greatest moments in my life was when I was able to tell him that.

FIVE

I don't know how I met Franz.

Franz was his father's name, and his grandfather's name, and we both decided that some sentimental slave-owner way back when wanted to honour his offspring with his own name.

Franz's mother, an incredibly pompous woman who insisted that I wear a hat on Sundays if I came with Franz to visit her, always pointed out to me as she served tea and crumpets that her ancestor had bought his wife off their master and freed her.

This, of course, was a mark of her class – several degrees above mine, I suppose – and her purpose was to cast aspersion on me and get her only child as far away from me as possible.

Franz could name his antecedents back to the mid-eighteenth century, and I didn't even know Dad's grandfather or great-grandmother. Besides, I had stopped wearing skirts and dresses and had the audacity to come to her house in jeans that weren't the cleanest. Worst of all, my hair was nappy. I hadn't put a straightening comb or straightener in it for a few years.

In fact, since that day in the late 1960s when I decided not to go to the hairdresser, I haven't worn my hair in any way except natural for over four decades.

I think that I disgusted her so much – I was also too dark-skinned – that Franz asked me to wear a hat on visits to her, to cover my head like you do when you see the Pope or an Ayatollah.

I felt violated but Franz was the nicest, sweetest person I had ever met.

He was handsome, too, a cross between Marvin Gaye and Sidney Poitier, loved to dance to soul, and he liked to laugh and make jokes.

He enjoyed Sam Peckinpah immensely. He would laugh his head off uncontrollably during the most violent moments in *The Wild Bunch*; *Straw Dogs* had him in stitches; and *Bring Me the Head of Alfredo Garcia* – I almost had to help him out of the theatre.

But his biggest laughs were reserved for *The Exorcist*. When that child's head started spinning and the rest of the audience – including me – started screaming, Franz spat his popcorn out and roared. He was a big man with a big laugh, and he giggled, too, in an attempt to stop himself. But it didn't work.

When Michael Corleone told his wife at the end of *The Godfather* that he hadn't killed anybody after we, the audience, had seen him kill everybody, Franz jumped up yelling: 'Yes, brutha!'

Of course everyone else felt that in themselves, but we hadn't admitted that we had bought into the life story of a mafioso and that our hero was actually the bad guy. But Franz knew. Franz knew what the journey was that we had been on and he had openly and willing taken it. Why I eventually left him for Danny and the North Side bohemian life, I'll never know.

I think that I met Franz that brief summer before I decided to study liberal arts, when I thought that I might be a lawyer.

The Civil Rights movement had not only been about marching, but about the law, and many young black people saw not only Dr King as our hero, but also Thurgood Marshall, the lawyer who had been a part of obtaining the 1954 landmark Supreme Court ruling of Brown vs. Board of Education, which declared segregation unconstitutional and opened the door to change.

We were a small group of people in between high school and university on a fast-track summer to see if we had the goods.

I loved the law, but my mind couldn't concentrate on contracts and torts, and after I'd seen a judge send a woman lawyer out of his court because she was wearing a pantsuit, and other women telling me that law profs were saying things like, 'women don't belong in the law,' I decided that I didn't want to spend my life fighting male chauvinists.

But Franz stayed with it for a while, as did Fabienne, a tall, beautiful fashion model-type whose fingernails and hair, alone, I thought, must have taken her hours to do before class.

She was the complete opposite of me in every way: model-slim and rangy, elegant as if she were ready to do a catwalk show for 'Fashion Fair', the haute couture show sponsored by black America's version of *Life* magazine, *Ebony*.

Fabienne was flimsy and flighty – a drag queen's study – but she had a mind like a steel trap and took no prisoners. She had no time for any man who did not match her in income and prospects. I was a hippie to her, and a hoot.

She had the mind of what the French call a '*fonctionnaire*' – a civil servant – but she added a twist to it: with her jangly earrings and vertiginous heels, her putdowns of men and her bright red lipstick, I was in awe of her.

Her world, like Felicia's, was black. Period. Black men, black food, black nightclubs, black talk, and she did not approve of Franz because he was too sensitive for her taste. Fabienne had no time at all for our big debates over cards in the lunch room.

Our main one that summer was over the writings of James Baldwin and Eldridge Cleaver, of the Black Panther Party for Self-Defense.

Like everyone my age, Baldwin was considered out of it. He'd been in France for too long, as far as we were concerned, popping over to be on the cover of *Time* as the 'black spokesman' and writing books much too lofty for ordinary people to read. Because 'ordinary' people were who we were going to serve.

We weren't going to be corporate lawyers. We were going to be storefront lawyers; fighting for the people; for political prisoners. We were going to be what the Panthers called 'the vanguard'.

Fabienne asked me one day in the corridor after class if I had actually read anything by Eldridge Cleaver. I had to admit that I hadn't. I liked his stance, his contrast from the leaders I had grown up with, and the fact that he had challenged Ronald Reagan – then Governor of California, who had tried to disarm the black Second Amendment advocates – to a duel on the steps of the California State House at Sacramento.

It seemed appropriate.

We had all grown up watching Reagan seated on a horse on TV, the cowboy presenter of a drama anthology series set in the Wild West, all the while flogging a laundry detergent called '20 Mule Team Borax'. To be challenged to a shootout by a black upholder of the right to bear arms was frankly something that we all wanted to see.

Cleaver had a stellar role-model wife, too, Kathleen, who sported a spectacular afro.

That day in the corridor, Fabienne thrust in front of me

an open page from Cleaver's memoir, *Soul on Ice*. It was an apologia for raping white women. He started by 'practising on black girls in the ghetto', then he 'crossed the tracks' for his 'insurrectionary act'. He felt he was 'getting revenge'.

She started yelling at me about how could I possibly believe in a man like that?

I couldn't. And I didn't.

Franz moved away from him, too.

Ironically, Cleaver went on to become a conservative Republican. In his obituary in 1998, the *New York Times* noted: 'He [Cleaver] demanded that the Berkeley [California] City Council begin its meetings with the Pledge of Allegiance, a practice they had abandoned years before. "Shut up, Eldridge," Mayor Gus Newport told the man who had once been the fiercest emblem of 1960s radicalism. "Shut up or we'll have you removed."'

There were a lot of endings like that for revolutionaries from the 1960s.

A lot.

SIX

The day after Dr King's assassination, the black community exploded (in spite of the fact that James Brown had come on TV to beg for calm). And after it was all over, the official count was thirty-nine dead. Thirty-four were black people. Thousands were arrested; dozens wounded by police gunfire. West Madison Avenue, around where Mamma had grown up, was reduced to rubble. A few areas haven't changed from that day. They're still the same.

The Chicago police, 10,500 strong, were the most aggressive of all in cities where revolts and uprisings broke out. A few months later they would be accused of creating a 'police riot' at the Democratic National Convention. After Dr King's assassination, looters destroyed shops; firefighters streamed in and were shot at. The Governor sent in 6,700 National Guard troops; President Lyndon Johnson sent in 5,000 US Army troops; and Mayor Daley gave a 'shoot to kill order' for arsonists and looters.

I worried about our cousins and uncles and aunts and probably family we didn't even know, who all lived on the West Side, in the thick of it. The area looked like Berlin right after the Second World War: burned-out buildings and shops and cars were everywhere.

I had a job in LaSalle Street, downtown. On public transport, I watched how white people looked at us, white women in particular. To this day, I never walked behind a white woman. I walk just a little to the side so that she can see me in her peripheral vision. The police stopped and searched people, as did the Army and the National Guard.

Our part of town, the South Side, was relatively quiet. The chief gangs, the Blackstone Rangers, etc., kept everything under control, having worked with Dr King in 1966.

The sheer grief in the air wherever black people lived or were was numbing. Tangible.

Churches were packed.

He was gone.

The community, the people, me … we simply didn't know what to do.

The rumour began to spread amongst the powers-that-be that the Black Panthers and 'Black Power' groups had fomented the riot. It was they who had infiltrated the community. It was they who were the clear and present danger. The outsiders.

It was the pundits, the talking heads, the police, the Mayor, the great and the good pontificating on talk shows up and down the land; it was they who were the outsiders, the strangers.

We were told to watch, be careful.

But the Black Panther Party was us. At least some of us. At least some of the young who had decided enough was enough. At least some of me.

We didn't want to wind up like our parents and grandparents, cowering in fear, roped in, held down.

We wanted it – the whole evil trajectory of it – to end, to stop with us. And we wanted it to end with justice.

Following the riot there was a food shortage. Which is how I spent a brief time working with the Black Panthers' 'Breakfast for Children' programme. There were kids going hungry.

These kids had seen soldiers in jeeps loaded with rifles cruising their streets. Policemen hiding behind cars, their rifles pointed up to the building where one of the Panther Breakfast children might have lived.

I met traumatised little kids, kids unable to sleep, to eat. I was very, very angry.

Franz and I, along with others – black and white – helped serve a traditional black breakfast from the Mississippi Delta, food we had grown up eating: grits (ground cornmeal, served hot with butter and a bit of salt); hot homemade biscuits, properly done with flour and water, kneaded, rolled out with a wooden rolling pin then cut into biscuit shapes with the lip of a water glass. And, of course, good pork sausages. All washed down with Florida orange juice, if there was any to be had.

There was no proselytising, no recruiting. There was nothing anti-white, nothing 'off the pigs' going on. They just sat and ate in a clean, calm, quiet place with other little kids. All we were doing was serving, sitting down and talking – just feeding and then sending these kids on their way out into the streets to who knew what.

This hardened Franz's resolve to be a lawyer, to fight the System.

Armed soldiers, the Illinois National Guard – the reservists – patrolled the streets.

But it was the CPD – the Chicago Police Department with their guns and shotguns – that really frightened us. If a Chicago cop wanted you, you were gone.

We knew that, as a body, they hated us. Many of them were of Polish and Irish descent, new enemies who were fighting for the same living space, the same jobs. To many of them, we were simply 'niggers', sub-humans to be contained at best, and if necessary to be put down like the animals we were.

Organisations sprung up that advocated going 'back' to Africa.

These were both black and white so that if you were thinking of emigrating to Africa you actually were spoiled for choice: the white racists offered passage but no settlement costs; the black organisations had no passage but plenty of clout in the Old Country.

There were African students serving breakfast and listening to the West African ones. When they talked, I thought I could hear that small timbre that sounded like my own voice, the voices of Mamma and Dad. I could hear the link. We hadn't lost everything. We, here across the sea, hadn't lost everything.

Franz had to stay in studies or he would have been drafted and sent to 'Nam, but what he wanted to do was become a community organiser, too, work in the community, anything to be with the people. I loved him because he wanted that, and we talked long and hard about how to do it.

But it wasn't possible. It just wasn't.

And then in June, Robert Kennedy was gunned down in the kitchen of a hotel where he'd just made a speech. I can still see the newspaper picture of him, sprawled on the floor in the glare of the camera flashes; a busboy touching his neck, the man's face turned in panic to the cameras; Bobby Kennedy's face stunned, as if he were about to object to dying.

The world waited a day. In the early morning the following day, we got the announcement of yet another Kennedy death: 'Senator Robert Francis Kennedy died at 1:44 a.m. today, June 6, 1968… He was forty-two years old. Thank you.'

The Democratic National Convention came to town. The CPD, still in the spirit of the Mayor's stance on disorder, came down hard on protestors. We stood there, arm in arm, and chanted back to the phalanx of law enforcement officers lined up the stretch of Michigan Avenue – seemingly to the horizon itself: 'The whole world is watching! The whole world is watching!'

Unknown to most of us, the various movements and student organisations had been infiltrated by the FBI's counter-intelligence outfit known as COINTELPRO (COunter-INTELligence PROgram).

COINTELPRO was the subject of one of Captain Shamazz's most unintentionally funny rants. Standing outside the university with his ubiquitous pamphlets and scowling face, he yelled like a Chicago Savonarola: 'Liz Taylor and Richard Burton, kiss my ass! You ain't got COINTELPRO to ask!!!'

We suspected it might have infiltrated the Black Student Union, and it made us wary of one another, uneasy. Partly because none of us could understand why anyone would become a spy.

The person we all looked up to was Fred Hampton, deputy chair of the Illinois Chapter of the Black Panther Party.

We were contemporaries: Fred was born in August 1948; Franz that October; me the following month in November.

Where Franz and I and most others like us debated and read and volunteered here and there, Fred organised youth gangs to stop them fighting against one another.

But he was like us, too, in that he wanted to study the law. He wanted to apply the law so that it worked for the poor, the working class, the young, ethnic minorities, all those outside the System. He joined the Panthers and rose through the ranks because, I think, he believed that it had the correct analysis of things: that black people could no longer turn the other cheek; we couldn't do passive resistance any more. We had to hold the Constitution to its honour, its word – for ourselves.

When we had our teach-in and closed DePaul down for one day, Fred showed up with a few Panthers to stand outside and make sure we weren't attacked. I don't know, maybe he heard about our action and showed up out of solidarity.

Sometimes he would be at the storefront where we served breakfast for the children, a kind of bear of a man, an athlete – he'd once wanted to play centre field for the New York Yankees.

He was a quiet, forceful man, who affected everyone he met. He was becoming nationally known, and we were proud of that. We didn't know that he was the subject of a massive FBI counter-intelligence effort.

It was discovered years later that the split in various black youth organisations had been created by COINTELPRO. Fred was on an official Agitators List, created by the FBI.

The FBI also sent false letters to the gangs that Fred had successfully brought to the peace table, and in July of 1969 the CPD and the Panthers had a shootout.

One Panther was left mortally wounded.

On 3 December, after teaching at a local church, Fred and his girlfriend – two weeks from giving birth – went back to the Panther apartment with another Panther to eat and debrief. Fred fell asleep talking to his mother on the phone.

At around 4 a.m., about fourteen heavily armed police burst into the apartment and shot Fred, Mark Clark, who was there as Panther security, and Fred's partner. Both she and her unborn baby, Fred's son, Fred Hampton Jr, survived.

Fred was finished off by a shot to the head by an officer.

A certain special agent Gregg York said: 'We expected about twenty Panthers to be in that apartment when the police raided the place. Only two of those black niggers were killed.'

This was the way the 1960s ended.

In the last month of the decade, those were the words that rang through us, a decade that had been filled with phrases like, 'Ask not what your country can do for you, but what you can do for your country,' and, 'I have a dream.'

When people wondered, therefore, a few years later, how Curtis Mayfield could write such a heartfelt, poignant lament to a junkie named 'Fred', in a movie about a pimp, I think that's because it wasn't for that Fred.

Curtis Mayfield was from Chicago, too, steeped in its racial story, its hopes and dreams and sorrows. He was a big recording artist and performer, but he stayed close to his people – to black people and poor people and the oppressed all over the world – until his dying day. And he admired and loved Fred Hampton like the rest of us.

Curtis Mayfield was singing about him.

WHITE RABBIT

ONE

Everyone has an era that has fundamentally formed them and from which it is not possible to move. This is the era that touches us. That is, if we were more than spectators or pawns.

At the time it's not possible to know this because it usually happens in the midst of adversity or some sort of miracle. Or when you are young and life looks like a long road with no end.

But if you're lucky enough to look back, you can see.

A map, a destiny, is as clear as anything could be.

My shaping era began after my high school graduation in June 1967.

I was eighteen and a half. It was then that I saw the possibilities for myself, for the very first time, of forming my own way, of moulding my own life.

This formative time, the fount of my politics and art, my world-view, my destiny, lasted until about the summer of 1974, when the newly ex-President Richard Nixon, after a blubbering farewell news conference in which he extolled the virtues of his late mother ('She was a saint!'), took off from the East Lawn of the White House aboard the presidential helicopter into what many of my generation fervently hoped was a well-deserved oblivion:

> Sometimes I have succeeded and sometimes I have failed, but always I have taken heart from what Theodore Roosevelt once said about the man in the arena, 'whose face is marred by dust and sweat and blood, who strives valiantly, who errs and comes up short again and again because there is not effort without error and shortcoming, but who does actually strive to do the deed, who knows the great enthusiasms, the great devotions, who spends himself in a worthy cause, who at the best knows in the end the triumphs of high achievements and who at the worst, if he fails, at least fails while daring greatly'…

Nixon was indeed 'The One' (to state one of his campaign slogans) – an imperial President: the only one to have a convicted Attorney General; the only one to have a Vice President make a plea bargain; the only President to resign; the only person to be an 'ex' Commander-in-Chief.

It was August, a hot afternoon. I had some iced tea as I watched him on TV. I drank a toast. Many toasts were drunk and smoked that August afternoon.

Nixon should have gone to prison for being a part of a conspiracy to break the law, but he was pardoned by his successor, Gerald Ford.

To me, this act truly began the 1970s – unlike the '60s, a time for many when the political was personal and the quest became not one for a just society, as it had been for many the previous decade, but a quest just for self.

Even though I thought that I was doing something else, I was a part of that quest, too.

TWO

By 1967, we young black kids had become promiscuous in our musical tastes and choices.

Our bebop/jazz-era mothers and fathers – who never really betrayed the jazz and blues roots of their parents, just took them higher – watched in horror as we embraced rock, folk and – the end of the world as we know it! – country. We had no idea that we were coming of age in an era of great songwriters in every genre: of course Lennon–McCartney; Bob Dylan…

In 1967, the Four Tops released a song called 'Bernadette', written by the label's in-house songwriting duo: Holland, Dozier.

'Bernadette' is simply superb.

The longing it expresses went way beyond the blues and became a kind of romance epic in the 'Lancelot' sense.

Here was a black man expressing his passion in a way that went beyond God and the carnal. This was Romeo, innocent and assuming that his girl is innocent, too, and there is nothing between them except the jealous Capulets and Montagues amongst their friends – not White People out there.

These friends, untouched by politics and the era, are treacherous and dangerous, lurking in the shadows of their own community.

And in that last section comes the revolution.

The great Levi Stubbs, lead singer, balladeer of black aspiration, pronounces the word 'friend' not like a black man with Southern roots, nor like a slick Detroiter, a citizen of Motor City, Motown, but with the cadences and the accent of – Bob Dylan!

Levi Stubbs – also a voice artist and therefore a man with a highly sensitive ear – had placed this aural nuclear bomb within a soul song, within the Empire of Soul itself.

Where Philadelphia was the capital of freedom, Detroit was the Empire, all because of Motown.

But there was more to come.

In the next stanza, Stubbs sings in a Dylan cadence, a kind of walk-down-the-country-road exclamatory thing.

No black man in mainstream anything had done that before because it was country, 'cracker' and 'like a rolling stone', and maybe even Ku Klux Klan and 'down home boys', waiting behind pitchforks and shotguns to dispatch you, nigger, to the next world.

But he sings it.

Finally, just to reassure you, and because he CAN, that beautiful voice soars with all its lyrical soulful power:

And so the ground, which had been shifting imperceptibly beneath our feet in terms of our identity and place in the land of our birth, was manifested at once in this feat of vocal transcendence.

In a soul/pop song.

THREE

I played 'Bernadette' over and over.

It reached that longing I had on the cusp of adolescence and adulthood.

I was old enough now to want for the power of the Beautiful Woman, a woman who could make a man destroy himself for her.

I wasn't beautiful, no matter how much Yardley or Mamma's stuff I wore, nevertheless, I wanted to try to see how far i would get just as me.

Not out of vanity, but out of that desire to exercise that brief moment when a woman can command by simply being young and reasonably attractive.

I was getting good reviews on the street. I wanted to see how far I could take it.

FOUR

In the autumn of 1967, Felicia and I began visiting Tom, a white friend from high school, at the University of Chicago. It was another world and something new to do.

I liked university life: listening to people talk, not about grocery bills and mowing lawns but about love and power and art and philosophy.

The campus of the university was the place where I could learn to be the Fatal Woman.

Just for a minute.

Then one day I heard the voice of a rock singer by the name of Grace Slick. Slick was the lead singer of a San Francisco band called Jefferson Airplane.

San Francisco was fast becoming one of those icon cities as far as I was concerned.

Along with LA and New York – which had always held that accolade – San Francisco was suddenly becoming somewhere you could go and be free.

You could wear what you wanted and, above all, protest the fucking war without having to run into unfriendly locals who threatened to tear up your placards and worse.

In those days, there was no trillion-dollar Silicon Valley full of tech industries, with buses full of workers driven out to locations enduring their ride with spittle and curses aimed at the windows by angry locals sick of the 'One Per Cent'.

There was no 'One Per Cent' in San Francisco then.

San Francisco meant beatniks (watch one of the worst films ever made, *The Sandpiper,* starring Liz and Dick [Taylor and Burton], to see the California scene in 1967–68).

That was it. And here was the Airplane, a band with Jerry Garcia of the Grateful Dead as spiritual advisor and a goddess of a singer. She was singing me.

Grace sang like a blues singer and a folk singer, too.

But there was something else: a Boudicca quality, a conquering queen who came out of the dark woods to lead her people to freedom. She herself was already there.

FIVE

In 1967 – the 'Summer of Love' – the Airplane had released a single called 'White Rabbit', loosely based on *Alice in Wonderland*. Very loosely.

The Airplane's Alice was not the perky creature we saw as little kids, wriggling with excitement at the Disney cartoon on our big fat TVs.

The Airplane and most specifically Grace Slick's Alice was a young woman making her way through a world that she had not built, had not constructed. And she took no prisoners. There was something ominous about her journey, something foreshadowed, forbidden, and it made you feel powerful to go with her, powerful now and in the future.

Forget Jane Austen because this was 1968. Time to gain wisdom AND power.

Grace Slick has retired from singing. She's a visual artist now.

Amongst her most sought-after subjects … are rabbits.

In one of the finest pieces of rock writing – or any writing – I've read, this piece by Scott Lucas, written in 2006 for Creative Loafing Charlotte, North Carolina's 'dominant alternative weekly newsmedia outlet', quoting Ms Slick, sums it all up: 'If I were still singing "White Rabbit" now, I would be like one of those old women with red lipstick and blonde wigs you see on Hollywood Boulevard.'

On the subject of Nixon:

> I got an invite from Trisha Nixon to attend a tea party at the White House. So few kids went to Finch, she must have invited like every class. She invited me as Grace Wing, my maiden name, not knowing I was singing for Airplane. I brought 600 micrograms of LSD and invited Abbie Hoffman as my date … I wouldn't have been caught, I planned to talk with the man, gesture with my hands – and plop, slip it in. But it never happened. A security guard recognized Abbie and escorted us both out.

And her verdict on Vietnam – on war: 'FUCK WAR. What would Jesus say to George Bush: "You're doing this shit in *my* name?"'

I had never heard such a daring white woman before.

SIX

'White Rabbit' begins with a drum and guitar flourish, spare, clean, like the Gil Evans arrangements for *Sketches of Spain*, created and recorded by Miles Davis between November 1959 and March 1960.

Slick has said the bolero Miles used was the inspiration and you can hear it.

In my mind's eye, listening to the song for the first time in some office organising a protest somewhere, my synaesthesia evokes a '*corrida de toros*' on a hot afternoon in Catalonia, a Hemingway afternoon, an arena where grace and courage are the necessary virtues.

Grace Slick brings this forth in her voice and Miles does this, too, in *Sketches*. He wants to 'make things, connect, make them mean something in what I play around it'.

I read this statement. He articulated what I was striving for: 'make things, connect, make them mean something'.

I started out to try out my new life.

SEVEN

Medication was a part of American consumer culture, what we Baby Boomers had been brought up on. Consume, consume, consume. No matter what the cost. No matter who pays. Your God-given right is to consume the resources of the earth and the sea and the sky; consume your dreams and everyone else's if you get the chance; consume your body and your mind and your soul; consume your talent and your will and your desire.

Make your story the world's story because it's all DOWN TO YOU.

I figured that my addiction to aspirin was actually driven in part by an aspirational urge amongst black parents to stay away from natural remedies, aided and abetted by the medical profession, Big Pharma, and insurance companies. Get ALL Americans taking prescription drugs.

That's why the typical American medicine cabinet contains more stuff than the Cabinet of Dr Caligari.

Medicate. Drug-up!

However, I'm lucky because I can't actually take drugs of any kind. Except aspirin. I don't know why. I tried. But one puff of a joint and I'm out cold, my head thrown back and my mouth open. That is it.

The first and only time that I had acid was on a very cold Christmas Eve. I was sitting amongst a few hippies, some of Tom's new U of C crowd. My new life.

Tom had gone from being a nice, quiet, white boy with the best knowledge of Miles Davis on the South Side, to the quintessential chorus member for 'Age of Aquarius'. *Hair* actually began in Chicago because Chi-town had become – in the summer of '68 – a hippie/Yippie haven on the Midwest prairie.

I had become a kind of hippie, too.

Braless, I wore the smallest military jacket ever created, with jeans and boots and no more 'fried, dyed, and laid to the side' hair, in the words of Felicia's boyfriend, Captain Shamazz.

I looked at the people around me, all these sons of doctors and bankers and businessmen and politicians and probably Mafia, too.

Where would they be in twenty years, I asked myself.

No doubt like their parents, I decided, except with a much more fascinating back story: on some spaceship heading for Mars, they would kick back and recite that speech from *Henry V* that suddenly came to my mind as I watched them eat their acid brownies:

> Old men forget; yet all shall be forgot
> But he'll remember with advantages
> What feats he did that day. Then shall our names,
> Familiar in his mouth as household words,
> Harry the King, Bedford and Exeter,
> Warwick and Talbot, Salisbury and Gloucester,
> Be in their flowing cups freshly remembered.
> This story shall the good man teach his son,
> And Crispin Crispian shall ne'er go by,

From this day to the ending of the world,
But we in it shall be remembered,
We few, we happy few, we band of brothers.

'Old men forget; yet all shall be forgot ... remember with advantages ... Then shall our names, Familiar in his mouth as household words ... in their flowing cups freshly remembered ... to the ending of the world ... We few, we happy few...'

What, I asked myself, would THEY remember?

This little black girl from the ghetto sitting in the same room with them?

I thought: 'If Mamma and Daddy could see me now, they would have a fit!' So I just had to make sure that they didn't. I changed clothes as soon as I had lost sight of our street on my way east and north to the university, and now here I was with these messed-up white kids. At a Christmas party without a Christmas tree!

I looked at the people around me. 'Fucked up!' I thought.

And I was reassured to hear someone echo me, someone say what I was thinking and feeling. Someone connected to me.

Suddenly, I heard it!

Somebody in this room, hiding in this gathering, was on my wavelength.

I could hear another person say what I was feeling, talking about all these privileged backgrounds, their working in the schools on the fringes of the university, risking life and limb to 'do good' or do field research, or escape from a Cape Cod upbringing, etc., free to travel back to the safety of their dorms and their demos and their drugs – just general 'dohickey' ('stuff'), as the country kids amongst them would say – at night.

It took more time than it should have but I came to realise that the voice I was admiring was my very own.

The acid had wiped my own voice-recognition mechanism out of my mind. So wiped me out that my brain had become disassociated from my voice.

My voice was out there and the feelings that I had suppressed about white liberals were suddenly there for all of them to hear.

One of the few black people there that evening said that I was hilarious. He laughed his ass off, he told me.

At least I was funny to him. He hadn't really recognised the voice that came out of my mouth.

It was Mamma's, telling it like it was.

And that 'proper girl' Mamma raised shrunk into the pillows of the couch; I literally hid my face away.

But it was too late.

I had told them all what I thought of them, and nothing I could do would assuage that.

And being what used to be called the 'bleeding heart' liberals that they were, they forgave me. After all, I was Oppressed. I couldn't be helped.

EIGHT

It was clear to me that Felicia and I were coming to a parting of our ways.

She was getting deeper into the life of the neighbourhood, preparing herself to be a woman like the other women, married and with children.

She was going out clubbing with other friends, new friends, instead of being with me, dressed in my combat clothing; she was going to places that were too boring to me, too staid, too full of routine 'oh baby, baby' soul music and – ugh! – cocktails, a preying ground for community courtships guaranteed to stay in the community.

I was going into the bigger world, after all, in my ugly clothing, my gender-free outfit except that I had breasts and men didn't have breasts the size of mine.

Her sister Maria was a much more interesting person to me now.

She was still in high school, yet she was fascinated by a wider variety of things than Felicia ever could be. That was clear to me.

Maria wanted to become a doctor and live abroad, maybe in West Africa.

She understood what I meant when I said that we should

work for Gene McCarthy and not Bobby Kennedy.

We would be different, go against the grain, have some adventure. Not be *Ebony* magazine clones. We would live the life that we just knew in our hearts Cicely Tyson was leading.

She was dating the Prince of Darkness himself: Miles Davis.

He had put her on the cover of his album *Sorcerer* and we both worshipped the picture of her with her short natural hair, clinging to her beautiful dark face, a face alert, curious – straight ahead.

I was really suffering inside because I knew that I was losing Felicia's friendship, her attention and love, but I suppressed it. I took Maria in hand. I was going to make her into the Felicia that I needed to know.

Maria was as shapely as Felicia, and almost as beautiful. Under my tutelage, she took those 'Get Clean for Gene' posters and blue-and-white daisy badges, changed into the tiniest of mini-skirts at one of my many new friends' apartments on the edge of Old Town, the hippie district, and became McCarthy's hottest supporter.

She stopped traffic.

She enjoyed the attention, too, although she was no more interested in white boys than Felicia was.

I could tell, too, that Maria was looking at me through new eyes, seeing me in a new way, and I liked that. Suddenly we were away from the comfy, black suburban enclave of our family homes and instead somewhere rich and strange. The North Side was the total opposite of our part of the South Side. And we revelled in the difference.

We went downtown to the Hilton Hotel where the Democratic National Convention was taking place. It was crawling with the CPD, known as 'the pigs' for short

Now with the white students and organisers, Maria and I joined in with 'the whole world is watching!'

And it was.

Every TV was tuned into our hometown and the week-long Democratic National Convention to elect LBJ's successor that was being held there.

The nervous and angry police chased and beat and drew their guns on hundreds of protestors, egged on by the Mayor himself, who had been offended by what he saw as the 'invasion' of Chicago. Many Chicagoans believed that this had been started by the late Martin Luther King himself during an effort – a few years earlier – to create 'open housing' for black and poor people. He had said then that Chicago had been one of the most racist cities he'd ever been in.

Three years earlier, MLK had been invited by local Civil Rights officials to march against the segregated school system and to help fight against the city's segregated housing.

He had lived not far from our old place on the West Side.

That summer, he had met our generation: the Black Power generation, Chicago division. No more cheek-turning, he had been shouted down with cries of 'Black Power!'

He replied: 'Whenever Pharaoh wanted to keep the slaves in slavery, he kept them fighting among themselves.'

Of course he was right. But we were young and impatient.

By my summer of 'rage', he was dead. Assassinated. I'm still in mourning.

At the Hilton, where the McCarthy campaign was headquartered, Maria and I made our way through the crowd, parting the waves. There were no black women in that hotel who looked like us.

I was practically topless, in a skimpy top with daisies around my neck, and Maria was in the shortest, tightest mini available. If our parents – or anyone from our neighbourhood – saw us like that they would have beaten us within an inch of our lives. We weren't trying to lure anyone; we simply wanted to be part of it all. We wanted to escape our careful upbringing and our careful mothers and see what the world was like, what was out there.

I looked like a rough boy because I wore no make-up. I didn't want to look like Lena Horne, or Diahann Carroll, chic and polished and utterly beautiful.

I wanted to feel like Jean Seberg at the end of *Breathless*, when she hangs Belmondo out to dry because it was never about him or True Love. It was about herself and transcendence.

I wanted to be Bessie Smith riding her big blues train through the South, complete with fine dining car and gold candelabra. She didn't need de-segregation; she ate in a palace on wheels.

I would be what I was looking for.

So I thought.

NINE

Maria and I found Carlyle, who had moved to a new place and was selling vintage clothing in a shop near the university. Together we decided to join the Yippie march through Grant Park.

We saw Abbie Hoffman, leader of the Yippies, and made our way behind him.

Suddenly Carlyle pointed to Hoffman's clothes. What looked raggedy from afar were clearly carefully designed rags. That summed up the Yippies for us.

The night of the Convention, we were out on the street. McCarthy had not got the nomination for President of the United States. The CPD was lined up Michigan Avenue as far as the eye could see.

What the courts later said was a 'police riot' broke out.

Cops and young people conducted running battles through the smart hotel lobbies, and up and down the wide and long boulevard, built to resemble the Champs Elysées.

We didn't see any black people in the crowd, which was really not good at all because it meant that they had been smart enough to figure out that any black folks in this raging throng would take the brunt of the ire of the police and maybe even get killed.

We quickly decided we didn't want that fate.

We made our way through a few alleyways, grateful for the dark, praying that we wouldn't be seen by the cops and blown away outright – just on general principle and business-as-usual for the CPD.

The streets were full of yelling, screaming people.

McCarthy's 'Children's Crusade', as the press called it, had hit the fan, and the Pied Piper couldn't control the kids.

And as for us, we had wanted a candidate who articulated what we felt, who wanted an end to the war, who wanted us out of Vietnam. And I had wanted Experience. But it was over. That part of my quest, anyway.

TEN

I was disappearing from home for days at a time. I had become a big liar by then. I had told Mamma and Daddy that it had something to do with university and it was too hard to come home. They believed it like they believed in Santa Claus.

I was staying with a girl named Stacey – from the Movement – who had met me on a march and taken me in.

Stacey was from the North Shore, the daughter of a surgeon. She had done something that I had not done: she had actually gone down South on a voting rights drive.

She fed children breakfast in the morning.

She marched and marched and marched for what she explained to me was 'my' freedom.

Eventually I came home to talk to Mamma and Daddy. They were frightened. I was in a world that they did not, could not understand. They had no idea what I was doing. All that they knew was that there was no guarantee that I would ever return.

Diane was away at Oberlin. She wrote me funny letters about boys and how she had found a cure for her eczema.

Sometimes I sat up in the girls' bedroom at home, in the window, in my old space, listening to the train.

I watched the quiet, normal routine of others, mocking them inside my head.

I was too stupid, too self-centred to understand that to the grown-ups in the neighbourhood – those black people – after all that they had endured, that safety and routine was a precious gift.

I was going off the rails fast.

I started to steal.

I wasn't a thief, but I wanted to steal from Stacey. I just wanted to hurt her on general principle. And I was poor.

She kept a small amount of housekeeping money in a cookie jar. It was wide open because she trusted everybody. We were all part of the same cause, after all. And no one needed that little bit of money. Except me.

I needed to buy books and bits of clothing. And a part of me was angry with Stacey. Angry that she had 'picked' me as one of the oppressed masses of Negroes out there.

I wanted her to stop me. But she never did.

She kept a small photo of King on the piano. That was the point. That was what she was trying to tell me. She was about peace. And I was at war. My people had worked for nothing for hundreds of years. Her money belonged to me.

All of them, safe white kids who had chosen us without our permission.

They were judging us all of the time, every moment, and we had no say, nothing.

They discussed us in great papers, put us in categories, and there we were, locked out of the corridors of power.

We were the ones dying. As one black woman told me later: 'Yeah, in the "Movement", all of the "black people" are men and all of the "women" in the Women's Movement are white – we're suffering a mini version of the Great Depression right with ourselves!'

So, I figured, historical permission: the right. I took her money.

I left her nothing.

We passed one another in the hall. She gave me her 'do the right thing' look and I gave her back nothing, either literally or figuratively.

The stealing had brought back my childhood headaches and nail-biting.

'They ought to do their thing in their own community,' Felicia had casually said one day as we watched a group of white students on TV explain why they were fighting for the 'Negro'.

At the time I thought that Felicia didn't really like white people.

Did I?

ELEVEN

One night, to make conversation, I asked Stacey about the Black Panther Party. She was deeply grateful. She handed me a newspaper. I don't know how she got it. Maybe she was one of them. My respect for her went up.

I was becoming a thug.

Black Community News Service
May 2, 1967, Sacramento, CA

A group of thirty young black men and women, dressed in black leather jackets, berets, and dark glasses, crosses the lawn to the steps of the state capitol. Many of them are armed with shotguns, though they are careful to keep the weapons pointed towards the sky. As they approach the entrance to the capitol building, Governor Ronald Reagan, speaking to a cluster of schoolchildren nearby, catches sight of their advance, turns on his heel, and runs. Still marching in tight formation, the group reaches the steps, faces the crowd, and listens attentively as their leader, Bobby Seale, reads Executive Mandate Number One of the Black Panther Party for Self-Defense to the startled audience. The mandate, addressed to 'the American

> people in general and the black people in particular,' details the 'terror, brutality, murder, and repression of black people' practiced by 'the racist power structure of America,' and concludes that 'the time has come for black people to arm themselves against this terror before it is too late'. Cameras flash as Seale finishes reading and the defiant group proceeds into the building. One wrong turn, and the delegation stumbles on to the Assembly floor, currently in debate over the Mulford Act, aimed to prohibit citizens from carrying loaded firearms on their persons or in their vehicles. Chaos ensues: legislators dive under desks, screaming, 'Don't shoot!' and security guards hurriedly surround the party, grabbing at weapons and herding everyone into the hallway. All the while cameramen and reporters run back and forth, grinning in anticipation of tomorrow's headlines. 'Who are you?' one manages to shout before the assembly is led into an elevator. Sixteen-year-old 'little' Bobby Hutton is the first to reply, and his words remain an echo in the hallway just before the doors slide shut with a soft hiss:
>
> We're the Black Panthers.
> We're black people with guns

Knowing Stacey, I knew that what she was actually doing was making sure that there were no Black Panthers in Her midst. She knew me better than I knew myself. She knew that she had a nice, middle-class, 'proper girl' in her house who was bullshitting.

The article was a cautionary tale.

I was part of the grey, aesthetic Senator McCarthy thing who couldn't possibly tolerate something like that Black Panther Party. I was with Stacey and the McCarthy people because I hadn't wanted to be a part of what I considered to be the Kennedy Plantation, even though Robert Kennedy was dead and Carlyle was perfectly happy there.

And McCarthy was still bragging about dragging the poet Robert Lowell with him on the campaign trail, implying that everyone else was a hick and uneducated … and what was I doing with a group like that?

I found out that I hadn't done enough research on McCarthy.

I didn't know that he had advocated the relocation of black people in order to quell urban unrest.

Martin Luther King was dead and there were six thousand Feds on the street and eighteen thousand National Guard to protect the Convention's premises. Rich people's property. I was with them, in a way.

TWELVE

I had two escape valves, two places I could go where I didn't have to grapple with what I was going through, where I could forget.

One was a restaurant called Ratso's, named after Dustin Hoffman's character in *Midnight Cowboy*, Ratso Rizzo.

Carlyle and I could eat for free because we dressed as 1940s MGM stars and everyone wanted to take our photo. Recently I found an old ad for the restaurant/music club:

With this ad:
Ratso Rizzo au Gratin
Broccoli, mushrooms, walnuts, onion, pepper,
soy sauce and brown rice
95 cents

From a site called *Long Lost – That was then. This is then*: 'Many of the nation's hottest jazz and blues artists played at Ratso's for a decade beginning in 1969 … one prominent food critic wrote that you could get a very good meal there … or you could also find a cigarette butt in your salad.'

Carlyle could get high while I took pictures of his various poses. Nobody could hurt us there. We were ourselves and the world was left behind.

The other outlet was Phil. He lived in Tom's dorm.

Phil was Polish American and from Detroit. His father worked in a factory, too, and I knew the price paid to get him where he was.

He had a beautiful, friendly smile, and maybe above all he was forbidden: a working-class white guy from blue-collar Detroit, a man whom I was taught – and shown – was my natural enemy.

While Tom was at class, Phil and I would meet up at the frat house and fuck our brains out.

Once Tom came back early and I had to lie under Phil's blankets and be as quiet as could be as they talked outside his room. He came back in as soon as Tom was gone and I have to say that I've never met a man as consistently ready as Phil. But maybe that's because he was young. I had nothing to compare him to. He had a beautiful body and was funny, too. He was in medieval studies and his speciality was the Black Madonna. He knew everything.

He told me about the Madonna at Rocamadour in France; the one in Munich; Dublin; Positano in Italy; Luxembourg; Poland (he said that it was the Black Madonna of Czestochowa that got him started – he couldn't figure out the racism in his family and the fact that they had a huge statue of a black woman on their mantelpiece); and Tindari in Sicily, which has the inscription '*Nigra sum sed formosa*', meaning 'I am black but beautiful'.

We were the sheer joy and pleasure of a male and female body coming together.

He was heaven and I hope that he's teaching his medieval studies somewhere or that he's retired and heavily garlanded and that he's very, very happy.

THIRTEEN

I didn't give Mamma or Daddy my number. They didn't know where I had gone. I called them when the trouble was happening downtown to reassure them, to let them know I was OK.

But they knew, like all parents knew, that their children had to get away from the safety. I had to get away, vanish.

Stacey was reading English and she had a small library. Her books were better than the ones that were serialised in *Reader's Digest*. She had Flaubert and Tolstoy, Zola and Proust when his masterpiece was called *Remembrance of Things Past*. I chose *The Sun Also Rises* because it was slender by comparison.

I read it in two days.

I had not been writing for a long time, not writing fiction or plays, that is.

I had already made up my mind to read history. This was the time of Truth, not lies, and fiction was a lie. Writing stories was making up things. History and the law and journalism were real.

I didn't understand Hemingway, but I could feel that he was practising a restraint, a kind of pull back that was the opposite of Daddy's *Reader's Digest* condensed novels. The very opposite. It was as if he was writing as I read him, the words appearing as if he and I were creating them together.

I found myself trying to understand how he was doing what he did.

My synaesthetic brain told me that he wrote all the way up to the point of greatest tension in a sentence, so that I, the reader, had to finish it.

I had to find the end of it. He wrote the word, the sentence that was the one just beyond what you yourself would form – just beyond it. He moved me profoundly, even though he used words like 'nigger' and his women did not exist except in the hearts and the minds of men.

I was reading a writer that the women on campus were calling a 'pig'.

I was living with people who were 'helping' me and also being used as a conduit or escape, an avenue of transcendence and clarification. I was their mirror, their 'good' side.

That, after all, is what a liberal is.

A liberal 'allows' you to enter their society, I concluded, become a part of their world. But they won't give up the world.

They still own it. They still shape it.

After the murder of Dr King, black men became 'brothers' to me.

I was so intensely involved with self-definition, with liberation in every sense, but especially that of my people, that black men lost their sexuality and erotic power for me. I was too busy working with them to make love to them, or to love them.

That changed. But it has never completely gone back to my teenage years.

Being a heterosexual woman, white men became my only sexual option. And they were completely available. They were easy to fuck, get release with, easy to test my erotic power on because I was starting to see that I had that. Even though I still couldn't see my face in the mirror. No matter.

I could see a face in the eyes of the white men who looked at me – no matter who they were.

The world was quite clearly chaos and I decided to plunge into it.

FOURTEEN

I knew immediately when I walked into his apartment that something was going to happen between Professor Dan and me.

He had a new baby and a wife about a decade older than me. I had seen her on the marches, and I admired her. She was a feminist, too. And I was about to betray her.

At Dan's house I first ate finger food, little sandwiches and cups of tea.

It wasn't enough food, although I was never a big eater.

He knew that. He served me himself as if there was no one else in the room and sat next to me on his couch. Right in front of everyone.

He sat across from his little girl, who played in her playpen and was definitely a daddy's girl because she hardly looked at Dan's wife. I think she was called Julie.

A person always knows when someone else has designs on their partner.

And I think that Julie knew right away that Dan was interested in me.

I didn't know if he slept with his students. Teachers did that then and no one said anything about it, so he probably did. I liked him.

He was cute in a thirty-five-year-old way. Plus he was very bright and talked about politics like the professor of politics that he was.

He linked up Republican candidate Richard Nixon with VP Richard Nixon who had been Eisenhower's Veep when he was a student, and told all of us that it was inevitable that Nixon would do something to disgrace his office.

Nixon was a paranoid, a neurotic. Avoiding disgrace was impossible for him.

He told us about the cloth-coat speech that Nixon had made in the 1950s, a speech made to evoke pity and assure the people that he was not a rich man.

He talked about Nixon and Khrushchev in some kitchen and how Khrushchev – the hero of Stalingrad, by the way – said something that was the equivalent to, 'We will bury you.'

Which Khrushchev actually did say. Dan understood Russian.

He talked about the fact that there was something inevitable going on with America, something the nation could not avoid. It had had one bloodletting during the Civil War. And there was more on the way. Without doubt.

I waited and came around two weeks later when Julie and the baby weren't there and had barely got through the door before Dan and I were at it. Except it was love for him.

I never loved him, although I liked him.

He was a good man, the son of an Irish labourer. Another working-class white guy.

His own father was like Daddy – a man who worked all the hours he could to give his children the best education he could afford.

Julie was from a higher class than him, a much higher one.

She was descended from someone who came over on the

Mayflower and was a Daughter of the American Revolution.

She was working on opening up the DAR, and told me once, when she invited me over to supper, that black women ought to be members, too.

After all, we were descendants of men who had fought in the Revolution – although not acknowledged – and we should be there, too.

I didn't know for a long time – not until after I told Dan it was over – that she had invited me over that day to try and transmit something to me, something that would go over the head of her husband, of any man, and come straight to me.

I was too full of my own narrative, the story I was weaving inside to understand her pain and anger.

It wasn't in the storyline.

After we talked about the DAR and she poured us a glass of white wine – which I couldn't drink because wine takes me out like drugs do, but I took it anyway because I sensed I'd better, I'd need it. She put on the great singer-songwriter Dory Previn's *cri de coeur* and lament about her husband, André Previn, who had left her for the much younger Mia Farrow, who was closer to my age.

Plus Mia Farrow was somebody I used to watch in a soap opera on TV, *Peyton Place*, and wasn't she married to Frank Sinatra, and bang! All my high-school movie magazine stuff kicked in as the wine went to my head, and I was pretty shocked that Mia Farrow would do something like that, but anyway I sat back and listened.

We sat and sipped and listened to Previn's quiet, ironic voice, her guitar strumming behind it, some of the strings in the background like an afterthought.

And my mind made a graveyard and graveyards are not good.

But I didn't want to marry Dan. I had no interest in that. I wanted to be worshipped and to know what it was like to be the centre of attention, the centre of someone's world.

I said thanks for the music and the wine and left. I didn't get it.

We all – minus Julie – travelled to Washington in a bus to protest the war.

I had never gone that far east before.

Dan gave me his key and asked me to come to his room.

Everybody knew what was going on. Everybody was talking about it, too.

These were friends of Julie's, women who saw her at coffee mornings while they were planning demos and discussing abortion rights. And I was there sometimes, too.

And I was fucking her husband. Solidarity.

But they never confronted me.

They shut down like their mothers would have done.

They said nothing, like good, middle-class women.

They watched me walk around in my interminable jeans and army jacket while they dressed in flowing dresses and had flowing hair and waited.

It ended because it had to.

I met some people who said that they were Weathermen and that Dan was a liberal and that I should be doing something 'real'. I didn't go down their route; I wanted to be a student. I wanted to escape into my writing, into books.

I had a student loan and the money was running out. The irony of it is that it was a National Defense Student Loan so I was profiting from the war anyway.

My headaches were coming back.

I read history books.

I had to go somewhere real. I spent hours and hours in the library, eating practically nothing. Sometimes I would go out with Carlyle looking for old clothes that we could clean up and sell to shops. There was a lot of 1930s and '40s clothing around in the early '70s and Carlyle had a great eye.

I was profoundly lonely but I didn't know why.

I had activity, friends, I could have had a boyfriend if I wanted. But I felt as if a long tunnel was opening up inside me, and something was pulling me down it.

Mamma and Daddy were in turmoil and I couldn't see them staying together, no matter how many kids they had.

Felicia was wrapped up in her world of black nightclubs and I know that she didn't approve of me. So I didn't tell her about my life, my choices.

I turned to writing plays again.

I was interested in chronicling the history of black people in Chicago, something that would combine my history studies and my writing. I began to study the 'Red Summer' of 1919, the race riots that left thousands of black people dead and homeless and injured.

When I came to see Tom, I stayed in the frat house.

One day I came back to his room and sensed that someone was there.

Suddenly a guy popped up from behind the bed, a black man, probably from Woodlawn, not far from the university.

He asked me where 'the white boy' was. I told him that no one was in the house. He stared at me. Then he asked me if I got high and I said 'yes'. He pulled out a joint which could have been anything and I had a puff. Gave it back to him. He asked me the question again. I gave him the same answer.

There was no money in the frat house and the place – besides the grandeur of the brownstone – was scruffy. He looked me over again. Then he left.

I watched him walk down the street. None of the students paid any attention to him. They didn't see him. To them, he didn't exist.

Somebody was playing 'White Rabbit' and screeching the song out of their window.

It was awful. Plus they kept singing the last stanza over and over, no matter where the song was:

> Remember what the dormouse said;
> Feed your head
> Feed your head.

LOW

ONE

If you live long enough to have known a song the first time, you can smile at the way it is used by later generations, the innocent reframing it to fit another time, another age.

When David Bowie sang 'Heroes' it was a time of recession, and we, as well as he, were children of the Wall.

Berlin was divided into two, and there was a grey, austere beauty about it.

Just an industrial, dingy grey in which there were shafts of life, generated not by home but from desperation, a strange sort of boredom.

No one had decent work, and yet there was glitter and glitz, a rampant and pagan youth intruded on by our elders who wore our clothing and pretended that they understood the party and the code of the party.

We who lived in the city prided ourselves on the city and its badness. American cities seemed to us to be exactly what Brecht had said they were: cauldrons of steel and smoke and slavery and broken dreams and trampled wishes.

There were too many of us alive. We knew that. Too many babies had been made after the war and there had been warnings.

Mamma and Dad had too many, too, and a part of me

couldn't bear to see their weariness and determination to do it all perfectly. They at once made me ashamed not to be home with them and be the proper firstborn daughter. And glad that I was gone. A vagabond.

Into my circle of bohemians, gay men, sissies and those who didn't know what they were came Danny and Ralph.

Danny and Ralph were two country boys from downstate Illinois who moved to Chicago because they had to. The countryside just wasn't big enough to contain them.

Danny moved into Frankie's building, showing up one day – Frankie said – like an angel dropped from the sky.

Urban legend had it that Frankie – one of the gay men I called 'the Boys' – had been engaged in a three-way when the doorbell rang and he jumped up, still fully erect, to answer it It may have been a potential boarder. Because in 1977 everybody needed money.

Another urban legend was that Danny from Downstate, Farm Boy, didn't blink an eye when Frankie flung open the door, not giving a damn that he was naked. Danny asked if the apartment advertised was still for rent.

How could he know that Frankie would have given him the place for free – that's how beautiful Danny was.

His real name was Michelangelo, named by a farm-wife mother who was also a painter.

She painted murals in between feeding the chickens somewhere on the Illinois/Indiana border where they had their farm.

She had the prescience to know that she was carrying an extraordinary child and named him – and his younger brother, too – before he was born.

Danny did look like something out of a Renaissance painting, a walking, breathing Caravaggio – medium height, thin but muscular with long, curly dark hair, milk-white skin that was almost translucent, and a magnificent face and eyes. His younger brother – yes, Ralph is short for Raphael – was even more beautiful and slightly taller.

To make matters worse, they had a band, Danny on drums and Ralph lead vocals, and they were superb.

They played a kind of prog-rock, downstate Illinois style which is impossible to define. I came to know that genre through Danny, after we became lovers, and often found myself the only black person at a Yes concert, for example, or holding aloft a candle for Peter Gabriel. It was a new adventure for me, a *terra incognita*. And I was looking for those.

The brothers played in bars and drank beer but never got drunk. Not in an ugly way. Nothing affected their looks or their sweet dispositions. Maybe that's what appealed to me.

They had slight country accents – a mild Southern twang – that we all found charming, and the Boys especially would have walked on burning coals just to hear them say a word.

They were unalterably straight but that was part of their beauty, too. They were not afraid of gay men, or outré black girls from the South Side. The most violently flamboyant sissy could be herself in front of them. And I was myself, too.

Whatever that happened to be at the time.

They never blinked an eye if they happened to walk in on one of Frankie's afternoon activities. They just did their business and left him to it.

I met Danny at one of Frankie's candlelit supper parties, a theatrical affair straight out of Georgian London (where, ironically, I now live).

We had to wear formal, vintage, slightly frayed and smelling of moth balls – absolutely nothing 'disco' or 'Farrah Fawcett-Majors'. We had to look as if we had stepped out of a Hogarth.

His parties were a great relief from my day job at the bank, counting out the dollar bills to people desperate to hold on to their money.

My immediate supervisor was black, and a few years older than me.

He knew that I despised what I was doing, 'propping up the system' in my own little way.

I think it amused him because we came from the same area, but I came in like a little black Janis Joplin – jeans, military jacket, afro, a feather boa around my neck, with my work clothes in a shopping bag: a blue skirt, jacket, blouse and heels.

I felt like a fraud and a fool, but lucky to have a job.

Gangs of people my age were robbing banks in Berlin and Paris and Rome, robbing them in order to bring down the system, and here I was working in one.

I daydreamed about being the Bonnie in *Bonnie and Clyde*, all for 'the People', but I wouldn't have got far.

All cerebration and no action.

TWO

This was the recession.

Not that it meant a lot to me. I was always broke. Living from pay cheque to pay cheque.

I think that Frankie pushed Danny and me together because he liked the look of us as a couple. It was a visual thing for him.

Also Danny was hard-working. He'd had enough of rural poverty to know that money did not come out of a hat.

I think that, somewhere inside me, I sensed that Franz was heading for domesticity – the little house and the little kids and the car and the dog and the cat and the mortgage and all of it. I didn't want that, although if I was going to do it, I'd better hurry up. I was on the dark side of my twenties.

But the wonderful thing was that Mamma didn't harass me about it. She didn't urge me to get married.

When I came over for the Sunday meal, I tried to talk revolution, I tried to tell her about Berlin and Baader–Meinhof and their activities, just a few years previous – kids who had taken the analysis into their own hands.

Bowie was there, I said stupidly to Dad, and when he asked me who was that – Jim Bowie, the man who had been at the Alamo; was David Bowie descended from him? – I knew that I had left the South Side far behind.

I tried to talk to him while he was repairing TVs, his workshop at the bottom of the basement stairs piled up with broken sets. But he had no time. Only his jazz records, playing in the corner by the bar, must have made any sense to him as he worked on the circuits in the backs of the huge boxes.

Mamma must have thought that I was hilarious, when I switched from time to time to wearing the platform shoes and shoulder pads of her own youth. They were back in style. But she never said a word to me about my clothes. Not once.

I don't know why, but I told her that I was leaving Franz before I told him, or even before I told myself. I knew that Daddy would be unhappy because he really liked Franz and was sure that, in time, he would lose the afro and beard as he came to confront the real world and it came to confront him.

I told Mamma what I was going to do and she said that it was my business and that I ought to be careful. She was terrified for me and about me, but wise enough and loving enough to know that if she gave me advice, I would take the opposite. So she was quiet.

But I think she prayed for me.

I needed praying for.

I can see now that she was being compassionate and patient with me.

My best friends were gone and in a way I was gone, too.

They were both relieved that I was at the bank; maybe I would stay there after I graduated from university; maybe I would settle down and wear respectable clothes and do something about my hair.

And if I had told them that I was beginning to listen to abstract songs about states of being, interested in bands with massive church organs onstage that conjured up King Arthur, and sat in crowded stadia amongst what they would consider 'hippies' (and they were), they would have rushed to the North Side to snatch me away.

Maybe they should have.

But I just would have run away. Again.

She told me later, much later, that she accepted me as a part of herself, as a part that hadn't lived itself out.

That was why she had tried to control me. She needed to keep that streak quiet, tamed, under control, or the forces out there that crushed all free, wild black women would crush her eldest child.

I was grateful to hear it.

But she told me twenty years after I had already figured it out. After I had already messed up bits of my life trying to reconcile myself, rein in what belonged to me.

And separate out what belonged to her.

THREE

I moved my trunkful of nothing to Danny's place while Franz was at work because that was how brave I was about it. Then I came back and told him that life had changed.

He looked at me with his beautiful eyes and thanked me for telling him. I realised that what he was thanking me for was not having to hear, on the grapevine, that I was sleeping with someone else behind his back.

Sleeping with a white boy behind his back.

By telling him, I had shown him respect. I was too stupid, too unconnected to him and his world, to see what I had done for him. I just thought that I should, that's all.

I didn't realise that that was what I was doing, but I'm glad I did it that way.

We remained friends. I shouldn't have ever broken up with him.

But I would have had another life, been a grandmother by now.

Maybe I am with him. In a parallel world.

I went from the potential perfect suburban housewife somewhere in the near future, after I had settled down, to Franz's 'Black Aspirational' to Danny's 'North Side Bohemian' in, as they say, one fell swoop.

Danny's tiny place was right out of *La Bohème* – with central heating – filled with paints and easels and huge portfolios and his drum kit.

His role model was Phil Collins, and he patiently explained to me what a spectacular rock drummer he was.

While he said, once, that Ringo Starr got lots of credit, he wasn't even the best drummer in the Beatles. The best drummer of all time was Collins. His precision, timing.

I listened and listened for hours after work, and I could hear it, too. Not like Max Roach, who I'd grown up listening to, but different, a rock drummer with an especially fine ability.

His bed was in the corner and it looked like he didn't change it very much, so I started doing that, just like I had seen Mamma at home. It was automatic, and I didn't even notice. His clothes were everywhere and so were his old meals. I turned into a South Side housewife, took charge and started tidying up. A mistake for both of us.

He was very loving when he wanted to be. And kind.

There was something secret in him, and this attracted me.

Behind his beautiful eyes there was something dark and lonely and fierce. He frightened me in that way that silent, beautiful things can.

I knew that he had been born and brought up downstate, which in many ways was the same as the South.

In the mornings, when I was a child, Mamma would comb our hair to the sound of the farm report, these alien voices talking about chickens and hogs and corn, playing their country music, and I would confuse them with the Southern people on the news every night, trying to run black folks out of town, deny us our civil rights.

Danny had a job as a graphic designer and he would work silently during the day while I was at work, making his designs, listening to his bands play.

When he smiled at me it was genuine and we talked for a while about having a child.

But this was early on, when we were in the aesthetics of our relationship and didn't know what we were saying.

He was the first of the occasional guys that I turned into romantic novel plots, men who only existed within my imagination, guys who had long ago ceased to actually exist and become part of the flotsam and jetsam of literature or film.

He was beautiful and we were beautiful together and being with him was a way to beat back the tedium of night class and the bank.

My manager – I guess out of black solidarity and to make me feel like the other black women tellers who fit into the place – asked me if I wanted to bring my boyfriend out after work for a drink.

Somehow they knew that I had a white boyfriend. But maybe it wasn't such a surprise because my address was on the Near North Side, where there were not too many black people.

I knew that they tolerated me, and in those times, in those tumultuous times of plane hijackings, of presidents resigning, of the loss of heroes, we all tried to stay together.

I was grateful to them for reaching out to me and ashamed that I was such a fraud. Because I was.

And I was hungry.

Our rent was very high and every penny went to it, so we didn't eat as well as we should.

Danny devoured hamburgers and spent his nights practising his drum combinations, and I tried to cook what was actually the Depression-era food of Mamma: beans and rice, some chicken, if possible. Every penny I made had to go for books and tuition and I was already over four years at university – I had to go part-time because I couldn't go full-time any longer.

I went home to eat and also to take some food back to the apartment with me. I certainly couldn't afford to lose weight and I was starting to. Mamma noticed it.

But I wanted to make a relationship with Danny. I wanted to be with him because he was complex, and unknowable.

I wanted Baldwin's *Another Country*.

FOUR

I soon came to realise that I could no longer communicate. Not to anyone.

I could talk a mile a minute, I was highly articulate. But I could not communicate what was going on inside of me.

I tried to write, but all I could hear was Danny's drums and his rock music, and his Eno ambiance.

I fell in love with that stuff, it stretched me, took me somewhere else, but I was an alien to my co-workers at the bank – people who came from the same background as me – and I was becoming a stranger to my parents.

I was also trying to be 'normal', although I would have been appalled if I had somehow managed to say this out loud. My body was telling me to hurry up and have a child if I was going to; hurry up and leave the Boys and the parties and get real, if I was going to.

The country-boy bohemian I was living with was a candidate; he understood hearth and home. Was I trying to lure him into something resembling what I had grown up in: a stable home, a mom and dad and kids?

A huge universe teemed and churned and boiled but I could not share that with anyone, I could not relieve myself of it, either.

If I drank or got high, I got sick, a cure, I thought then, but I know now that it wasn't. Then I could see that while I lived on the outside, inside I was in awe of something that I couldn't make real.

I wanted to be that which I had fled, that which I had ridiculed and pretended that I didn't understand or like.

Mamma and I had never really talked. She'd been too busy when I was a child and a habit of that had never developed between us. But I needed to speak to her. I was in my mid-twenties and I needed her wisdom.

I started volunteering at the local settlement house, a kind of community centre run by the Quakers.

I had the sense – inherited from Mamma and Dad – to know that I needed to balance myself out. That was what I inherited from Mamma, too: stay in the world, be in it as it is.

When you know what it is, then make your assessment, your journey, your change.

But always be in the world.

And the Quaker Centre was the world, the real world of people who didn't live with rock drummer/illustrators and go out bar-hopping with drag queens.

At the centre, I worked with little kids – my favorite people and my connection then when I wanted children so much. I don't know. Maybe it was hormonal; or somewhere I felt that it was the proper thing to do.

Danny was Catholic, too, and we could marry at my parish church. With all of his downstate country relatives coming upstate in their pickup trucks, carrying their guns, loyal but appalled at his choice. And my relatives, trying hard to be polite but huddled in the corners of themselves, rolled up in balls of fear and outrage and disgust with me for marrying a 'hillbilly'.

In my arrogance, which is really a part of the theatrical bit of me, I saw myself making some kind of Martin Luther King type of appeal to the angels of their better natures.

The children were all complete anarchists and I watched, crying inside at what was happening to them. They were being 'civilised'. They were being made to sit still, and to queue up, and to eat at certain times, and to be quiet, and to sleep when they were told to.

I would sit at their little tables, listening to them talk amongst themselves about their drawings and their toys. I understood them completely and I wanted to be their knight against the well-meaning idiots who were smashing and grinding them into the dust.

They were black, white, Hispanic, Asian, Native American. Well, that's what they were classified as. These titles and terms meant nothing to them, not even male/female because there were just as many boys playing with dolls as there were girls playing with trucks, and in my corner, nobody was told which toy to pick up.

I became them, trying to get in touch with that time when I was them instead of now, worrying, worrying, frightened.

I was having a mini breakdown.

But in that time with them, I learned that I was actually silent.

Not only silent inside but outside, silent before the world.

I was silent looking at its phenomena, and I resented the interruptions from this.

I made supper at home after work: roast beef when we could afford meat, and butter pudding like Mamma used to make.

I even had an apron and tried to keep in my head the things that she did.

Danny announced that he was quitting work to concentrate on his music.

We didn't talk it over; he just said it one day.

I wanted to write plays, I had a play in me, but I couldn't just stop to do that.

I didn't understand that at all.

But I didn't say anything.

I just worked in the bank, went to classes at night, came home and cooked if it wasn't too late, read my texts until I fell asleep over them, went to bed and started all over again in the morning.

With him.

I felt trapped.

But I had trapped myself.

The strain of the masque that I was wearing was beginning to take its toll.

FIVE

I don't know when Danny began drawing David Bowie.

There were hints in his record collection; stuff started creeping in, mainly from the Ziggy Stardust era.

Inside myself, although I loved much of his music, I was fighting reality: I was strictly into disco and glamour and soul. When I wasn't being a 'wife', I was out with Frankie and the Boys dancing at all the gay bars. Trying to make all of what I was work.

I was starting to draw again – secretly, I didn't want Danny to think that I was in competition with him or anything – and listening to Eno, in particular, opened a door inside me that I couldn't get open before. But Bowie was something else altogether.

Besides his Ziggy thing, I had serious issues with him.

'The Thin White Duke' was offensive, everything that my political life had been opposed to. Where was Bowie, the Man Who Fell to Earth, the guy in Berlin, the one I could relate to, in this Thin White Duke, this cynical whatever that Danny seemed to like, contradicting everything I thought he was.

While the rumour about Bowie having done a Nazi salute in an open-top car in London was untrue, what he had done was make a point about Hitler being the first rock star, how that monster had 'staged a country'. I saw Bowie's interventions, even though in his past, as still dangerous for the times we lived in.

The jolly, kind of happy, flower-power hippies I knew had been cast aside in favour of something darker and deeper, like the anarchists who were attacking the Italian state; and in America, the void left when Nixon took his helicopter ride, in disgrace, away from the White House.

Danny was drawing dark and fierce stuff now, and I was, by virtue of living with him and loving him, in his world.

At one of the Georgian suppers, which by now Danny was refusing to attend because he considered them decadent (that was the point, actually), Frankie had a 'guest of honour in from West Germany' by the name of Hans or Fritz or whatever. I suspect that this was not the man's real name. No one was named 'Hans' or 'Fritz', unless Frankie had hired a comedy German. My half-glass of red had made me as drunk as the average person would have been drinking a bottle.

And I was glad to have it.

We didn't have much food at home.

There was much, too much, wine flowing and I suspect that he was just another international Pretty Boy that Frankie had met at a bar or something.

Those who weren't drunk were wiped out on hash and coke. It was all pretty jolly and then Hans started telling us about his hometown, Berlin, and he started talking about Germany.

First of all, he intoned, Bowie was there. Bowie was in Berlin. Somebody piped up – in typical Chicago fashion – that 'it was in safe hands, then'.

Hans told us other things, too.

His monologue was all about the Red Army Faction, an

organisation many young Germans supported, even if they didn't say so, he assured us.

The media, he told us, called them the Baader-Meinhof Group or Gang, after their two leading lights.

And I'll never forget what Hans said because of its understatement. I think he was quoting something: 'The Red Army Faction's Urban Guerrilla Concept is not based on an optimistic view of the prevailing circumstances in the Federal Republic and West Berlin.'

Frankie had become a big, bad Chicago Italian and told him to shut up, we had a supper to finish, but Hans couldn't shut up because, to him, here was an opportunity to speak to a group of clearly quite stupid Yanks – Midwest Chapter – which meant that we were the second *smartest* Yanks, who after all were from the East Coast Chapter, so he had a duty to inform us.

He told us how his generation was alienated from both their parents and the state, legacies of Nazism. The media was conservative and biased. And a former Nazi had actually run government in a coalition a decade before.

We must never forget that the older Germans were the 'Auschwitz Generation'.

If we wanted to read, he said, looking at Frankie's excellent 1930s collection of *Life* magazines – the ones with movie stars on the covers, of course – then we had to read Franz Fanon (who I had read in my Black Student Union days), Herbert Marcuse (Angela Davis's teacher, I knew about him, too), and of course Ho Chi Minh, Che Guevara, Gramsci.

We had to 'burn baby burn', be 'right on', and 'off the pigs'.

Danny stormed out of the party, saying that he had to go home.

When I got back, he was listening to *Heroes* and drawing.

He didn't say anything to me. I started dancing to it.

He told me that it wasn't actually a dance thing. The title had quotation marks around it. Anyway, why did I always have to dance to everything?

Then he took it off the turntable and put on *Low*. Then he turned his back to me and went back to his work.

And I couldn't believe that I had arrived at this place. That I was here.

There was one other thing: I wasn't sure how we – I – was going to survive the winter.

SIX

I could have gone home to eat. But that would have been hell. The street reminded me too much of Felicia and Diane and I couldn't face that.

I started going to the cinema. Not to see the first-run flicks that Franz liked, no Peckinpah or Pacino.

A friend of Frankie's worked in an art-house cinema and got me in for free.

There I discovered Pasolini and Bertolucci and Fassbinder. Especially Fassbinder.

I saw as much as I could. *Why Does Herr R. Run Amok?*: something I felt like doing at the bank, counting money day in and day out, the utter boredom of being a teller.

All of his films: *The American Soldier*; *The Bitter Tears of Petra von Kant* – the Boys' favourite and the subject of an impromptu recreation at one of the suppers – and, above all, *Ali: Fear Eats the Soul*, which I talked about more than I did *Roots*, the TV programme the entire country was watching and talking about.

In fact, I was growing tired of *Roots*. Not because of it, but because I realised that some white colleagues at work were suddenly staring at us – the black tellers – as if they had never seen us before. Which I suppose they hadn't. I wanted to urge them to see *Ali*, too, but that would have been too much.

I was very quarrelsome. I was very hungry.

The great thing about going to the cinema was that popcorn could fill you up. You could do things with popcorn, too – make it with other toppings – and it wasn't expensive.

But above all, I admitted to myself finally that, in spite of it all, I wanted a life with Michelangelo from downstate. I knew that he was tiring of me. But I had nowhere else to go. And maybe I loved him, too.

I retreated into a tale that I was beginning to build into a play. I began thinking of telling a story from black Chicago, not on an epic scale like *Roots*, but the way Bertolucci had told the story of Italy in his film *Novecento* (1900). I knew that I could make this great, tell the story of my people and through it tell something shocking and surprising about Chicago, about its eternal Mayor.

When I was reading history, I stumbled across some information regarding our eternal Mayor, Richard J. Daley.

It seems that Daley had come of age in a gang – an Irish gang known as the Regan Colts.

It was they who had been one of the instigators of the violence that erupted in the summer of 1919, when black soldiers, returning from the First World War, combined with the pressure of black workers competing with Irish workers for jobs and housing, created a toxic mix that exploded into a series of race riots across the country.

The black community were the principal victims and I wanted – needed – to write about this.

I wanted to centre it around a love story between a young, educated, sheltered black girl and a rough doughboy – a GI – a black guy who had never been anywhere before going to France, and who had been gassed in the trenches and was probably dying.

He was a man who wanted to show that he was more than a butcher in the stockyards; an ex-sharecropper with no education come up on the train from the Mississippi Delta to find freedom.

He was not the lowest of the low, but a human being with a depth of sensitivity and perception that only needed love – true love – to release it.

I thought that the girl was me, and the domineering mother, Lorraine, was Mamma.

But all of the characters were me, especially the soldier, standing outside and pressing his nose against the window of life.

Lelia was living a beautiful life in the suburbs with her house and big, friendly St Bernard and her two children and beautiful husband. It was settled for her and she was thriving.

I wanted that, too; I wanted the safety and the reassurance, and maybe, deep down inside, the routine. The routine that would anchor me to life, give me something else to do besides constantly exploring myself and the world around me. I wanted release.

And there was the play. My lifeline.

Most people didn't live like me, I told myself; most people went about their lives, they were happy to do that. Even proud.

But I woke up every morning and began again with my paper that was always unrolling itself in my head, always writing. I had to walk through the brambles and the bushes, hack through the undergrowth. Search, search.

I came upon a photo of a sparky, intelligent young black woman director by the name of Jackie Taylor and I knew instantly that she was to be the person involved with my play.

I put her picture inside of my notebook and looked at it

every day. I was drawing inspiration from her. Because things were finally, without question, breaking down with Danny.

He seemed to be withdrawing more and more inside of himself.

We barely spoke.

His brother came over and they'd go out, leaving me alone, not telling me where they were going.

I started telling myself that they were reverting to type, becoming 'downhome boys', and now stuck with a black chick they couldn't shake.

That was going on round and round in my head. I had to go, but had nowhere to go.

And, somewhere inside of me, I thought that if we had a baby, if I got pregnant … But why did I care? Was it love? My ego? Insanity?

And if Dad knew that I was effectively humiliating myself with a white man, he'd haul me off to the middle of Lake Michigan and leave me there.

One Saturday, when Danny and his brother had driven off downstate to see their parents for the weekend, I realised that I couldn't leave the house.

I couldn't go outside.

Outside seemed like a big, hostile void, ready to suck me in. Destroy me.

I stayed with my play, writing it over and over again, imagining myself in the world of post-First World War Chicago.

I was glad to be there.

Because I wasn't fit for where I was now. The time I was in now.

My work was all that I had.

And popcorn.

SEVEN

I retreated into my play, which I called *1919*, a kind of homage to the English translation of Bertolucci's *Novecento*, and further into movies.

There was a film I watched over and over called *The Best Years of Our Lives*, a major Hollywood picture when it was released in 1945, which has now fallen out of fashion but was considered a milestone in cinema when it was first released.

It tells the story of three returning servicemen – one of them disabled, played by a real disabled actor from the war – and their troubles and triumphs on the home front. I liked the documentary feel of it. It made me think about the play, think about how I wanted it to feel. Not 'culinary', as Bertold Brecht called much of theatre, but direct, as if it were happening. There were two moments in the film that I went to see it for: the end, where one of the three protagonists – US Army Airforce Captain Derry – looks across the room at the end of a wedding to another main character in the film. She is the woman he's in love with, who he had to separate from because he was still married, but now divorced, he can come to her.

I loved the moment when they saw one another across the room, Gregg Toland's famous 'deep focus' allowing the viewer to see what they see. There she is, standing there, and he walks over to her. He tells her that things will be hard, that it will all be terrible but – and he doesn't even have to say this – they will have one another. They will always have one another.

And then they kiss so hard that her bridesmaid's hat falls off as the scene fades.

I needed that ending. It shamed me to feel that way, that I was sitting somewhere in some gazebo in my mind, covered in ribbons and lace, waiting for Prince Charming and True Love to find me. The 'David' I had created in my childhood and who I was sure would understand me.

The other scene – the one that haunted me and haunts me now – is right at the beginning.

Captain Derry back from the Front, from War, is waiting in a small, regional California airport to go home. A porter is carrying the bags of the rich man who has bumped our hero out of the queue of available spaces.

The porter – not an actor, but a real person, a civilian – momentarily glances at the camera.

He looks directly into it.

He steps out of the frame as if to say that he won't be erased, he won't be an 'extra'. He is a flesh and blood man, a black man – and not a lad, either – who has to fetch and carry for a fat cat who has no idea what this black man's life is about.

It lasts about three seconds. But within it is everything about how things had not changed after the war, that he and men like him would have to fight for everything all over again – and they did.

I tried to put that black porter into my young black soldier, Emmett. I wanted Emmett to confront the older generation, the Booker T. Washington generation, who said, 'Cast down your buckets where you are', or something to that effect.

While my life was crumbling around me, I was finding something in this world of post-First World War Chicago, something in the artefacts and the more genteel time and its rhythms and the will of a defiant mother who was determined to bring up her child as best she could.

The central character of my play *1919* was the young girl, but the force of nature, the fulcrum around which everyone revolved, was the mother, Lorraine.

I didn't make her a weeper or someone who copes, or a battleaxe, as I had seen so many older black women portrayed.

No, this woman would be vital, fighting all of the way; she would not weep, or cry, or have an imaginary violin on the soundtrack when she appeared onstage.

She would be a contradiction, a mystery, the thing that you would not see.

Maybe, in creating her, I could become that, too.

I could escape the bank and all of the banks I seemed destined for.

I needed to find a way out, if only in my mind and in my work.

EIGHT

One of the tellers in the bank used to be a student radical.

I had seen him a few times in Grant Park.

I recognised him, and if it had been known that either of us had been there at the time of the Convention in '68, we might not be at that bank.

He had considerably cleaned up his act: his hair was cut, the beard was gone, etc.

We would exchange a few glances sometimes at the water cooler, or when the lines of customers snaked around the counter after they had filled out their deposit and withdrawal slips every Friday like clockwork.

I counted the money out, smiling at each one. And each person had a signature note, some music that played in my head whenever they stepped up to the counter.

One day, tired, I heard the overture to something Russian and operatic that I couldn't put my hand on, mixed in with something that I had heard while working at my new part-time job at the Crazy Fools Pub on weekend nights – probably played by the avant-garde group of musicians dedicated to black liberation and also liberating you to what jazz was, or as Ahmad Jamal called it: 'great black music'.

It was running like that.

Or in other words, the day was a kind of chaos.

Maybe that's why I messed up.

I counted out at the end of the day and was five hundred dollars short.

I was called into the office and questioned. My black supervisor tried his best to ameliorate the situation. He knew that I hadn't taken the money. But no one knew where it was and I was the only one who had access.

I went over and over all possible explanations. I was shaking like a leaf. I didn't know what would happen to me.

The supervisor couldn't help me.

I was told that I would have to take a lie detector test in order to keep my job.

The way it worked was: they asked you obvious questions, questions you wouldn't lie about, in order to see a pattern and shape.

Then they asked the questions that they wanted answers to. If there was a deviation, the conclusion was that you lied.

I was asked if I had ever taken drugs.

I couldn't say, 'I have never taken drugs,' and then go on to explain that a puff on a joint or the bite of a hash brownie is not 'taking drugs'. The test didn't allow for that kind of nuance.

So if I was to be technically correct, I had to say 'yes'. Otherwise the machine would record my wavering as an attempt to hide something … or as lying.

Then I was asked the direct question – whether I had stolen the money – and I said no. That was the truth, according to the machine.

The test was taken during working hours. After it was over, I walked out and back to the floor. They tried their best, but everyone was looking at me.

The old student radical gave me a power sign, very small, but who needed that right now?

I looked across the floor at the customers and the shiny surfaces and the System.

Two days later I was called to the office and told quite casually that the money had been found, stuck at the top of the drawer in one of the mechanisms that made the drawer slide in and out.

I burst into a big smile.

But, my boss said, I was being fired because I had admitted to taking drugs.

And I had to go right away.

My supervisor was nowhere to be found.

I got my things and walked out into LaSalle Street and got myself lost in the hustle and bustle. I found a movie theatre and bought some popcorn. I sat on the lip of a public fountain and ate the entire bag. Then I went home.

Danny was there and said, without any preamble, that he and his brother were forming a band and that they would go on the road. They had written a collection of songs and wondered if they could get an audition at the place I worked at on the weekends.

Frankie was giving one of his Georgian dinners and I went on my own.

He held – for me – what he called 'Bette Davis Moments' in his narrow galley kitchen, based on the moment in his favourite film *All About Eve*, when Bette Davis talks to her producer in the kitchen.

I was the only female at the supper, filled to the rafters with drag queens. Some were professional and, of those, some were stars.

I had a glass of champagne and told the assembled throng, come to worship at the shrine of Frankie, what had happened to me that day and what was happening between Danny and me.

The advice was unanimous. As one South Side drag queen told me: 'Get my grip … and tip!' In other words, pack my suitcase and walk away, my head held high.

Frankie took me to his pantry and told me that essentially these guys were dull boys and he would have told me so but had been surprised at how far things had gone.

He had never seen me as a housewife and what point would there be in me becoming one. I was a playwright and a wearer of the clothes that could be found for me.

I was the mascot of the gathering and they weren't going to allow me to walk around in thrall to a dull country boy.

After it was over, the biggest drag queen, from the state of Oklahoma, Aphrodite Welles, stood up to do her rendition of Cher. It was a medley: Cher, as Sonny and Cher debutante, singing 'I Got You, Babe', all the way to the glory days she was experiencing now.

Aphrodite danced and pranced around the room, all six-feet-three inches of him.

He had captured the construct of woman, objectified it, and gave it back to all who would receive it.

I had lost my principal job that day and it was snowing outside.

But I had found a family that I had had for some time now but without understanding it.

Aphrodite gave me her big gypsy earrings.

I put them on.

GYPSIES, TRAMPS AND THIEVES

ONE

I decided that the language option I was going to study at university would be French.

I think that it had something to do with Daddy's time in France during the war.

Sometimes he would tell me that he recalled sailing from 'Marseilles, France', which he would elongate like something he wanted to savour for a long time.

I didn't want to study Spanish because I had studied it in high school, and anyway, Spanish was all around me. Everyone spoke Spanish.

I had also discovered Rimbaud's *A Season in Hell.* I wanted to read it in the original, not go through the portal of a translator.

I wanted to know exactly what he meant with the line: '*Les blancs débarquent. Le canon! Il faut se soumettre au baptême, s'habiller, travailler.*' 'The white men are landing! The cannon! We must put on clothes, take baptism, work!'

There was much more there than the translation.

I hated *Les Enfants du Paradis* because I simply could not understand it, and the images looked banal, the translation banal. I had no basis for knowing that somewhere it was not quite right.

I knew that translating a language is not the same as the language itself, its terrain: the hills, the valleys, its plains and particular pavements.

And on some level, it was about Baldwin.

I couldn't understand why he hadn't been on the podium at the March on Washington a few years earlier. He seemed to me the perfect orator – a man who had escaped, who lived elsewhere and could cast his eye over his native land and report what he felt and knew.

Baldwin was a man who existed in two worlds, a man who had found his feet abroad. I read everything he wrote and I loved the outlaw about him, and also, he seemed to me to be a kind of dancer, someone fleet of foot and full of grace.

I discovered decades later, when LGBT history began to be known, that Baldwin had been kept off the podium along with A. Philip Randolph, the great Civil Rights activist and Father of the March itself.

At the beginning of the Second World War, Randolph and others had gone to the White House to inform Roosevelt that they were prepared – as union organisers – to send the sleeping car porters (black men) out if they did not have decent pay and conditions.

Of course Roosevelt could not allow a strike and march on the Capitol on the eve of war, and so he signed an Executive Order that eased the porters' conditions.

Some say that Randolph was helped by Eleanor Roosevelt, the First Lady and, it is sometimes alleged, a closet lesbian.

Randolph, however, was anything but closeted.

He was arrested on an indecency charge with another man in a car off the roadside. He never explained nor apologised. He considered homosexuals as part of the community of the oppressed, but he came up against the homophobia of the black community, and the black church in particular.

Moves were made to keep him out of the spotlight, keep the March as 'American as apple pie'. After all, the television networks had cleared the afternoon schedules of soap operas, game shows and stuff for the after-school set, and ran wall-to-wall coverage of the event.

A television first.

Movie stars were brought in and Burt Lancaster read a poem by Baldwin, instead of Baldwin – quite notorious in the Movement by then for his best novel, a chronicle about the love between two men: *Giovanni's Room*.

The reality of the Movement suppressing others, particularly some of its greatest champions, has yet to be uncovered, talked about, and heroes and heroines restored.

Even though I did not know this as I bought my French books, I did know that French seemed to hold its own kind of liberation.

So French it was.

I sat in the back of the class behind a long, tall boy with a big, uncombed afro and trouser legs that stopped well above his ankles.

He was very assiduous, taking down every note, everything that was being said. He caught my eye when we stood up to move on to our next class.

I found out later on the grapevine that he was from Alabama, a state with a terrible and undeserved reputation for being the home and the haven of hicks. To be 'Bama' or for something to be 'Bama' was quite simply to be relegated to the bottom of the totem pole.

His beauty and his otherness were the talk of the campus.

A few women I knew suggested that he should be taken in hand, made into a Chicagoan.

At least get longer trousers and a haircut.

I disagreed. I liked him the way he was.

He was younger than me by a year but was a great deal wiser. He was a beautiful boy and very, very different.

He took to me right away. We were the only two black students in class.

I liked him because he didn't expect me to be a 'sistuh' or a 'handmaiden' to the Cause.

That kind of burden is how I perceived what most black men then were about, very driven people with lots of women and the Mission.

Carlyle was a Robert Kennedy supporter and still had his Robert Kennedy stuff. He talked about the slain senator from New York and brother of JFK with great affection, even when talking to various clusters of students about moving on, how we all had to move on.

Students of all colours and backgrounds were beginning to gather around him. To say that he was charismatic is an understatement.

He had a very strong and strange Southern accent, like a country and western record gone bad. He laughed a lot, too.

Not the cool half-laugh that we Chicagoans had, the kind of laugh that makes you wonder – if you're the recipient of it – if you are actually the joke. It was the laugh of a man who felt lucky, lucky to be where he was and who he was.

That's what I felt about him.

The black students kept pretty much to themselves on campus. They played cards in the lunch room in a tiny clique that sat right in the middle of the hall, their intensity and hostility sucking all the energy out of the room.

I told Dad about them once and he just simply couldn't understand why they had gone to a white university; there were plenty of superb black ones about.

Mamma said that it was because quite obviously they

wanted to start trouble. And nobody needed their nonsense.

I was torn – as always – between sitting with the BSU (Black Student Union) or the general population.

If you did that, you were made to feel that you were a traitor. If you didn't know how to play gin rummy and talk about 'offing the pig' at the same time, you were one, too.

But Carlyle ignored them. He was friendly, but he never engaged with their arguments and their running commentary.

I was intrigued by him, mesmerised. Who was this 'dad-gummit' from 'Bama?

Spindly as he was, he seemed to be able to fend off trouble.

Then I didn't know about his weaknesses and the lie he had lived for so many years.

TWO

I realised that I was becoming more and more estranged from the BSU.

I supported more black studies and raising the number of students of African descent in the school. But there was something absurd in what they/we were doing.

Here we were, most of us brought up quite genteelly, walking around looking like we came from the 'hood.

There was a haughtiness from some, these sons of doctors and lawyers. I couldn't stand them, and in many ways, still can't.

Carlyle stayed away from them.

I wanted to tell these revolutionaries of the BSU that Carlyle was a man born and brought up in the cauldron of the South while many of them hadn't gone further South than Joe's Rib Shack or its equivalent somewhere on the Far South Side.

Or to the 'hotel/motel Holiday Inn' thing that Franz liked and I participated in sometimes with him on Friday or Saturday night in some lakefront hotel full of middle-class black kids getting off away from Mamma and Daddy.

Things were moving on and I wanted to move with them.

Angela Davis had surrendered to the police; the Symbionese Liberation Army – a black/white group of Movement people – had kidnapped Patty, the Hearst heiress, and held the nation enthralled with their broadcasts, and she seemingly turned terrorist, too, by making broadcasts in which she called her mega-rich parents 'pigs'.

The wind had changed. But I had no idea, nor had anyone else, which way it was blowing.

Carlyle and I were the outsiders, the two people who seemed to straddle both the black and the white students, Carlyle mainly because he was being seen as a future student leader – the first black person ever to be considered for something like that.

His star was rising, but I could tell that he was uneasy.

When the BSU took over the university and shut it down for a series of teachings on black history and imperialism, Carlyle and I went to the Assistant Dean's office, where he was being held hostage in a kind of suburban way.

He was allowed to give his wife and the police updates.

The students who were holding him gradually forgot why as they formed themselves into a Council and debated.

Carlyle and I watched their mounting excitement as they rifled through the Assistant Dean's files, not sure what they were looking for or what they thought they might find.

The ROTC – the Army's student cadets – were outside in the courtyard, waiting to come in if need be. We really didn't have a leader, just that Council trying to decided what to do next.

The Dean refused to press charges and demanded that the police not set foot on campus.

Carlyle talked to a small group about growing up in Alabama, the uncertainty of it, the terror.

Gradually he gathered a crowd, including the Assistant Dean.

He seemed to be the guy I was looking for without knowing I was looking for him.

He was a kind of mirror of me, I thought, that part that I couldn't quite see yet, that I didn't understand.

That night I did give some thought to spending the night in the county jail and that made me want to give up my protest, I admit, and go home, but the gauntlet of demonstrators and counter-demonstrators would have been intimidating and then who knew what would be waiting for me outside. So I stayed where I was.

I talked to the Assistant Dean – a great chat about American Revolutionary history, his speciality.

He saw the need for the revolution to continue, to never stop. He talked about the Right and its ascendancy. He told us that he understood us.

Then, suddenly, Carlyle announced that he was leaving the sit-in.

I was shocked. To leave would be tantamount to deserting the Cause, whatever our Cause was. Besides, what could lead him to walk out of the sit-in?

As he picked his afro with a comb he explained that he had a ticket for *Hair* and he had no intention of missing it.

And then, from what seemed out of nowhere, Janet appeared.

They left together.

I watched them walk across campus, she clinging to him as he sang the score to the show. At the top of his lungs. While the real thing was going on all around him?

Or was it real?

Was his leaving it, hand-in-hand with the dullest girl on campus, his way of saying that this was some kind of theatre? That he understood this and none of us did?

The police stopped him just as they were about to leave campus.

A small crowd gathered around.

This was, after all, Chicago, the city that Martin Luther King had called the most racist he had ever visited. And here, right in front of the police, was a black man walking off into the night with a white woman.

Janet lost her temper, the first time I had ever heard her raise her voice. We were all gathered at the windows. This was going to be our student president.

But Carlyle got through, and continued on his way with his dull white lady.

How could he pick her over me?

I said this to myself out loud. I shocked myself.

THREE

I was moving away from the world of education, academia, and going somewhere else. I knew that I would stay on to graduate, I knew that I was going to do that for Dad.

And for a professor, too, a black man also named Ben, who standing behind me once at the cashier's office, and seeing me staring at my tuition bill, asked me if I had the money to pay it.

I said no.

He wrote a check and paid for my semester.

I will never forget him.

But in spite of that, the joy of learning, of school, a place I really loved, all of that was over.

Formal learning was a series of dates, an empty chronicle that had nothing to do with me, and what mattered to me. Soon, I knew, I would have to stop day classes and go to school at night. I didn't mind; I thought there would be more 'real' people there.

I was on the fringes of student life, mingling, but not there.

I watched the other students, so intent, so focused on getting their scrolls at the end. As I watched my generation, I heard in my head a kind of Brahms. I think it was Brahms. Something being played in our baby rooms, in our cribs.

Look at us, I thought to myself.

Our generation's paediatrician – our baby doctor, the man who wrote THE book to tell our mothers what to do – even he was at our demos, marching, protesting.

At our age, early to mid-twenties, back in the old days, we would have been parents and Army colonels and parts of businesses, but what were we doing now?

Being students, eternal students, listening to yet another speech about changing the world.

Carlyle and I were not there any more; our demo days were over. We were going through the motions of it, just as I was going through the motions for my classes.

Later, Carlyle and I spent our afternoons talking about art at Ratso's over a bowl of soup and homemade bread.

McDonald's was just beginning to go mega, and I lived on the soup and bread and the Filet-O-Fish.

Carlyle told me that he intended to be student body president and asked would I help him, would I be his campaign manager?

This was going to be conventional politics, the real thing, the thing that made up the democracy itself. Debates and campaigning and voting.

I could see that politics might change things and I began to think that I might want to be a part of the political process.

I worked hard on his campaign, running the mimeograph machine, standing outside handing out leaflets. I sat up all night debating his point of view, his worldview.

And I was proud, too. Proud of this brother.

Carlyle came across as 'down home', not some middle-class black kid equipped with a mountain of theories.

He was also elegant, reasonable, funny in a world becoming less so.

Plus he had other things he was doing. Things in which I

was the rube, the hick.

In between classes I was going to the rep house to see films. Carlyle often went with me and we'd do a running critique on the dresses and the make-up.

We could understand why Bette Davis had been our mothers' favourite.

Carlyle was easily elected and I worked with him on the Student Union's business. On the surface. But we weren't really doing that.

Carlyle was slowly becoming a collector. I began to spend more time with him and his antiques; rather than politics, I was getting an education in his fine taste.

He never talked about Alabama. But he was old enough to have known about Little Rock and the school desegregation there that had made headline news.

I wanted to know what he told himself about that, what he had seen and felt. I knew, too, that there was an issue with his father. He hinted at that one day when I talked about Dad.

He sounded bitter.

Anyway, he would rather talk about the Bauhaus, Cedric Gibbons and the way that Garbo used her key-light.

His sister came up once from Mobile to visit him and see if he was OK. He was her baby brother.

They sat and put their heads together and I was a bit jealous. But I really couldn't be.

She was a gentle Southern woman, and cooked for us in Carlyle's small place the size of a shoebox.

She wasn't shocked when she stayed over and saw the state of the place, half student, half artist. All clutter.

I was sort of living there, halfway between Mamma and Dad's and this black bohemian world.

Carlyle was collecting boxes full of art deco photos: Duke Ellington caught in a silver sheen – he could have been no more than thirty – and Bessie Smith, her mouth thrown open in triumph.

Carlyle went to junk sales and boot sales when he wasn't studying and gradually the collecting overtook the politics and he resigned as president because he was an honest guy. And also, because he was bored.

I went on an anti-war demo to Washington D.C. and learned an enormous amount about Kris Kristofferson at the farm I stayed at in Northern Virginia.

I had never been in the countryside before. I was taught that the woods were a scary place for black people. We disappeared; we died in the woods.

There was something that I knew walking through the grass and sniffing the air.

After all, I was from country people and somewhere in me I still knew it.

When I got back, up to my neck with my professor from the U of C and trying to dodge his wife, Carlyle made me a big pasta dinner. We had some wine, which knocked me out – he knew this would happen – and he told me that he was getting married to Janet. The most boring girl on campus.

I couldn't understand what he was saying as he spoke to me. He. Was. Getting. Married.

I hadn't even seen it; I hadn't even known it.

I pretended that I was happy for him. I told Franz about it, and he said that it didn't surprise him. If Carlyle was going to marry at all it would be somebody like Janet. I demanded to know what he meant.

He didn't tell me.

I pretended that it was all OK, and continued collecting antiques with Carlyle.

To make conversation one day, because I had stopped speaking to her, Janet asked me if Franz and I were going to get married and have children.

I said no.

I said that I didn't want kids to bore me.

I looked out of the corner of my eye at Carlyle. I waited for him to applaud me. But he didn't do a thing.

The wedding was quick, and big, a Polish-Catholic working-class thing.

Only Carlyle's sister could afford to come up from Alabama for it.

To say that his new wife's family was not pleased that she was marrying a black man is an understatement.

The whole thing was like something out of a bad movie, with big Polish guys as the heavies who looked like they might, at any moment, run amok and kill Carlyle and all of his family and friends. And me.

Franz came with me and insisted that we sit by the door. He had a big afro and a beard. But I was a part of the wedding so I couldn't.

I could hear doom-laden music.

And this was the first time that I questioned the music in my head.

I was sure that I was simply jealous. How could I think that he would be happy with only me and not anyone else?

I decided to bury myself in the Middle Ages.

I needed to get my degree for Dad's sake. I couldn't mess with this. I had to leave my day classes when my grant money and then the loan money ceased. I had to find some kind of work that would enable me to continue my classes.

I didn't know if I could study at night, after night classes. Night school was another world.

I would have to stay up at night; I would have to be serious.

One of the people in the Student Union organisation was

an affable guy named James, who had bright red hair, which I loved.

James was studying to be a doctor and he had a job selling cars. I was convinced that he fancied me.

He had come to the wedding and danced with Janet and Franz and then we – Franz and James and I – left together to find something to eat and drink because we couldn't eat the food.

I cried my eyes out.

Franz left me to it.

About a week later, James said that he was going to Europe for summer vacation and had an extra ticket to Amsterdam, the coolest place on earth.

Maria was having a gap year in London and maybe I could take a ferry over to see her.

James told me that I could pay him later.

I didn't know how that was going to happen, but I said I would. Somehow.

I ran out and got a passport and told Mamma and Dad that I was going to Europe. What could they do, I was gone.

I didn't say anything to Carlyle, and Franz just waved goodbye. He couldn't stop me, either.

The only food that I could afford to take on the plane was Toblerone bars. I ate a great deal of them.

There was a stopover in Iceland.

As I sat waiting for the flight to Holland, two little white kids walked up to me and stared.

I smiled and they smiled back.

They made me cry.

FOUR

I had never seen so many dog turds in a street as there were in Amsterdam. Big, massive ones, and they were everywhere and could turn up anywhere.

I kept my head down whenever I went out, searching the ground.

We stayed in a student hostel, a huge people-warehouse for those on the European leg of the 'hippie trail'. Because (make no mistake about it), for some reason, Amsterdam was the place where you could sit on the ground at the Central Station, panhandle and live for ever.

You could go into a tiny 'mom and pop' shop with the smiling proprietors greeting you and look down on their rack to see the most intense porn I had ever seen available for sale. Those old folks didn't blink an eye.

They didn't blink an eye in the quarter where the women sat in the windows, advertising their wares and specialties. I tried to speak a bit of Dutch but was told that even the Dutch have a hard time with the language, so I gave up.

I had never in my life seen so many 'white'-looking white people. They all looked like one another to me: blonde, round faces, friendly.

In the 'brown cafés' you didn't have to buy dope. Just sit in the doorway and inhale.

I saw *The Night Watch*, which was illustrated in one of Dad's encyclopaedias.

I burst into tears at the sheer scale of it. I had no idea it was so massive and I was moved by it, especially having seen a film with Charles Laughton at the repertory cinema house in which he portrayed Rembrandt, and the suffering, the humility of that genius.

I did learn one Dutch word, '*blumen*', for flowers, because, like Mamma, I had to have a fresh flower near me no matter what.

I learned to collect the *blumen* that fell from the stalls and lay in the gutter. We danced in the Dam Square to travelling troubadours.

I had to go to Anne Frank's house, to the Secret Annexe. Like every girl of my age who had read the book or seen the movie version, I was moved by her story.

As I walked in, I saw Shelley Winters' Oscar for Best Supporting Actress for her role in *The Diary of Anne Frank*. That really disturbed me; it seemed like a sacrilege.

I didn't know that Miss Winters was Jewish and dedicated her win to the victims of the Holocaust. I didn't know how spontaneously passionate she was until over a decade later, when I was a member, while living in New York City, of the Actors Studio Writer and Director Unit. I knew later.

One afternoon, Norman Mailer was presenting an excerpt from his Marilyn Monroe play *Strawhead*. Norman got Marilyn wrong and the way that we knew this was that, suddenly, from amongst the group watching, Shelley Winters jumped up and yelled that Marilyn had been her flatmate and friend, and that the Marilyn Monroe known to the public was an act. Maybe one of the greatest acts in show business.

Shelley Winters started me thinking about Marilyn Monroe in a serious way, and set the groundwork for the fact I stumbled on in 2005: that Marilyn had not only helped Ella Fitzgerald's career, and Ella said so, but that Marilyn was a politically committed woman, a very complex and naturally intelligent woman whose beauty had become a burden.

I wrote my first version of Marilyn and Ella's story in 2005, and I've written several versions of it since.

Theirs is a beautiful and amazing story.

As I climbed the narrow stairs up the Annexe, I thought about this girl, this profound writer who had found her destiny, her purpose, in an attic, hiding from a monster.

I saw her movie-star pictures still plastered on the walls, and felt how cramped it must have been for a growing girl, for a girl whose mind, whose human capacity, was infinite.

I looked out of the same window that she had and saw the canal and the trees and the Westerkirk over that same canal, and the bells and the sky.

You didn't talk in there because it was a shrine even if it didn't have the air of one. James and I came out into the grey Dutch light. It was not possible to talk after that.

Later that evening, just out of curiosity and because I felt 'international', I took a ride on the back of the scooter of a guy I met at the hostel.

I had to fight him off at a vacant lot, and I realised how utterly stupid I'd been, and lucky, too.

I took the ferry from the Hook of Holland over to London to see Maria.

I don't really remember where she was, but after having lived in London now for almost thirty years, I think that she was in the East End, Tower Hamlets, because there was talk of the Tower of London.

I had never seen such poverty in people's faces before,

that look that lets you know they haven't eaten properly for a long time.

Some guy called me a 'Yank' playfully, and for the first time I knew what that meant. I had no money at all, as far as an American was concerned, but I could still move around.

Maria was cooking, washing and lived in a small attic room.

The entire house smelled of urine and everything seemed so dark, the sky was so dark.

This was nothing like the candy-coloured London that Maria's sister, Felicia, and I had read about, dreamt about. The 'Swinging London' of the Beatles and Jean Shrimpton and James Bond and Shirley Bassey and the Queen.

Maria and I didn't talk about Felicia.

She had moved away from both of us.

I went back to Amsterdam to meet up with James and catch our flight back home.

James had been high the whole time, which was very strange because he was an incredibly straight-laced guy.

One night, over a beer (I was drinking Coke, I didn't want to be unconscious), James went on and on about Carlyle and the wedding and the mistake he'd made.

We spent the whole evening talking about Carlyle and it was very intense.

When I went to sleep at the hostel that night I realised that I was in love with Carlyle.

And James was, too.

We'd both fled to get away from Carlyle's new life.

Both of us.

FIVE

I had to concentrate on getting my undergraduate degree.

I was in my mid-twenties; I didn't want to be an undergrad much longer. But I wasn't going to let my father down.

But it was like going to church and no longer believing in God. There were people at the bank where I worked who had degrees and they were counting out big pay cheques to electricians whilst they themselves took home nothing. This was before the frenzy for degrees, before people piled them one upon another.

We were told that the Arab nations were going to starve us of petrol. Watergate was in the air and every young person felt that there was a shadow government, something out there that controlled all of us. Every major film seemed to say this either overtly, like *All the President's Men,* or covertly, like *The Godfather,* in which Coppola brilliantly subverted the good guy/bad guy trope by making Mafia chief Michael Corleone a hero because he wasn't a hypocrite.

Just a killer.

We wanted to get out to work but there was no work.

I saw my old movies: *Casablanca* a thousand times; I developed a mania for *Robin Hood* and decided that he was the only guy who could actually sort the world out.

I was well and truly heartbroken when someone told me that Errol Flynn had been a slave-runner in Tasmania or somewhere, and I felt like I had to prove that this was a lie. I was greatly relieved to discover that it was, and also that Errol had offered his services to El Commandante, Fidel Castro.

I learned at the cinémathèque that Orson Welles, instead of being the big, fat guy on TV who sold cheap wine, was actually a genius, a true *enfant terrible*, who had suffered the tragedy of all *enfants terribles*.

Louella Parsons had called him 'Little Orphan Orson' in a parody of Little Orphan Annie, in an attempt to destroy his career after *Citizen Kane*, the most audacious film ever made by a young filmmaker.

Hitchcock was no longer the fat, creepy English guy who made good television and *Pyscho*, but another genius, maybe the greatest in the history of the cinema. Chaplin was back in favour and Joan Crawford's last film was about about a mutant killer.

All the great movie queens of Mamma's youth – Davis, Crawford, de Havilland – were making horror flicks. Men of their era, such as James Stewart, could play the dignified older man.

I was in between Franz and Danny, whom I hadn't yet met. I had some job sorting magazine subs. I was temporarily back home. The air was heavy around me.

Franz and I finally knew that we weren't going to do anything permanent. Dad was very disappointed. He really liked Franz. And he wanted me to settle down.

But I hadn't found a black man like Lelia had and I figured that I never would.

They would run a mile from me. I didn't know who I was.

And then, about six months later, Carlyle asked me to come over to his and Janet's apartment on the North Side.

Their apartment was lovely, completely decorated by Carlyle to look like Marlene Dietrich's boudoir from her 1930s golden era.

When I came in, Janet was in the bedroom crying her eyes out. They didn't even try to hide this from me.

Carlyle was high on something. He looked about thirteen years old, scared and perplexed.

Suddenly he started playing Led Zeppelin and lit a joint. He asked me to go for a walk with him. I didn't want to leave Janet alone, but I wanted to find out what he wanted to tell me.

We went to Lincoln Park, which was near their apartment. I had no idea why we were going to a park at night; what could you see at night?

He wouldn't answer my questions, not that they made any sense; I just needed to understand.

Suddenly, he stopped in the dark. It was as if he was listening to something far away. Then I noticed that the bush next to us was moving. Two men were having vigorous sex.

Suddenly I could see that the whole park came alive, all of the bushes moving, quivering, trembling. Where the hell was I?

Carlyle explained that this was where he had spent a lot of his time the last few months. This was why everything was a mess.

Before that evening, I was the last person who would know that someone was gay. Anyone.

Maybe because I didn't want to know.

But here it was. He told me that he and Janet were through, but because she was Catholic, she wanted an annulment. He agreed. Which meant he had to go and see a shrink who would certify him with a mental disorder: homosexuality. In that way she could get an annulment.

He had six or seven sessions. They were extremely aggressive, almost like exorcisms, I thought.

Because the shrink was attached to the archdiocese, the shrink was also trying to 'cure' Carlyle. The type of work he used left some peripheral damage, I'm sure. It dug up his relationship with his father, whom I'm completely convinced assaulted him as a child. It was his father's way, Carlyle said to me once when he was very high, of trying to 'make a man out of me'.

I can never forgive the Church for what it did to him or other gay people.

I truly believe that these sessions, this destruction of his being, began the assault of his demons.

Janet was too busy making sure that she remained in the bosom of Holy Mother Church than to tend to someone she had once loved and who was now being stripped away.

Nietzsche said that what doesn't kill us makes us stronger. This shrink work didn't kill Carlyle, but neither did it make him stronger. A thin black duke, he got even thinner, and I moved in with him after his bride's burly and triumphant older brothers moved her out.

My pitiable efforts at cooking got the response they deserved: we ate out.

Somehow there was money. He was a star. Mamma and Dad really liked him.

But I didn't think that either of them saw him as a potential husband for me.

His nail varnish was a bit too garish for them.

One evening he said that he wanted to take me out and asked me to wear a dress, and not to forget.

I only had one, so that was simple. He took me to a bar full of men, all kinds of men: the beautiful, the ugly, the ordinary, the extraordinary, the tall, the short, the black and white.

A democracy of desire, and no one blinked an eye when I came in.

One evening there I met all of the guys I call 'the Boys'. They changed my life.

SIX

In the bars that Carlyle now frequented, he met a set designer who worked at the Goodman Theatre: Frankie, a beautiful, muscled Italian American with a gorgeous moustache and the most rampant libido I had ever seen.

He had several properties on the Near North Side, beautiful brownstones that he had bought with the help of an inheritance and his own hard work.

In one of those brownstones he created a kind of haven for a flamboyant junior version of Auntie Mame known as Helen. A brilliant party-giver and restaurant hostess, she was Frankie's alter ego, the female version of him.

She wore nothing but vintage Chanel, which was interesting because she was a plus size with tremendously large breasts. But she had a very tiny waist and somehow she got into a sample size 6. To this day I don't know how.

Helen took my hand and led me to her wardrobe, where she kitted me out as a miniature version of one of the Andrews Sisters, the American singing group of the Second World War.

Helen's live-in partner was Donald, an accountant who lived in a permanent state of bewilderment at everything around him.

Helen, Donald and I were the only straights in the environment and, aside from Donald, our world was so completely surrounded by gay men that we cruised men like gay men do, unconsciously, until one day one of the Boys pointed it out and suggested we stop.

Frankie's main friends were in the theatre.

One of the actors, a brilliant interpreter of Beckett, had had a part written for him by the playwright.

The Boys were utter and complete hedonists; they had sex twenty-four hours a day, wherever and whenever they could. They were at the bar every night until dawn; and then hard at work in the day after a few hours of sleep.

I fell asleep in a pile of these guys once, all of us nude and on our bellies.

The next day at brunch, one of Frankie's new house guests saw me come into the brunch room (Frankie had a room for everything) and breathed a sigh of relief.

I asked him why.

He said that when he came back in the morning, he had seen my backside and thought I was some boy that Frankie had picked up: boys were not Frankie's taste.

The guest said that he hadn't seen Frankie for a while and was very relieved that he hadn't changed.

Through Frankie and his friends, I began to understand what the theatre was, its dedication, its focus.

I would sit for hours watching readings and rehearsals that Frankie was busy lighting, and listen to him and his friends talk about Ionesco and Brecht, Ibsen and Miller and Williams on Sunday afternoons, when they did not drink.

I met Nino through Frankie. Nino was later to invite me to stay with him in New York.

The other group of the Boys were drag queens.

By day they were labourers; some were truck drivers,

driving chickens out from Iowa to market.

Most of them were muscular, deep-voiced and total dudes until 5 p.m.

After that they prepared for the evening. This took hours.

Each of them had a speciality and a speciality that existed in a particular era and time: one was Diana Ross at the height of her time with the Supremes; another was Barbara Streisand – there were three of them, actually: one for the *Funny Girl* era; another for her Central Park concerts; and another for *Hello Dolly*.

And there was Aphrodite, the leader, whose speciality was Cher in her incarnation as the singer of 'Gypsies, Tramps and Thieves'.

Aphrodite was about six foot three, and built like a wrestler who could break a door down with one blow.

I never knew her real name.

All I knew was that it took six hours for all of the shaving and the make-up and the long, black, curly wig, and the girdle and the pantyhose and the bra and the heels and the flouncy gypsy dress and the huge earrings.

She was also MC at the drag club and, for her finale, she'd leap onstage in all of her massive glory, shake her skirts like a cut-price Carmen, throw her head back, throw out her chest and mime 'Gypsies'.

It was utterly tremendous and, like all of those drags, it was also amazingly delicate and nuanced.

Aphrodite – another aficionado of the cinémathèque – loved Hitchcock's *Spellbound*, especially the moment when Ingrid Bergman realises that she's fallen in love with Gregory Peck and Hitchcock creates this bit where doors open in her mind as she closes her eyes and surrenders to her infatuation.

Aphrodite would always scream out something lewd at that part of the film and we'd all roar with laughter.

His motto was: 'It's all drag', meaning that we are all in costume, whether we know it or not.

Even though he loathed the cinema, he was terribly serious about it, and when he wanted it to be quiet, he'd literally stand up and yell for silence.

He told me one day that with Carlyle I should be careful.

That I should go find a 'real man' and stay away from 'sissies' like him and Frankie but, above all, Carlyle.

Through the drag queens I came to see the artifice that is 'woman', the way we are painted and preened, invented largely by others, whittled away and shaped and stamped down.

When I would sometimes go home with Aphrodite after the club, he'd talk to me while making one of his 'Betty Crocker Queen of the Kitchen' breakfast feasts, about how most women have no sense of themselves; we don't know how we're being manipulated from the moment we can walk until the day we die.

He was a student of women; he knew what constituted this construct called 'woman' that had very little to do with the real person beneath.

I was living in this world of drag queens and gay male bars and grappling with my feelings for Carlyle. Even after he met the love of his life, Lars, a guy from Minnesota and an incredibly gentle soul.

Lars was a Buddhist and he collected the pictures and sayings of great black women heroines. Sojourner Truth was most important to him. He told me that he thought about her every day.

Lars was an office clerk. He wasn't an artist or a drag queen, he didn't collect antiques or stay out all night. He wasn't a crazy.

He worked quietly at his job and came home at night.

He and Carlyle set up home, and I was happy about that.

Before that, Carlyle and I had lived together briefly over a restaurant that Carlyle was decorating.

While living there, in basically a storeroom with no real privacy, I got word that my sister Lelia and her husband Harry had just had their first child, a daughter whose middle name was the name of Mamma's mother: Nora.

I cried with joy as I sat amongst the costumes and the boxes and the artefacts that Carlyle was collecting in order to decorate the restaurant.

My question, the question I couldn't shake: What was I doing, and what was to become of me?

SEVEN

Carlyle became a photographer, his speciality young men.

He became a kind of Oscar Wilde to a generation of tin-pot Bosies, who treated him just as callously and cruelly as the original had Wilde.

I was trying hard to settle down into some kind of domesticity – some kind of 'straight' life with Danny because I thought that I might want to have a baby before it was too late.

I had a non-paying job at a rock magazine writing profiles and I was also writing a commission for a small black theatre company.

It was good to write again, although I had very little confidence.

One summer's day, when I delivered a draft of my play to the company, I went to the artistic director's office to say hello – and there sat James Baldwin.

I knew that he was in town for a conference, but I never thought that I would meet him.

I could barely speak.

He asked me to ride in the taxi to the airport. He was on his way to New York.

In those days you could almost sit on the runway, so I

could stay with him until he walked through the gate. I was really looking forward to it.

In the taxi Baldwin sat drinking something out of a paper cup – bourbon, I think – and he began to tell me, out of the blue and with no warning, how he couldn't write any more.

Here was my idol, the man I had been reading since I was a young girl, and now he was confessing his fears to me and asking for advice.

I sat there as calmly as I could, but inside I was speechless.

All that I could say was how much he meant to me, and others like me.

We'd never let him go. He'd never go out of fashion with us, no matter what American-centred commentators or academics thought.

He, James Baldwin, was our godfather, and I for one intended to go to Europe and live in Paris like he did.

He cried a bit and kept drinking as he listened to me babble about how much he mattered. I didn't know what to do.

He asked me to sit with him at the airport until his flight.

He talked about the state of affairs in America, the state of letters, the state of black people.

I listened, but what was going on in my head was this: how could a man like him, loved all over the world, be so lonely?

As we sat waiting for the plane, he pointed out another man in a kind of high collar with his hat pulled down over his eyes.

He told me that the man was Richard Pryor. And indeed he was.

In time, Carlyle became a kind of aesthete, something out of the age of Aubrey Beardsley.

He began drinking and taking drugs as his obsession for young men grew.

I think it was a kind of Dorian Gray thing, a pursuit of youth. He had a great fear of growing old.

Lars couldn't take the booze, the drugs, the infidelities, the narcissism, the lies and the waste, the sheer waste of everything. He left.

The last time I saw Carlyle was a decade ago in the South of France.

He hadn't changed much, except that he walked with a limp and used a cane. I never asked him what was wrong. I was too scared to find out.

He told me in his cavalier way that he was in love, and of course it was with a young man, someone thirty years his junior, a kind of dandy.

He had copied my locks, but kept his after I cut mine off and stored them away.

I never throw my hair away. He cut his hair and he kept it, too.

By the time I saw Carlyle again, most of the Boys were dead.

I lost them all between my early thirties and early forties, the victims of the first wave of AIDS when you died from the disease.

I had friends in New York, where I was then living, who were dying, too.

I changed adult nappies, read to them, fed them, helped them take a list of pills as long as their arms.

And I didn't wear a moon suit when I saw them. I held their hands.

I watched beautiful, strong men turn into sickly-looking seventy-five-year-olds, prone to every ailment out there. Utterly defenceless.

I gave friends what few pennies I had to go to the Pasteur Institute in Paris, where they were conducting trials of new drugs. Go anywhere and try anything. Just stay alive.

There was a time when I couldn't go to any more funerals for a while.

I think it's one of the reasons I left New York in the mid-1980s. For me, it had become a city of death.

Aphrodite, who had moved home to her sick mother in Iowa, stood up in a local movie house one day and told someone to shut up.

After the movie was over, Aphrodite left with a friend.

The person she told to shut up came up alongside her and stabbed her in the heart, killing her instantly.

Carlyle was found dead in his apartment near a university where he had gone to teach.

They found him completely naked, his entire flat stripped clean.

There were no clues. At least not any that the local police bothered to investigate.

To them, he was just a gay black man.

A student acolyte made a video of him teaching and posted it on YouTube.

I saw it once.

I won't be looking at it again.

Carlyle told me once about something he called 'Negro existentialism', the rebellion against fate, the status quo, the way it's meant to be – for us.

The idea, he explained, is to go off the rails, and go off so completely that you are left alone to mumble into oblivion.

That's where the ancestors and the ancient gods from the Old Country dwell.

There, will be discovered purpose and meaning.

Not before then.

PART THREE

HORSES

ONE

In spite of the fact that I was born and raised in one of the greatest capitals of culture on the planet, I didn't have the chance to partake of much of it.

I guess that most white Chicagoans would say that, too: admission to museums and other things was expensive.

But what they didn't have to face was the city's de facto segregation.

That made downtown, where most of the great cultural institutions were, a no-go area if you were black. You didn't feel welcome. That's because you weren't.

Middle-class and upper-class black parents could just thumb their noses and take their children elsewhere or build their own institutions, or instil in their kids some sense of entitlement based on their education and background.

But if you were working class and you had just enough money to make ends meet and a little bit more, forget it.

Nevertheless, Dad didn't let this stop him one bit.

Armed with his encyclopaedias, and other books and writings that he found, he broke through the barriers and took us with him.

I knew, for example, that the Art Institute of Chicago, which I did not see for real until I was an adult, housed one of the greatest collections on earth and I felt proud of that, as did Dad.

It owns and displays that great pointillist masterpiece on which Sondheim was to base his brilliant musical *Sunday in the Park with George*: *Un dimanche après-midi à l'île de la Grande Jatte*, painted in 1884 by Georges Seurat.

This is considered by all Chicagoans to be a Chicago painting, and we don't care where it actually came from or who painted it. That's a detail. This painting is us.

High Western art was still something that mattered when I was growing up.

The *NBC Nightly News* signed off with Beethoven, but what I was doing was writing. And I wanted to know more about the Chicago writers.

I knew about *A Raisin in the Sun*, Lorraine Hansberry's timeless masterwork, because you did know about plays like this growing up. It was part of the Canon.

The play was us, about our parents, struggling to find a home and a place in the American Dream.

I knew about Gwendolyn Brooks, too, who would become Poet Laureate of the State of Illinois. We knew her poem 'We Real Cool', published in 1959, because it told so much truth about folks we knew, and I loved it because of its complex simplicity, and its attempt – and success – at putting in the poetic universe a voice we could hear at school, on the street and sometimes inside.

And I knew about the others, of course: Hemingway, above all.

But somehow – and I don't know how – I stumbled on the books of Saul Bellow.

He didn't talk about my world.

I'm quite sure that he took little interest – if any at

all – in the black upwardly mobile working class of my neighbourhood. Yet in *Herzog* I heard something. I heard something that spoke to me … that kind of writing all the way to the end of a sentence, fighting against its ending, too, but pushing through to the end and beyond.

Bellow wrote like Chicago felt when you went downtown and looked up at the skyscrapers clawing their way out of the flat, flat prairie. So much steel and glass, robber-baron stuff, but there it was all the same. It was Chicago and it didn't matter if the 'Windy City' chased you away; Chicago blew everyone and everything away.

I could see what Bellow and Brooks had in common, even if their admirers didn't.

They both have something to do with talking to the elementals. By that I mean the things that Chicagoans have to face, like the snow and the great wind, the oftentimes blistering hot prairie summers, and a kind of disconnect from the East and the West.

There is that great, beautiful lake, as big and all-encompassing as a sea, and the railroads, where America criss-crossed the city, meeting itself going backwards and forwards. Backwards and forwards.

There was Route 66 going all the way to the West Coast, through the desert, and it was there – that Big Country – in the words of Brooks and Bellow, just beneath the surface, and in the words of others, too.

Bellow especially. I liked him because he wrote like a journalist. Like Hemingway did.

He reported back from a place of carnage and irony. We couldn't see it. We didn't want to. But we knew it was there.

My own aim was typically modest: to take what I understood from them both and make something new, the admonition of all jazz creators 'in the tradition', and that was something I held close to me in the early 1970s.

I wasn't ambitious. I had no ambition other than to be able to write what was going on inside.

I re-read and re-read Brooks and Bellow, seeing if I could find my way inside of my own work.

But they were old people, from another time.

I needed someone who could speak to me.

Now.

TWO

I told myself that I needed to study playwriting, that I had gone far enough on my own: reading other play scripts, seeing things on TV.

But I also needed to escape Carlyle's marriage.

He had actually settled down into some kind of domesticity, very 'Young, Trendy, Interracial Couple on the Near North Side'.

You can see that kind of aching trendiness everywhere: Islington; the Village; the Left Bank – it's the same. I just couldn't believe that Carlyle was buying into it.

I decided to study playwriting formally with David Mamet, the King of Chicago playwrights, at the new theatre space for his company, St Nicholas.

Already he was creating interest on the East Coast.

Even those of us on the edges of Chicago theatre, have to laugh every time New York comes calling.

It's as if when New York finds you, then you exist, and while it's true that every writer, actor, director wants to 'make it there' – I moved to the Big Apple – it takes a certain degree of distance to understand the relationship between what we call, with irony, the Second City and the City that Never Sleeps.

Mamet was a year older than me, as were his compatriots, William H. Macey and Joe Mantegna – a pantheon of super actors you could watch and learn from every week.

I've never had an experience quite like it again, not even at the Actors Studio, whose Writer and Director Unit I belonged to in the 1980s after I moved to New York.

Mamet and his associates' theatre, the St Nicholas, was not only brimming over with talent, it was almost a religious experience.

These were Chicago actors, Midwest actors, red in tooth and claw, who took pride in their accents and attitudes and the stories they could tell.

When New York City claimed him and showered him with prizes and productions as if he had come to them a raw piece of meat to be shaped, Mamet had already written and received acclaim for: *Squirrels*; *Revenge of the Space Pandas*; and later, *The Water Engine*; *Sexual Perversity in Chicago* – which put him on the map – and *American Buffalo*, which ensured him a place in the lexicon and a host of parodies.

The first professional production I had ever seen was at the age of almost twenty-two – about twelve years after I started writing plays. During an anti-war trip to New York City, I saw *The Two Gentlemen of Verona*. Joe Papp's musical version with an interracial cast, something then taken for granted.

The music was by the same team who had written *Hair*. It even included a song called 'Bring All the Boys Back Home'. Not quite sure how that anti-Vietnam War song fit in, but the music was so good nobody noticed.

I would go on to work for Papp after I moved to New York later in the decade, and sit in his office with him and others after work as he puffed on his big cigars, talking about life, and referring to his library of Shakespeare always to his right hand.

However, I didn't write musicals and neither did Mamet.

His playwriting class was flawless, a textbook in Shaw and Shakespeare and of his own driven talent.

Once two little old ladies, who always sat in the front row, disagreed with him when he lamented the fact that he couldn't get his plays published.

One of them said that it was easy, everything she had ever written was published.

Mamet exploded and told them that what he meant was PLAYS! – not what *they* wrote – and went on to insult them to the point that you wanted to go and put your arms around them. But these women were sturdy and had a great sense of humour.

I think that they liked it.

I think that they enjoyed being told off in that Mametian tongue and language (without a pause).

I came home to Mom and Dad's after work – I stayed there when I didn't have rent money – and wrote on lined paper in my room.

I tried to apply what I was learning from Mamet, but I didn't want to write the clipped, crisp dialogue that he wrote, although I learnt a great deal from it.

I wanted to put that language into some sort of black destiny and shape. Tell the story of MY people against the big set pieces of history.

I had been reading about the Bertolucci film project that would eventually become *Novecento*. It was to be about two men, born the same day: 27 January 1901, an auspicious date. It was the day that Giuseppe Verdi died.

In the final version of the movie, this is announced at the beginning.

The two men, Alfredo Berlinghieri and Olmo Dalcò,

come from opposite ends of the social spectrum, a powerful symmetry.

I really envied the 'permission' that Bertolucci had to write about his people and their history, just as Coppola had done in *The Godfather*.

I wanted to put Chicago black folks into some sort of epic work. Not a big, sprawling play, but a play that embraced some of the ideas and themes of a certain time and also of today.

A post-1919 riot investigation named some of the Irish clubs – one of which Mayor Daley had belonged to as a youth – as the instigators of horrific attacks on black people.

And since Mayor Daley had given Dr King a hard time when he came in 1966 to head up a desegregation drive, I thought that he (the Mayor) could – without being in the play – be all over it, and possibly help audiences understand some of his positions vis-à-vis black people.

I wanted to capture the time now and then.

The area that the play's young black ex-doughboy, Emmett, worked in, was a hotbed of racial trouble. Known as 'Back of the Yards' (the mammoth Chicago stockyards, one of the nation's centres for the slaughter of cattle), it had begun in the 1850s before there were any meatpackers or stockyards in the area.

Notorious for its poverty, and for the diseases of the poor, it was chronicled in Upton Sinclair's *The Jungle*, written in 1906. Jack London called Sinclair's novel 'the *Uncle Tom's Cabin* of wage slavery'.

The cauldron that was race relations exploded, the clash coming after a young black man was hit on the head with a stone and died on a de facto segregated beach.

The Irish, who held the political power in the city, patrolled their areas, and since most of the police force was

Irish, they didn't bother to investigate, just as they didn't enforce the law in relation to violation against person and property in the black community.

Added to this was the pressure of returning black vets from the First World War who simply were not going to put up with any of it after they had fought for their country in the killing fields.

This could be my *1900*, a way to respond to what was going on today, to make a big play.

There would be a daughter, trapped between her loyalty and love for her strong, protective and elegant mother (I had no idea at the time that this play had anything to do with Mamma and me!) and her own will and need to live as she pleased.

This is symbolised by her love for a young black soldier, crippled as a result of a gas attack. They would start a new life.

One day, in the newspaper, I saw that picture of Jackie Taylor, the young black woman actor/producer who had her own theatre.

She looked sparky and defiant.

I would take my play to her.

I was working with Carlyle, who now had a small shelf in a shop. There he could display and sell his antiques.

One day, while I was dusting some of them down, a guy tall and thin and like something out of an effete Victorian drawing strolled into the shop.

It was the beginning of my going in yet another direction.

THREE

I keep thinking that his name was Julian because this name suits him.

I suspect that Julian grew up in some small Midwestern town filled with the inevitable, and made a decision to become outrageous.

I can imagine Julian dressing like Lytton Strachey in this Kellogg's Corn Flakes town he was born in, and soon everyone got used to the shock of him and welcomed him inside their homes. And then he became normal and that simply would not do.

Try as he might, he could never shock the people he wanted to, and soon trying became a kind of pastime in itself. The Art of Trying.

The nearest big, ugly city full of the wages of sin was Chicago. Everybody's Sin Town.

Before he left his small town, he saw *They Shoot Horses, Don't They?*, a very gloomy, doomy pic about marathon dances during the Depression. That someone could actually dance for money must have perplexed him since dancing was vulgar anyway.

Of course, Julian had grown up in a Calvinist household.

He had a million square dances in his brain, lots of 'dosey

does'; you could see that in his eyes. But Julian never danced. He barely moved. He had a kind of Frankenstein shamble that he thought was cool. He dyed his hair deep black, a bit like the dad from *The Addams Family*, but no one pointed that out because Julian had a power. He could sway things. Influence events. Make the markets move.

He quickly formed a collective in his own mind, although what was happening around him – a real club called Horses – had nothing to do with him. He had decided that his fantasy group was essential, I guess for his own sense of self. Those were the times when people still thought that collectives were necessary.

This was really a curious thing because, in his subgroup, the one away from the real Horses – let's call it 'Shadow Horses' – he surrounded himself with very enthusiastic people, very sunny and optimistic people. Maybe they were punishing themselves. Maybe he was their mea culpa. But they were too young to have very much of a dissipated life.

Maybe Julian did not see any of this as a curiosity, which was really a curiosity in itself.

No doubt he surrounded himself with those who thought he might save them.

They had nothing to declare but their art, a phrase they learned from Julian. He told them that he had made the phrase up, that this revelation was all down to him.

They bought it – the 'Shadow Horses' – and just climbed aboard the bandwagon he made for them and waited for instructions. And of course, the best instruction of all: himself.

These examples included being amazingly thin and having the capacity to eat what he wanted. And also to do impromptu concerts of slowed-down rock hits. That was key to this 'Shadow Horses', this was important.

Julian liked singing 'Whole Lotta Love' by Led Zeppelin

in the manner of a funeral dirge. Which, actually, it kinda was.

This deconstruction, this presentation of the everyday in a way that theatricalised it, Julian explained to Carlyle and me, was the very heart of his Horses, everything it was about.

The avant-garde was not enough and besides it had been hijacked, co-opted, years ago. He saw everything in the possibility of his transcendence of this, the getting rid of the old notions of 'the new'.

He wanted to climb mountains, but to do that it was necessary to go where the whole thing mattered. Chicago. The Near North Side.

Which is why, he explained to us over tea, he had chosen Chicago.

No one is impressed here, he said. Period. Chicago is a big deal, Chicago can close a big Broadway show, close it right down and couldn't care less what the critics say.

Carlyle and I slotted in right away, into his group, because we were black and that was fascinating. Plus we weren't coming with any agenda, we just were. Which made things much more interesting.

It was the first time that I had actually been objectified. I had never seen myself as an opportunity or a gateway, nor heard someone express me in that way. There was the boring bank, and maybe Sunday meal at home, and then back to my shared house with Stacey and then up to go out to the bank, and then…

Julian, of course, had very fine things. Very beautiful pieces of cloth and dresses, coats and shoes, hats and handbags. He had more experience than Carlyle had in hunting out treasures, and, being a white guy, he could go into people's homes, sit and rifle through boxes and old suitcases. Carlyle wouldn't be allowed to do this.

Sometimes he'd sit out in the car – something given to him in perpetuity by one of Julian's people – and patiently wait until Julian had made his assessment, taken his gracious leave, and brought the loot to the car. He'd always get away pretty cheaply.

During the day, counting out bills and working a calculator machine and being helpful, and accommodating, I'd think of what had been purchased that day, and if I would be wearing any of it soon.

I looked for my own image in the photos of Josephine Baker made in the '20s, and those, too, of Anna Mae Wong, who wiped everyone off the screen and was a living lesson in the genius of chiaroscuro lighting.

A world that I needed at the time.

FOUR

The woman next to me at the bank had become a Buddhist.

Not a chanting Buddhist.

Nor a Buddhist with a statue, or a ritual or robes. Just someone who had decided, all on her own, that this life was it.

And after we died, that was that.

Who knew whether holy books hadn't been compiled by some crazy person, she would ask in her quiet Buddhist way. St Paul made Christianity, not Jesus, and that went for the rest of the religions. As far as she could understand it all.

'Work out your own salvation' was what she took away from what the Buddha allegedly said, and I liked that.

'Work out your own salvation.'

Which was a good way to start because I was growing weary of righteousness.

The entire country was growing tired, beaten down by the oil crisis, by the recession and the little wars and the stuff going on in the streets at home, big and small. And discovering that our President might be a crook, might be a guy involved with a robbery, might be part of a grand conspiracy.

It made you go home after work not wanting to hear the news. Made you not want to read newspapers. Nothing.

I recalled being told that Nixon would one day disgrace

the nation and there he was disgracing the nation, and the prophecy was suddenly eating the nation alive.

I'd go home for Sunday supper, Dad not talking about Nixon deliberately, I think, because somehow there had been an inevitability about it. It was all part of his feelings about the potential for certain white people to wreak havoc on the world.

Right in the White House, right there, 'Tricky Dick', as he was known, sitting in imperial splendour and actually manipulating the body politic to make it resemble what we wanted.

So work out your own salvation began to make sense to me, began to hold some kind of resonance that I needed to work out, needed to make tangible.

In a little corner of the shared house I lived in, I began work on my play.

I wanted to make it art, wanted it to be fragile, to have a fragile heroine, someone who on the inside was like a piece of glass. But on the outside she was a lady's maid, someone who people assumed would have no feelings.

One summer, a decade earlier, I had been sent to summer school up on the North Shore as part of a desegregation drive.

I had ridden the train north with women from my part of town who worked as maids in the posh houses in the neighbourhood where my summer school was located.

They used terms like 'my lady' to refer to their employers, and looked at me out of the corner of their eye. I didn't quite fit. I wasn't elegant enough.

But I was a writer, and so I listened, I listened to their real lives, I listened to them dissecting their 'ladies'. I knew that I was being made privy to the inner lives of people of service.

I never forgot them.

I wanted to build a precious black woman, make her

important within her universe. Give her a universe.

I didn't know if other black women writers were doing that. Because this is how I was beginning to see myself: as a black woman writer, as a woman, a writer who came from a matrix, one that I wanted to make visible and real and open.

Sitting in the space of Julian's group, his 'Shadow Horses', I watched them recreate over and over that scene in the film *They Shoot Horses, Don't They?* in which only Jane Fonda's character and her partner are left, dancing in their exhaustion and despair, dancing against the poverty and the helplessness; you can almost smell her unwillingness to live (that's how good Fonda's performance was) as the spectators in the film watch, eating their sandwiches and smoking and pointing and laughing and making bets on the human specimens on the dance floor, dancing for pennies in the depths of the Depression, dancing until they dropped. Literally.

As I built my play, I also began to read, not Depression-era literature but *The Great Gatsby*, because Jay Gatsby fit the black woman in my play with big dreams, and heading for disaster.

The novel had been recently made into a film and we were being bombarded with images of Mia Farrow, wet-lipped and doe-eyed, staring into the middle distance, glittering cap on her head, made of a thousand beads, and her wide-eyed acceptance without question of everything that was glamorous and beautiful. That seemed to me the spirit of the maid in my play. Her parallel life.

I could drop out of the cycle of being what I was supposed to be in the world and remake myself, remake who I was. Through the play. That was what the play could do, that was what it would do.

It was a way to see Bertolucci's film as part of a bigger picture. And within that bigger picture was the story of a young black girl, the daughter of a maid with ambitions, who turns her back on those ambitions and decides instead to strike out on her own terms.

This play would take place in the midst of the Red Summer, and the choice would be for the girl, 'Annise', to stay in the safety of the northern suburbs, in the big place where her mother worked, or to return to where she and her mother lived, a small flat in the ghetto, in the midst of the mayhem and the death.

Her mother, Lorraine, would see her daughter's going back as an acceptance of death. But for Annise, it would be an embrace of life, of her own life.

Standing for eight hours, counting out money, looking at the landscape of counters and teller windows and grey people coming back and forth in an effort to hold on to what they had, all that allowed me to shape Annise.

Because she would be my own yearning, my own wanting to escape.

The Great Gatsby begins with Nick remembering his father and his 'younger and more vulnerable years', and his father's admonition that 'all the people in this world haven't had the advantages that you've had'.

I remembered this as I rode the 'L' home, looking into the people seated across from me, going back to lives of routine and dreariness.

I was going back to take a shower, change into one of Carlyle's art deco gowns, and head out for the evening.

FIVE

I had no idea, until I began to write this memoir, how many different groups of people, how many 'crowds' I existed in at one time.

When I step back and look at it, I can see it, but then it all seemed to be a group of people I knew. I had no idea they were all so different.

But if I place them side by side, they were as different as could be. The only thing that they had in common was me. A 'me' they all thought they knew. And I was trying, through them, to understand who I was.

Franz and I were still friends after I left him for Danny. Through Franz, a few years earlier, I'd met a Honduran banker by the name of Fernando. And through Fernando, I met Chris, with whom I had late-night telephone calls for years in which we told each other everything, but we never so much as held hands. The tension that created between us allowed us to be candid and open with one another. We knew what we were doing. It was a kind of abstinence.

Fernando lived in an apartment on the Gold Coast, the area off North Michigan Avenue, one of the richest areas in the entire Midwest. The streets were, and still are, quiet and tree-lined and full of elegant and very expensive brownstones.

It was possible to leave the clamour of North Michigan Avenue, with its shops and restaurants and tourists, and turn into a Gold Coast residential street with its air of deep and profound quiet, another world.

All major cities have, in their centres, surprising areas like this. Only the most privileged can live there. Or in the case of New York, only those who lived under 'rent control' and whose rent remained stable had a right to be in these urban havens. In the case of a rent-control tenant, that right existed until the end of their lives.

Not far from Fernando's apartment was the Playboy Mansion.

Playboy and Hugh Hefner created and dominated a kind of consciousness in Chicago. Before Hefner moved to LA in 1971, he had made a Chicago that revolved around a prototype: the man who could have everything he wanted.

Playboy was all about the all-night party; the beautiful girls with the big hair and big tits; men smoking pipes and great jazz singers and comedians existing just to entertain you.

Playboy was aspirational because anyone could be a part of it. It was about grown-up fun, and, although we feminists fought against everything Playboy represented (Gloria Steinem had made her name a decade or so earlier by going undercover, working as a Bunny, and emerged to write about it), it appealed to a very human trait: hedonism.

Hefner also managed to champion freedom of speech into the bargain.

He published, sometime in the 1950s, a short story about a heterosexual man trying to live in a world in which homosexuality was considered the norm, his aim being to get heterosexuals to understand the discrimination that gay men experienced.

And not just gay men: Hefner gave the black comic-activist Dick Gregory his break.

Gregory was very much in the Lenny Bruce mould but much more dangerous: Gregory was a black man saying the unsayable.

His act involved challenging Hefner's largely white parties at the Playboy Mansion. Gregory slapped down any lurking *noblesse oblige* on the part of any white person who sat there and politely smiled.

They were going to understand his reality, or risk getting their feelings hurt.

'I named one of my daughters "Miss", so she'd be called "Miss Gregory"' – my favourite 'joke' of his, his daughter's name both a statement of fact and a take-down of that overly familiar first-name basis on which black women were too often addressed by white people.

Hefner hired black women for his clubs. I had a friend who worked at the main one.

You had to perfect, above all, the 'bunny dip', a kind of swoop and curtsey which gave the customers a chance to see your breasts without having to touch them.

My friend enjoyed the club because the customers tipped well, which helped towards university tuition and fees, and books, my former paramount concern.

I had, at last, graduated from university a year or so before with a BA in American history, after six years of going to classes full time and part time, night and day. Franz sat with Dad at the commencement ceremony and later told me that Daddy had wept when I walked across the stage to receive my diploma.

The president of the university murmured something like, 'You got it at last.'

Now I had bills to pay. Fernando hinted that he could help me. I knew what that price was.

Fernando made a great deal of money as an international

banker. He loved display. Everything was big, shiny, designer, OUT THERE.

He believed with all of his heart and soul that the solution to any problem was what he called 'a dose of General Augusto Pinochet', a man he had enormous respect, even love, for.

He said that his office needed a 'dose of General Augusto Pinochet'; his cleaning lady, too; the United States, the world, all creatures great and small could benefit from the dictator's firm rule.

Fernando, comfy in his world of dictators and big dollars, would swan around his huge flat in the evenings, swigging from a bottle of champagne, oftentimes only clad in the underwear made for him by Honduran nuns, which he would show off with every chance he got, praising Pinochet when he wasn't praising Elton John. Whom he was unshakeably convinced he resembled.

Fernando had no interest in my play or anything artistic for that matter.

He was only interested in capitalism, cocaine and sex, and if they came all together, all the better.

He called me 'the Catholic girl' because I wouldn't join in with him.

As for coke, I think that everyone has an idea what their drug of choice might be. You don't have to take it to know, it just calls you. I had an idea that coke might be my drug, and so I ran away from it as fast as I could. My primal fear of domination and control from outside forces made me stay away from it. I didn't want to trawl some back street at 2 a.m. looking for it, be enslaved by it.

Whenever I came over, Fernando always fed me, and this was good because I didn't always have regular meals. Danny was trying to get more hours at his design job and I could see that his drumming was going to come to an end. And us, too.

The Vietnam War had ended in defeat and retreat, the images of people hanging off helicopters as the Americans left Saigon played over and over on the news. There was an energy crisis; the boom in wages was over, never to return, and all people could talk about was the price of gas.

But inside Casa Fernando, all was well.

I didn't know if I was feeling the general malaise, or whether it was peculiar to me, my own sadness.

I was temporarily living in the back of a shop with Carlyle – how I got there I'm not sure, but it was shortly after his de-homosexualisation therapy had come to an end.

We had rooms – cubicles, actually – with no doors, and we washed in a sink in the storeroom of the shop/'country kitchen' of an eccentric millionaire who owned half the farmland downstate. He had come upstate to Chicago to build a replica of the barn and the farmhouse he had grown up in during the Depression.

Carlyle and he had met when Carlyle sold him a few antiques, and somehow, after his marriage collapsed, Carlyle went to live in the back of the rich man's shop.

I was there, two years earlier, washing the face that I couldn't see in the mirror, when Carlyle told me that Lelia had given birth to Kelly Nora. Now, two years later, another baby was on the way, and for some reason, I mentioned this to Fernando and he looked at me and asked point-blank and in the most innocent voice why black people had so many children. There were too many black children.

This was my bell.

Ten years earlier, I would have walked away from a person like that – after punching them – but by now I had developed the 'splinter of ice in the heart' that Graham Greene believed was a prerequisite to being a writer.

Now, spouting out reams of racism, Fernando was a specimen, Another Human Experience. I had to study him. So I let him speak.

Fernando was friends with Chris, heir to a huge pharmaceutical fortune – a very good painter, who also owned part of a family yacht.

In that summer of drought, while Danny was figuring out what to do, and I had been fired from the bank and started waiting on tables in a trendy Near North restaurant, Franz and I would be invited to go sailing on Sundays, on Lake Michigan, in Chris's yacht.

Mamma didn't like to take us to the beach, or to the lakefront in general, because the beaches, when we were children, were de facto racially segregated.

The beach and the water were always sinister and sources of angst, so I never learned to swim.

Now I was on a yacht, slightly seasick but watching the shoreline slowly disappear as the boat sailed leisurely on the Great Lake.

Franz smoked a cigar and pretended to be a mogul.

I think that we were both marvelling at the fact that we were even on a boat like that.

Out of the blue, Franz asked Chris, as we headed for shore, if he was Jewish.

Not for any other reason than that Franz was fascinated by people and wanted to know everything about them that he could.

Unfortunately, Chris was offended and, I should think, a bit alarmed.

By the middle 1970s, the alliance that black people and Jews had forged, particularly during the Civil Rights era, was destroyed by the Black Power and Black Student Union movements of the late 1960s and '70s, when young black people – and quite a few Jewish kids, it turned out – took the side of the Palestinians and the Muslim world.

Our allies for justice became not Jews but 'white people', and for many, perhaps, white people who should have been watched all along.

Franz explained himself when it became clear that Chris was offended by the question. They remained firm friends. I think that Chris felt he could trust him, but it was hard to say.

Sometimes I spent the night with Fernando. I wanted to be somewhere different, somewhere where money wasn't a source of constant worry, where I could wake up in a huge bed, and look out of a window and see a tree-lined street and hear nothing, nothing but birds.

He gave me a key and said that I could stay there, to write the play … and pretend.

One afternoon, while I was wearing his dressing gown and nothing else, working on a scene of the play, the front door opened and in came his girlfriend from Brazil, Estella, along with her little girl – a law unto herself known as Estella Two.

They were followed by a shaken Fernando.

It was clear by her tone of voice that Estella didn't have a clue about the life Fernando led in Chicago.

I jumped in the bed, hid under the covers and held my breath.

The bedroom door opened and Estella Two strode in like she owned the place.

She couldn't have been more than six years old. She walked over to the bed, turned down the covers and, peek-a-boo, there I was.

I made a 'ssh' gesture to Estella Two and she smiled at me. She was up for the game.

Estella and Fernando were having a furious argument that

Above: My photo of Mamma and Dad, taken at O'Hare Airport during one of my visits home from NYC in the 1980s.

Below: My sisters, Gina and Lelia, and me, in the mid-1990s.

With Mamma in the early 1990s.

Above: My favourite photograph of Mamma and me, taken in 1994.

Left: Dad in the early 1990s.

London in the 1980s.

London in 1987.

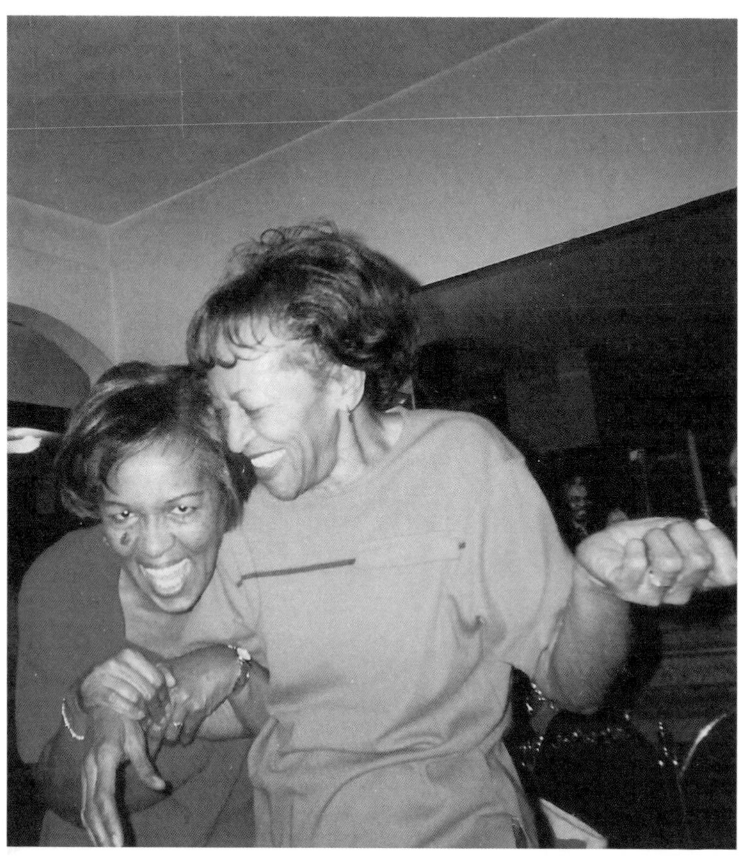

Mamma and her baby sister, Aunt Ernestine, in the 1990s.

Right, Father Malette, the priest who baptised me. Still part of the family. Photo taken in the mid-1990s.

Mamma in the 1990s.

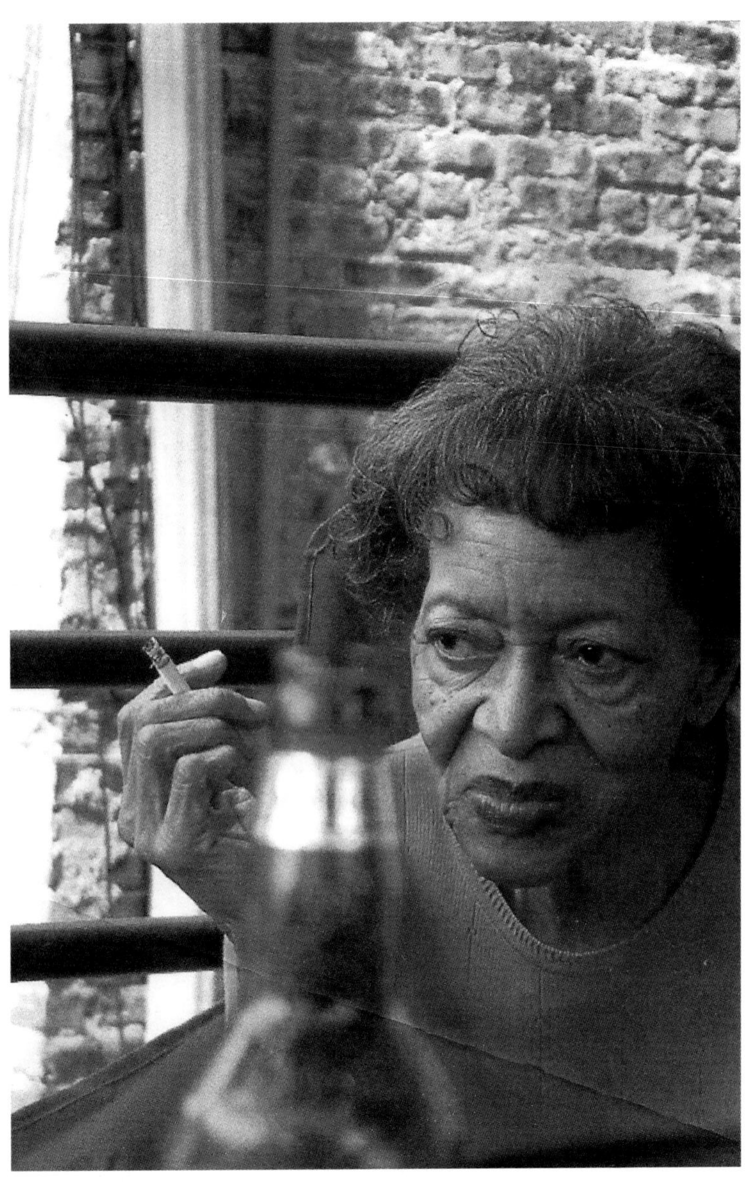

Mamma.

I couldn't understand, and I was desperately trying to keep Estella Two amused until they left.

After what seemed like an eternity, Estella and her child departed.

Fernando came into the bedroom, laughing. For him, it had all been great fun.

Then he said that a friend from work was coming by.

She was a black woman, an attorney by the name of Claudia.

It was clear to me – and I'm sure to Claudia – that Fernando wanted us all to climb into that bed together.

Claudia was a South Sider, like me, and after telling Fernando off she ordered him to take us out for a huge meal. Which he did. He spent the evening trying to persuade us to have a three-way with him, but Claudia hailed a taxi and waved goodbye out of the window.

Chris rang me the following night. We just talked about life, and painting.

He had a girlfriend from university who was going to New York to become an agent for emerging artists. There were deserted factories and warehouses below Houston Street. It was very bleak there, we were in a slump, and buying one now might be an opportunity.

The nation and most of Western Europe was about to begin the long drought of 1975 and '76.

I would sit by the window in shorts and a T-shirt, looking at the street outside the window of the flat I shared with Danny, listening to Chris for hours and hours. I recognised myself in some of the things that he said. But I wondered where we were going.

His brothers tended to marry 'shiksas' – tall, blonde, elegant women with naturally thin, straight noses who practically had a *Mayflower* pedigree. I'm not sure that it was conscious. I didn't know if Chris had one in his life, and here I was, a kind of 'mammy' for him to offload on before the Big Day when he had to tie the knot and couldn't pretend any more.

Besides, I felt that Danny had someone else. I was waiting for him any day to tell me. Apart from being my boyfriend, he provided the roof over my head. There was no way – with my lack of funds – that anyone would rent an apartment to me. Who would give me anything?

I had nothing, was going to be nothing.

At some point that summer, I was involved – either mentally or physically, and sometimes both – with about seven men.

Most of them knew one another, but none of them knew that what they had in common was me. I was amazed at their ability to keep me secret, keep me out of their conversations while they watched baseball together or talked about the heatwave; or whether we'd have the first Deep South President in Jimmy Carter after the general election; or when they went out to the bar or to get their cars washed on Saturdays; or had Sunday supper with their mothers; or at the barbershop. Would some of them come to blows if they knew about the other one? A man could.

And, also, I was trying to figure out what I was going to do about my relationships: I was becoming addicted to Chris and his life; I was becoming an enabler of his melodrama and I was still caught up in Carlyle.

Lelia was settled with a lovely family.

And I had nothing except a jumbled, whirlwind, mess of a life.

Donna Summer's 'Love to Love You Baby' rang out of every shop and on every dance floor; on the radio, everywhere.

And the tinny sound inside my mind's eye, inside my head

as I struggled with my play, let me know that I had turned something off. That I had locked away the Little Kid, the one who held all of the music that unlocked the world.

That summer, I discovered Rimbaud.

I was reading about a poet-singer by the name of Patti Smith. My age.

She was a devotee of Arthur Rimbaud, who I had never heard of. But because I liked the sound of her, I bought a book of his poems, *A Season in Hell*: 'And springtime brought me the frightful laugh of an idiot.'

I was almost at the end of my twenties. And I had nothing.

SIX

The years 1977 and 1978 seemed to meld into one for me.

I've tried to pull them apart, tried to separate them, but I can't.

I think it's because at the end of '78, I would turn thirty.

And this shows you the arbitrary nature of these deadlines or goals. But there are several phony lines of demarcation that can create existential panics in life. Now, when I look back, I can see that I was in one.

My life was changing – for the first time since the end of high school, almost ten years, I was facing the possibility of not having a 'husband'. I didn't realise that I saw my boyfriends that way, a kind of permanent fixture who was at home, and lovers, etc., were outside and the ones you had fun with.

Maybe this was because it was the '70, and not the '60s, that actually invented sex and experimentation with it and relationships, and if you hung out with gay guys for a good deal of the time, like I did, this kind of analysis, then, was easy to come by.

They didn't put me there, put me in that state of mind. I was always there. Somewhere within this 'proper girl', raised so carefully by my parents, was someone just like 'the Boys', who incidentally all had 'husbands', guys who lived with them, some of them earnest dullards no one in the straight world would suspect.

Carlyle's husband was very beautiful: Lars.

Lars was Minnesota Swedish, but tall and ethereal, graceful, quiet. And he loved Carlyle more than anything in the world.

His apartment became a shrine to their relationship: pictures of the two of them, and decorated in exquisite art deco that would fetch a fortune now.

There was a photo that he had taken of Carlyle posed in the black-and-white world of Cecil Beaton, a '30s Hollywood meets Berlin-between-the-wars that Carlyle would have been at home in.

Since everything revolved around Carlyle, he came and went as he pleased. Lars tried to speak to me discreetly, tried to have someone close to Carlyle know what his feelings were, but I never allowed him an opportunity. My allegiance, my obsession, was with Carlyle.

The song in the air – even for people who weren't into that kind of music – was Fleetwood Mac's 'Go Your Own Way'.

I sang it to myself (largely because the owner of the restaurant I worked in played it over and over again while we set the place up for the day) and I thought that this was a good idea.

I came back to the apartment I lived in with Danny – because it was no longer a home to me – changed and went out clubbing with Carlyle.

I knew that he used me as a kind of bait, that coming into a club, particularly a gay one, with me gave him many options. Especially with the men who didn't quite know yet how or where in the bar to test the waters.

They were the most interesting because they were in limbo (almost wrote 'no-man's-land'), in which a woman can be a kind of stopgap before the plunge. I was always on the outside of this, watching the eye contact that Carlyle and the man made, the first tentative steps.

Helen continued to give her incredible soirées, each one with a theme, each one unforgettable.

I danced with Iggy Pop when he came to town, fighting my way to the front of the stage; pulled on by the muscular and wiry little Iggy himself.

And we all went to everything that the real Horses gave. Even Julian, who was bitter that his kind of 'Shadow Horses', even with its acolytes, never really caught on.

The Horses building was an old warehouse. The entryway was dark.

Carlyle always found sheer, skinny 1930s dresses for me to wear there.

Neither of our 'husbands' was allowed to go with us. They wouldn't have liked it; that's why we chose them.

There were cocktails, and dope for the dopeheads, and the theme song was Bowie and Lennon's doom-laden paean to the age, 'Fame', featuring Lennon's whiny vocals and Bowie, cold and instructive, posting a warning that they both know no one will heed.

SEVEN

In that arc of time, between the Tall Ships sailing under the Verrazano-Narrows Bridge in honour of the bicentenary – that boiling summer of '76 – until I left Chicago in a blizzard at the end of '78, I know that I was in some state of self-destructiveness.

Not suicide, but a kind of gradual disintegration, a breaking up of everything. I wasn't looking for the smallest components in order to rebuild them. I was aiming for dust, something that you could put into an hourglass and turn upside down.

I had ancestral angst – the burden of being 'good', of being a 'role model' and pedagogical and always making sure that people either looked level at you or looked up. No black woman must ever allow herself to be looked down upon. Too much of that happened outside of our will and our prevention to voluntarily bring that on ourselves.

It was important to go forwards, to aim high ('Keep your eye on the sparrow,' Sammy Davis sung like an angel for the cop show *Baretta*), and that was what had to be done.

My mother, my aunties, their mothers and grandmothers: none of them had gone through what they had gone through, and endured what they had endured, to have me folded up in a seat in a movie repertory house, watching over and over and over Errol Flynn swinging through the trees as Robin Hood. Putting myself *there* instead of with Miss Jane Pittman or inside of a Toni Morrison or Alice Walker.

They couldn't have cared less, but I was shocked.

A part of me was looking at me … and was appalled. I could have done something sane and constructive with my time and gone to the improv club Second City (a term that Chicago embraced after an article appeared in the 1950s calling Chicago just that), could have seen live onstage (and pretty cheaply, too): Harold Ramis and John Belushi, John Candy and Bill Murray, Dan Ackroyd and Gilda Radner, improvising – obviously stars in embryo – right near where I lived. 'Right here, Toto,' Dorothy says in *The Wizard of Oz*. 'We don't have to go anywhere!'

Black girls didn't have existential crises; we were supposed to deal with this by being geniuses in the kitchen like Vertamae Grosvenor, cooking by vibration and having a strong back and ready will. I envied her more than I could say. She had a daughter, and had been to Paris, and could rustle up a five-course meal out of one pot and a gas ring.

If we cracked, it was some kind of moral failing that only the Lord could solve, or there was something in the blood. A curse from way back, something that had double-whammied back from some ancient who had intended someone else ill.

'What goes around comes around' was the old saying – the old saying about double whammies and boomerangs.

I buried myself in *1919*. I dramatised everything that was going on and put it in the pages of that script. A go-getting young black woman was going to produce it and Carlyle was designing it, right down to our shoes.

I was in safe hands. Because I needed to be.

While I was making salads in the restaurant, I overheard

one of the waiters talk about a theatre magazine called *Performing Arts Journal* (*PAJ*). It was edited by, amongst others, a man called Michael Earley. It talked about theatre in a kind of scientific way, a way in which the theatre could be created to go forwards, a way in which it was not a repertory house, nor Brecht's 'culinary', off-Broadway type of theatre.

I imagined the whole scene in New York 'downtown' theatre. I read over and over the text for *Einstein on the Beach*. I longed with all my heart to see Robert Wilson's work, hear Philip Glass live. I wanted to see Wilson's *The Life and Times of Joseph Stalin*; *A Letter for Queen Victoria*; *I Was Sitting on My Patio This Guy Appeared I Thought I Was Hallucinating*.

I bought the magazine and read the play scripts they published over and over.

I wanted *1919* to be new. Like all jazz should be. I wanted to do something new. But, I wondered as I chopped vegetables in the restaurant kitchen, what made me think that I was good enough?

Plus I was getting old. 'They,' I decided, like black people to be young, like Renaissance paintings – a means to enhance the canvas. No need for an old black person at all. Age was not useful in a black person. To those, that is, who see black people as commodities. Any way that you want to define that. Plus getting close to thirty was pushing it for a black girl, and yet…

One arctic-cold day, Robert Wilson came to town with his protégé, a young lad on the autistic spectrum.

I didn't know or understand until very late in life – i.e., recently – that my job is to make, to complete, to do.

To be not a chef de cuisine, but a cook, a good cook.

To put simple fare on the table and be grateful for the bounty. As my ancestors had been. And that's all I want to do now for the rest of my life.

I have the ability to smell rain coming if it hasn't rained for a while.

The air goes moist, you smell the wet earth and there's a kind of gentle Northern Lights in the air.

By late 1977 I had shut all of that down, put that to the back of me.

But I knew that something was coming. That I was going to be on the rack.

Again.

EIGHT

Frankie lived across the street from Danny and me, in a house like something out of a dream.

I called it 'Black Girl Antique Chic', or 'For Colored Girls Who Had Found Sanity'.

Frankie was an actor and a painter. She was a few months older than me, taller, with a huge Angela Davis afro and a little girl, Cody, whose dad was third-generation Irish, which gave little Cody a massive afro, almost too big for her tiny head.

Frankie's house was decorated with her late grandmother's things – a woman who had graduated from Oberlin College and whose mother had been a 'conductor' on the Underground Railroad, that system of safe houses used to get runaway slaves to safety in Canada.

It was like the bedroom of Charles Foster Kane's second wife, the opera singer, full of incredible bits and pieces from every era: a stove from the Second World War that still worked; art nouveau cutlery and plates; things handmade on looms and spinning wheels; drawers full of beautiful linen.

Cody could already speak three languages at five: English, French and Spanish. Frankie worked her butt off to pay for lessons.

Frankie could tell that I was eating mostly at the restaurant, so she fed me her home-made meals: good, thick soups and bread, chicken, salads. She had a nose ring like the young black woman I admired above all then, the poet/playwright/performer Ntozake Shange.

Her 'For Colored Girls' had become a mantra for all of us. Her words had reached down and pulled something up and out, stuff that we couldn't articulate but knew and felt as black women coming on stream, about to pick up the mantle of our elders, of those who had gone before us.

But not in quite the same way.

The titles of the poems that comprised what she called her 'choreopoem' said it all: 'dark phases'; 'graduation nit'; 'now I love somebody more than'; the already classic 'no assistance' – about how no one helps a black woman; 'no more love poems #1'; the terrifying 'a nite with beau willie brown'; our second classic, 'somebody almost walked off wid alla my stuff'.

Even the way they looked on the page: in bright colours, the language like razor blades, free from any of the balm of Holy Roller religion and organised politics and the inducements of our elders.

And the end of the play, when everyone comes together and the Lady in Red intones:

'I found God in myself/and I loved her/I loved her fiercely.'

I saw Frankie's marriage with her husband, Bill, and he seemed to me to understand her, to know who she was. But Bill was a teacher. He wasn't a frustrated rock drummer.

Danny and I moved to a slightly bigger place not far away, the place that I would eventually move out of.

I made my bed near the heater, and worked on my play.

If I had had enough pride, I would have packed my bags and moved back home. But I couldn't go back home. I knew that I had left.

I erased everything and just went to work, and rehearsals, and when I could afford to, go look at an old movie.

The Boys were up to their usual rambunctiousness. A few of them were going to the doctor a bit more often with slightly stranger than usual STDs, but everyone accepted those as the wages of sin. And life.

I met the company that Jackie Taylor, the young founder of the black theatre that was going to put my play on, had assembled. They were bright and eager and perfect casting.

Jackie herself was going to play the mother. And while she was way too young, she had the gravitas. And anyway I wanted the play done. No point arguing with the money woman.

Carlyle went scouting for props and created a poster and programme that looked exactly like something out of 1919.

I think that I told Mamma and Dad.

I had made up my mind, on the threshold of my thirtieth birthday, that they wouldn't ever understand what I was doing. Mamma certainly didn't. All that she cared about was whether I was eating, and Dad had the other, younger children to be concerned with. I was a grown woman. I had gone.

Dad and I didn't talk much when I came home on the rare Sunday for lunch.

He was repairing TVs and going to fairs to scout for things to sell, in addition to his hours at the factory. He and Mamma were under enormous strain with my youngest siblings growing up at home and going through the usual things that teens do.

Except that this was Mamma and Daddy's second round with a bunch of teens.

I couldn't understand how they coped.

That summer of 1977, Mamma had turned fifty. A month before Dad had turned fifty-three.

Ancients to me then.

They had both become closed, locked in their own worlds.

I didn't know anything about the lives of my three youngest siblings. They were a generation and a world away from me, and still are. I suppose that deep down inside, I couldn't understand why Mom and Dad had had so many children.

They still had so much life left.

The house was tense, and at the same time it felt empty, not the way it felt when I was growing up. But maybe it was just me. Just where I was.

If a writer has done any kind of halfway decent job on a play, then it takes something away, it never adds. Writing never gives, it takes away. Sometimes writing can be a sloughing off, a stripping away of layers of accumulation, of other people's 'stuff'. But it never really replaces. It may offer insight, but it never gives back.

You stare into the abyss and try to bring words out of it. How can that be giving?

Jackie's theatre was poor and in a poor community, surrounded by some of the most notorious estates in Chicago. She had put her storefront theatre – the Black Ensemble Theater Company – right in the middle of it. And I liked the difference between this and the effete world of the North Side that I existed in – 'Horses', with its arch evenings, and some of Helen's soirées, throwbacks to another era in which Carlyle would be serving the drinks and I would be in the kitchen.

But Jackie's theatre was urban and we were going to make a piece of theatre that spoke to the community. I felt like I had a purpose.

The restaurant I worked for had a kind of elegant upmarket version of the place I earned my living in. I was asked if I wanted to work in the cloakroom there, which was a great gig because you got tipped a dollar every time.

Malcolm Wilson somehow got a copy of my play and tracked me down at the restaurant.

Malcolm was the most exciting black actor in Chicago. Tall and beautiful, he was the toast of the town and, in some ways, the kind of black actor that white critics liked: edgy but not too; doing the kind of roles expected in the ways expected: Othello, etc.

Malcolm wanted to do the play. He wanted to play the young soldier, Emmett.

Except not with Jackie. He was doing an Athol Fugard play at the Goodman, the Valhalla of Chicago theatre, the stepping stone to NYC.

Mamet was being produced there. He had left the St Nicholas and was now in partnership with the young, ambitious assistant director who theatre folk were calling Eve Harrington in relation to the older, established director of the theatre.

Malcolm told me point-blank that no critics were going to go to the 'ghetto' to review the play and that I owed the script and my own career this chance.

After he finished the Fugard, there was no way that he wouldn't be allowed to have *1919* considered.

Of course I knew that he was right. Jackie's theatre had no money. And it would have taken Sidney Poitier – or Malcolm – in the lead to get the audiences into the neighbourhood.

There was no one to talk to about this. Not really. Frankie urged me to 'stay with the sistuh'; Carlyle was neutral, although he favoured Jackie because he liked her energy.

Who did I owe this to?

If I pulled the script, it would collapse her theatre, I knew that. But I also knew that if I wanted to have my plays produced, I had to think in terms of a career.

But I had given Jackie my word; and also, what she was doing was part of my ethos, what I was trying to do. If I walked away this time, telling myself that when I made it 'big' I'd be back to help her, that would go against everything that I thought I was.

Mamma would say that I have to think about myself. But I had given my word. Daddy would have said that black folks will never get anywhere if we don't help our own.

I told Malcolm that I couldn't. I wasn't going to go with him.

The play opened in a blizzard. A comedy opened the same night. The critics chose the laughs, not a tale about a black family trying to survive in the midst of a race riot.

Maybe if I had to go out on a cold Chicago night full of that fierce wind and driving snow, I'd go for the laughs.

The critic of the main paper, the *Chicago Tribune*, came. While she had reservations about the production, she thought that the acting was very good indeed. And she quoted a line from the play, a line in which the soldier, Emmett, talks about the barbed wire in the trenches.

I can't recall it now, something about the barbed wire growing up and out of the ground like something…

At any rate, what she said after she quoted that line meant everything to me. It was something the equivalent of: a writer who can write like that will go far.

I had written plays since I was nine years old. I wrote them because they gave me pleasure, because I was fascinated by the interaction of human beings and the recreation of that. And now a critic had said that I could do it, that I had the ability.

But where was I going to go with it, with myself?

And another thing.

The piece of paper that I always carried with me, the scrap of paper that I wrote things down on, to make into stories or plays or books.

I stopped carrying it.

I couldn't write.

I suddenly saw that it was an industry, a kind of monster in which you had to create this vehicle called a 'career' into which you put your writing because it was the only way that you could survive, could eat. So that you could go on.

It had nothing to do with writing, with the hard slog of it. It was luck, it was graft, it was being in the right place at the right time and being with the right people, having the right people notice you, the right critics and journals.

Samuel Johnson had said that only a blockhead wouldn't write for money, and maybe that was true, but what did it mean, at the end of the day, if you could vanish, disappear, be nothing because the right people didn't see you, the right people didn't notice.

Malcolm had quite simply told me the way of the world, told me what it was.

What difference does it make, he had said in his way, if you were the best writer in the world and no one saw it? What's the sound of one hand…

Maybe I was growing up. Maybe I was seeing the way the world worked and this was the way it worked. And everybody knew it. Except me.

I had never gone a day without writing down something.

But after *1919* had opened and closed, I began to think about exactly who I was, what I was. Was I willing – was I able – to play this game?

This transcended colour and gender; this was human stuff;

this was about understanding the world and being in it. Or out of it.

And I had to make up my mind about Danny. It was obvious that this phase of my life was coming to an end.

NINE

Every writer knows that just because you've stopped writing, it doesn't mean you've stopped writing. A writer is always writing.

Inside I was writing two things: a book to be called *Social Expulsion and Social Change*, and a play called *Vigil Part Two*.

As far as I could make out, *Vigil Part Two* was to be an examination of ghettoisation. The book was to examine the effects of being 'inside', of being effectively trapped in an area of, say, a major city from which you couldn't leave.

It was becoming clear to me that what I was writing about in *1919* was this escape. I wasn't interested in the glamourisation of it, the finding within in it the ways in which people coped, survived.

Of course black people – all people who weren't 'white' (that was coming to mean, to me, not just white skin, but of being the status quo, the norm, 'what is expected') – were in some kind of ghetto, an invisible concentration camp built by mores and customs and practices.

For example, the other day I had seen a black woman shoplift downtown. Normally, she would have been followed – as a rule of thumb, black people are still followed around certain shops, no matter what you look like or how old you are – but she wasn't, for some reason.

At any rate, she started taking things, and putting them in her bag. Stupid, inconsequential stuff: bland potholders; little key rings.

She didn't look to me like anyone who needed them, but watching her I thought of myself in Stacey's house and the era of my petty theft from her. Consciously I might have known what I was doing, but unconsciously?

And that lie-detector test at the bank.

I was terrified and did what I was told, but there was also an atmosphere. It was as if they knew that there was some criminality there, something that they could get me on, and I wanted to give them something – anything – so that, just maybe, they'd let me go.

Puffing on a joint being passed around at a party certainly didn't fit into the category of 'taking drugs', but I had been terrified in that room. There was all the terror that must have been bred in me, that I must have seen and felt anytime I saw a cop, a law enforcement official of any kind. These people were not my friends; these people I couldn't go to for help or to report a crime because THEY WOULD SUSPECT ME, TOO.

What kind of tension/trauma did that create inside of a black person? What was passed down in their mother's milk, in their father's voice, from the grandparents?

I knew that I would have to go back to school to get the credentials to do this sort of book; it couldn't be a pop book. Not then, anyway.

You can do that now without an academic background, with loads of field research and years of practice, but you couldn't then.

Besides, Franz Fanon had written the masterwork, *The Wretched of the Earth*, and there was no way that I could improve on that.

The thing that I was writing in my head and finally did write and get produced was *Vigil Part Two*, my version of a play text that I had read in *PAJ* by Franz Xaver Kroetz, one of Germany's most important playwrights. It was called *Wunschkonzert*, translated as *Request Concert*.

The play is completely silent and chronicles the last moments of a woman's life before she commits suicide.

My version of this play was to be called *Vigil Part Two* and was not about suicide, but homicide – the last moments before a maid goes to work for her white employers.

We see her little indignities, the things that she has to do in order to get ready to go to work.

At the end, the television that's been playing in the background with its banal programmes becomes something else.

As she is walking out of the door, we see a news bulletin about the murder of her employers. We know then, that the maid is on her way to do this.

It was performed in New York in the mid-1980s at an avant-garde space in Soho. Of course.

On the imaginary table by my imaginary bed (actually on the floor away from the heater in what I was increasingly seeing as 'Danny's place', not mine), I was reading *Song of Solomon* and *Meridian*.

They were beautiful books and I was grateful for them, but they were the terrain that I knew.

I needed 'the street', the outlaw, the unbeautiful.

I was selling salads and quiche at a posh restaurant – I wasn't flipping burgers at Micky D's; or cleaning toilets downtown; or hiding my husband's shoes from the welfare people; but it was the condition that I was in, inside of myself.

1919 had left me stateless, more homeless than I had ever been.

The Boys; Carlyle; Mamma and Daddy: it all seemed to be not empty, but a kind of Eternal Return.

If I stayed as I was, maybe I would eventually have kids like Lelia and move to the suburbs and have a dog and a garden, or my version of it: a black bourgeois bohemian existence; maybe married to a black artist or musician or a lawyer with artistic leanings; or to a white professor or artist; have children that I would send to the Latin School and then to the University of Chicago and maybe then to Harvard for postgrad; and I would grow old wearing caftans and have locks.

This was an option, and I had been brought up to aim for this safety.

But I couldn't do it, although I wanted more and more to have children. My body and my mind and my heart were telling me that, at twenty-nine, it was time to do it, and do it fast. The possibilities of a healthy baby diminish with age. That's nature. And I was listening.

I continued to spend my spare time watching old movies in the rep houses, sitting in seats that smelled like unwashed old men, discovering that Fred MacMurray, who played a doofus dad on TV in the 1960s was actually an enormous presence in Wilder's *Double Indemnity*. Orson Welles in *The Third Man*, which I watched over and over and over. Bogart; Bette Davis; Garbo; the work of the great directors. I rediscovered *Gone with the Wind*, a film that I had refused to engage with, and suddenly I could see that it wasn't about black people: it was about Scarlett, it was actually the meek creator of the novel's alter ego; it was about the South and how it saw itself against the evil North. It told me more about the Dixiecrats than any politician could.

Although, like everyone else, I was glued to *Roots* as it unfolded on TV – and, like every black person, mildly amused at how white people were beginning to see us, the questions they asked at work about slavery, the whole eye-openness of it – it was *Gone with the Wind* that told me much more; it told me about Myth, the animating power of it.

I watched *Vertigo* again and again when it was considered still just a big fail. But to me it had captured the drive in men to remake women, to see, in women, an extension of themselves, the Thing Not Acknowledged, and how – maybe – that's what a woman's life is: a series of male projections in the guise of something else.

Looking out of my bedroom window, on to the yard, listening to the Illinois Central train in the distance, I tried to work out my destiny, the way that you do between twenty-six and thirty when childhood and girlhood have, without a doubt, come to an end, not to return – I hope – until you are very old. The 'sea of possibilities' was over.

Mamma and Daddy were telling me this in their own way.

They were watching me, I could tell.

Later that year, at another restaurant where I worked in coat check, the star attraction was Miss Alberta Hunter.

I had never heard of her.

Miss Hunter was, quite simply, along with 'Bricktop', another queen making a comeback, the Harlem Renaissance personified.

She was born in Memphis, Tennessee in 1895, and left for Paris – her second time – to make it big the year Mamma was born, 1927. She played with everybody. Lately, she'd been a nurse in the '50s until, in the early '60s, she was 'discovered' again and urged to sing once more. Miss Hunter, ever shrewd and wily, held on to her nursing job until she was forced to retire. She turned down some gigs at prestigious venues because they weren't on her day off.

I knew that she had been in Robert Altman's latest film, a movie I had seen called *Remember My Name*, about a deranged woman, played by Geraldine Chaplin, who was determined to get her husband. She looked so much like her dad, Charlie, that it was actually unnerving to see her with a cigarette in her mouth, planning to off her ex. And on the soundtrack was a killer-woman blues, sung by Alberta Hunter. The album cover of *Remember My Name* shows Miss Hunter clothed like a housekeeper, looking out of a screen door as if she knows what will inevitably happen, and Chaplin looming behind her in the shadows.

Remember My Name, on which Miss Hunter is joined by the best, including Doc Cheatham on trumpet, is considered one of the major studio sets in the jazz/blues genre.

She sang in a club in Montparnasse in the '20s where Langston Hughes worked as a busboy. They were great friends and, I can imagine, a great support to one another.

Miss Hunter was a lesbian, something she never hid, but never was 'out' about it. Langston was gay and closeted.

I watched her every night.

She was glorious, her hair combed back, a shimmering, simple gown. She was an enormous superstar on the New York nightclub scene with its various cognoscenti, everyone designed dresses for her. She said goodnight to me as she left. She always spoke to us workers.

I didn't dare say anything more to her than 'Goodnight, Miss Hunter,' but she was burned in my heart along with all the great queens and my newest, Ntozake.

At one of Helen's soirées, this one a kind of Bloomsbury Set thing, Nino was there with his boyfriend Nathan from New York.

Nathan was a self-styled 'New York Jew' who couldn't stand Chicago because – as he said to me once – 'Where are the Jews?'

I didn't know what he was talking about until Nino explained that the Jewish community in Chicago was quite sedate compared to New York. Chicago made Nathan paranoid – there were too many trees and not enough Jews. He couldn't find anywhere to eat, it was all much too quiet, etc.

As we all sat there being entertained by Nathan and his account of his Chicago uncle ('All the Jews here marry shiksas, explain that to me!'), Nino said something that made me think that he was inviting me to come to New York.

I knew that he lived on Charles Street, the last street that Delmore Schwartz had lived on before he died. I was obsessed with Schwartz's work after a new biography of him had recently been published, and because of Saul Bellow's latest novel, *Humboldt's Gift*, a roman à clef about his relationship with Schwartz. The novel chronicles the relationship of Charlie Citine with his mentor, a washed-up poet called Von Humboldt Fleisher.

In his short story, 'In Dreams Begin Responsibilities', Schwartz writes about a man in a movie theatre watching the story of his parents' first meeting unfold.

The man knows the ending, and tries to stop his parents coming together, tries to urge them to go on and live their lives, be free. It was beautifully written, and poignant, and Schwartz died unrecognised, a shambly old man on a bench in Washington Square Park.

I didn't, and of course I don't know if I'll wind up that way, too, but above all, I recognised his work, the quality of his heart and his mind, his search.

And when Nino, in the midst of one of Nathan's tirades at the table, asked me if I wanted to stay with him for a few months in New York, he could use the rent because he was going to start on his cabaret career and leave the office work … I said yes.

ON BROADWAY

ONE

I thought somebody had slipped something into my Coke.

There was the famous drag queen Wanda Lust, whose speciality was Cher in all of her glory, now dressed in a tie and tux, and surrounded by drags dressed as Las Vegas showgirls while she channelled Frank Sinatra in his 'fill 'em Joe', one-for-my-baby and one-more-for-the-road era.

She was singing that Drifters classic, like a farewell gesture to me, even though I hadn't told anyone that I was leaving Chicago.

No one came to our storefront theatre on the second night – just a few friends. The worst thing for actors: an empty house.

And you aren't a playwright if you're not produced. Plays are living, breathing things. They have to get off the paper.

The actors went on, as they would do, because they were pros. And it snowed and was cold outside and the theatre was cold inside.

I didn't ask Mamma and Dad to come.

I had decided that they didn't know anything about my work. Not that I helped them to know. Mainly because I didn't know much about it myself, it was just there as it had always been, ever since I was a child.

I watched the actors in the soft, Edwardian light onstage.

The girl in the play, Annise, I thought, was me, longing for an artistic life.

The beautiful, domineering woman was Mamma, manipulating me so that I would keep my feet on the ground, not because she didn't want me to be happy, but to save my life.

I walked home from the theatre in the snow. I picked up a pen like I always did but couldn't write.

There was nothing there, or, there was plenty, but I saw no reason for it to emerge.

THEY had got me, the powers that be; the gatekeepers.

They had worn me down.

And there was always the possibility, the probability, that I wasn't good enough and that's why no one came.

We were just a little storefront Negro theatre in the ghetto and who cared? I had to face that fact.

I had to face the fact that I might always be mediated – black and a woman, always designed by others.

And gradually, you think that this mediated thing is you and maybe it should be you because that was the only thing that was going to get through.

When it becomes you, then you can make up your own reality about it. Fool yourself.

I began to think that if I stayed in Chicago this is the way it would be; it couldn't be any other way.

I saw this little kid that was once me with buck teeth and pigtails, sitting in a corner reading that play script over and over again. I loved the way it looked on paper. I remember what Sister said to me when I told her that I wanted to write plays. She said just write them.

I watched *Playhouse 90*, the great evening TV shows that broadcast live plays. The actors were actually doing them live.

They were caught in the shadow of the boom mic; the glare of the studio lights bounced off jewellery and caught you in the eye momentarily. The writing, the great writing!

Even though I was a little kid, I knew it was great. Like *The Twilight Zone* was great when Rod Serling wrote it.

I copied down the words as I heard them and the gestures and incorporated them into my little school plays.

I loved – and still love – the making of plays, the construction of them: the rehearsal room; the script changes; watching actors build and refine and the director shape them; the set.

Opening night is an anticlimax. Not interesting.

I was like Hitchcock. He said that he enjoyed storyboarding. After he'd done that, the picture was done, as far as he was concerned.

I sat in the back of the auditorium at school and watched the audience. Which I still do. I wanted to see if the machine worked.

I had a pen at the ready all of the time, stuck in my white uniform blouse.

Mamma was so tired of bleaching my blouses, but I had to have my pen.

I wanted to write something now, watching that amazing transformation of Wanda. But I had nothing to write with.

That's the way I wanted it.

At the end of 1978, I would be thirty years old. I used to yell that age at my profs during our anti-war/black students' demos: 'Can't trust anyone over thirty!'

Soon I would be the distrusted one, the one to watch, to disbelieve.

Soon I would join that battalion of adults in adulthood and walk that path to milestones that would only be about deterioration.

Not progress, not going forwards.

I went to Crazy Fools at night, wiped the tables down as usual, made sure that the candles were lit, the chairs in proper alignment.

I even, for the first time, allowed myself to think who might be coming in that night. Who, amongst the regulars, came and sat in the back in the dark, drinking shots in a steady line, unseen by anyone else but me, their waitress.

Sometimes I would run into them in the day in the street, men out in broad daylight and they expected me to know them, call them by name.

I wanted to, I wanted to remember.

But they were a drink: a Jack Daniels on ice there; a double Scotch here.

For the first time that spring I realised that one or two of them had tried to talk to me, make conversation, make a connection.

I had a quota to sell every night and so I was focused on that, and the banter at the bar.

I liked the bartenders and the owner and never paid attention to the customers because it didn't pay to do that. They came to drink; they came to get lost. They came to listen to music that for a moment in time made them heroes, co-creator with the musicians on the tiny stage.

I knew, because I felt it, that there was something tender in each of these regulars, something that they had once shown to someone and had been rebuked, tossed away.

I knew what they could not – that they all had the same face at around 2 a.m.

It was vulnerable and bitter and calculating. These men were drunks and professional at it. They had spent a lifetime concealing from themselves and from others the reality of what they were.

They came to the bar to unseal themselves, take themselves out of the coffin of their own making.

And I, by virtue of being a black girl, I gave them a kind of permission.

They did not expect me to have feelings except in song or movement. It wasn't because they thought I was not worthy or capable. It was simply because their only true relationship was with the bottle.

Their being out in the daytime was to be in search of the bottle and that they could not hide.

I always knew more than I was saying as far as those guys were concerned.

There was a line, even though they pretended that there wasn't.

You smiled and laughed and, as the night wore on, you could call them by any name you chose; they couldn't remember, either.

And yet, as I thought about myself, thought about not having that piece of paper in my pocket, thought about what this meant, I started to find one of them.

I wanted to sit down and talk and it didn't matter if I didn't drink. The drunks at the club didn't notice.

I knew and they knew that there was a fount of wisdom, a thing that could be tapped into, and the drink was the machine that kept it at bay.

If the drink had not, they would be prophets walking the land, surrounded by fire created by others. There was a wisdom that drove them to drink and a pity, too.

One man in particular was never sober.

He would saunter in at six, as soon as the bar opened, and he was there to talk, to connect, to listen. I wanted to ask him about being unlucky.

The play that I had meticulously researched, the precision

that I had put into it, had been blown away by a big snow and a comedy opening across town in the good part of the city, on the same evening.

No one reviewed it, of course, except that *Tribune* critic. Like all playwrights – those most exposed of writers – I clung to that quote and read it over and over again. I wanted to ring up that critic and thank her on my knees.

Her review had meant that much to me.

But that's not done, and all of this I wanted to sit down and talk about to one of those drunks, listen, maybe be consoled.

Instead I wiped down the tables in the bar, and lit the candles on each table, and made sure that the seats were well apart. I was grateful for this job at this time.

When I got home, Danny was at his drawing board, his head down, barely speaking to me. I called his apartment 'home' because it was where I slept.

He was preoccupied, silent.

This was it. It was over. It had been over a long time ago but now there was the little matter – again – of where I was going to live.

I only did waitressing and sometimes telephone sales, not occupations that would allow you to have a place of your own.

I was down to being primal, basic here. I had to stay with him because I had nowhere else to go.

Nowhere else to live.

I made myself a little corner, the same shape as the one in the bedroom that I shared with my sisters. I sat there and slept there and waited.

Danny already had another girlfriend, someone from work who I am sure he explained the situation to. She would have been a compassionate girl and would have listened in rapt attention as he talked about the black girl living with him who could not afford to leave.

I thought about one of the guys at the bar, a very quiet man who slipped me a note once asking for my telephone number.

Maybe I should give it to him, maybe I should tell him tonight that I had nowhere to live. Nothing to write.

I sat in my corner, I sat silently, reading something, but I had nothing to read, nothing important, nothing that mattered.

Dad would have been outraged if he had known that I was effectively at the mercy of a white boy, a country boy, a boy whose people might belong to the Klan or whatever its equivalent was where he came from.

I was on the North Side, that terra incognita; that place my brother Ben would say almost in hushed terms when I was asked back home where I was, as if I had gone and vanished and become someone else.

If only I could write it down.

But nothing came. For the first time in my life, I stared at a blank sheet of paper and it stayed that way.

Chicago, that spring, had a hostility that I had never known.

The city seemed to shut down, roll itself up and vanish before my eyes. I would reach out and it would disintegrate, I would walk towards the high rises on Michigan Avenue – those great skyscrapers straddling the flat prairie – on my way to Marshall Fields and they would seem to recede, repulsed by my approach, by my being.

The voices, the manner, the movement of bodies: it was as if I was watching a movie.

What would I do now?

I had been a writer all of my life, every waking second, and now that part of my life was over. I suppose the truth was that I had never put myself forward as a writer, I didn't like the idea of the 'professional writer'; I just wanted to write. But that was not how the world worked, at least if I wanted to eat and for someone to say that what I was doing was real.

I watched people walking along the lakefront off North Michigan Avenue, one of the poshest parts of town. I watched them laugh and talk to one another, or be alone.

I wanted to jump in, and since I can't swim, the jump would be fatal.

What stopped me was Mamma and Dad.

They wouldn't understand why I had done it, even if I left a suicide note.

Nothing in themselves nor their upbringing would have prepared them to understand. I could have killed them, too, if I had killed myself.

They condemned me to live.

I lived from pay cheque to pay cheque.

It was impossible to save. I didn't make enough money to do that.

I had never made enough money to do that.

What was I going to do?

Two actors who had auditioned for the play and kept in touch were heading for New York a few weeks after my thirtieth birthday.

They were fed up with Chicago. I asked if I could hitch a ride. I could contribute to the gas. They jumped at my offer.

The 'Crazy Fools' gave me a send-off, telling me that I'd be back.

I told Danny and I thought I heard him breathe a sigh of relief. That hurt, but maybe that was the way it was.

I was already packed, practically living out of my suitcase by now. There was nothing left to do.

I called Mamma and Dad and I could detect alarm in their voices, but what could they do?

The day came like a cat stalking through the house.

I looked around for a bit and then said goodbye to Danny and thanks.

We hugged each other and he closed the door behind me.

He didn't look out of the window as I walked to the car. It wasn't necessary, I suppose.

I paused and looked at the street.

This was the North Side, the place of adventure, the haven, the New Life.

I looked at the brownstones and the trendy shops just starting to become a fixture, and the students and the old people, too.

I was leaving the city of my birth and even then, standing there as the snow began to fall, even then I knew that I would never live in Chicago again.

Leanne and Bobby's car was packed up to the roof. Literally.

For some reason, Leanne had packed every vintage fur she owned and boxes and boxes of stuff. I seriously doubt that any of it was Bobby's. The only place for my suitcase was crammed in the back seat.

The only place for me to sit was on the hump in the space between them. That's how I'd have to sit for the twelve-hour-plus drive.

They stopped by home so that I could say goodbye to Mom and Dad.

Mamma gave me some pyjamas.

She kept that tradition for decades until she became ill.

I glanced at all of the family pictures she kept arranged on the mantelpiece: my grandmothers and grandfather, my great uncle. I was on the move like they once had been.

I watched my parents standing together on the porch as we drove away.

Mamma waved goodbye.

I know that they were scared to death.

Twenty years later, after Dad died, I found out that he had taken a burial policy out on me.

Always practical, he wanted to make sure that he could give me a decent burial.

He'd never known a woman like me. Anything could happen.

As we headed for the highway, the snow began to fall. It was December, after all. Normal.

Leanne turned on the windshield wipers and Bobby blasted the radio.

Then they passed the coke.

I didn't know what to do.

I couldn't believe that they were actually going to snort coke on an Interstate, in what was becoming a blizzard, all the way to New York.

Dad had always told us that the main reason that so few black people travelled on the Interstate was because it was dangerous for us.

There was no protection: you couldn't count on the state troopers to help if a pickup truck full of 'Dwayne' types decided to have some target practice.

All of us had grown up on tales about black folks getting killed on highways: our neighbours the Robinsons had died that way.

Plus they were snorting coke in a car full of mink coats.

I could ask to get out, but to get out in Indiana, which still had an active Ku Klux Klan – Jackson family or no – would have been stupid.

And we were in a blizzard, a proper Indiana snowstorm, and soon it might not be possible to see, let alone pull over.

Leanne was also, besides a cokehead, an obsessive/compulsive whose malady manifested itself in constantly wanting surfaces to be clean. In the car. While she drove.

I had forgotten that once she'd stayed overnight with Danny and me after an audition.

I woke up hearing the sound of running water in the bathroom.

It was 3 a.m.

I walked into the bathroom to find Leanne washing everything that she'd worn to the apartment, including her raincoat and umbrella.

I stood there watching her scrub and scrub her raincoat, talking to it, arguing with it, commanding it to do what she demanded.

Now in the car she was obsessed with the coke getting on the car seat, the dashboard, the radio.

Bobby certainly didn't have any intention of spilling the coke, but he was a big, bumbling fool at the best of times and stuff was getting spilt, especially at the turns.

And what about me?

What would happen to me if the Highway Patrol pulled us over? I'd be thrown into some *Deliverance*-type jail complete with good ole boys wanting to rape Leanne and me and string Bobby up.

Why couldn't they see that?

One reason was that Bobby was snorting so much coke that I seriously doubted he would know that he was about to be lynched.

I thought about a myth I had read about the Guardian of the Threshold and how there is always one more obstacle, one more test for the Hero before he/she wins the prize.

Earns the prize.

This was mine.

In the early morning, as we headed into Pennsylvania, Leanne began to tell us her greatest wish: it was to play Desdemona in *Othello*.

Bobby almost snorted his coke out laughing, pointing out that the entire message of *Othello* is that he's a black man married to a white woman who loves him…

It was clear that this was a running argument between them and no one else could join in.

Leanne stopped his analysis with that mystical index finger kind of thing that some black women have, a combination of command and control, and holding back the Dark.

No, he didn't get it, she said solemnly to me. He just didn't get it.

I didn't, either, but I was much more interested in the road, how fast we were going, who was behind us, in front of us.

Every time a car full of white people passed us going the other way, I envisioned them stopping in the woods somewhere to connect with like-minded travellers and come and get us.

I saw a car full of people laughing as deeply sinister, people glancing over at us as threats, and I wasn't even doing any coke.

It was to go to New York to escape this Midwest/Southern paranoia that mattered to me most.

I covered it up with the theatre, etc., but it was really to not have that feeling again, not hear those voices again, those accents, those intonations of a prairie state with Southern links. I just honestly didn't want to know anything more about the South.

Suddenly Bobby became quite melodramatic and began to

tell us a story straight out of Poe. It seemed that his father once made the trip on this very stretch of highway and, stopping over, he was invited into a small room where the gas station owner played cards to pass the hours in between customers.

Bobby's father had a friendly face – 'like a butler', Bobby said – and the man unburdened himself after offering Bobby's dad a glass of whiskey.

The gas station owner wanted to make a confession and he had to make it to a 'nigra' otherwise his soul would not be at peace.

There were bodies out there, he said, black bodies, buried in the vast lot he owned just around back.

Bobby's dad had grown up in the bad old days on the Mississippi Delta, like Dad had, so he knew when white folks were telling the truth or just bullshitting, or worse still, waiting to see if they could get a rise out of the black person they were talking to.

Bobby's dad decided that the gas station owner was bullshitting, and continued sipping the booze as a way of appeasing the guy and making sure that he got out of there.

Years later, bodies were found, black bodies, and the gas guy explained it all away by saying that the men were robbers and he had dispensed justice.

Which, under Indiana law in those days, was a defence that people accepted.

Parts of Pennyslvania – which we were going through right now – were bad…

I asked as politely as I could whether they would consider not snorting for a while.

For a few hours.

Besides, I said, the concept of a black Desdemona… I pretended to be interested, anything to keep her from the coke.

A white Othello would be the revolution, she said, a white actor playing the part – which was the tradition anyway – but this time without make-up and everyone else around them black.

She saw this Othello as if he were a negative photo. I listened as intently as I could. She was whacked.

Bobby got into some nonsensical argument which he thought was philosophical. And I wished that I still prayed.

At 5 a.m. we stopped – I remember the time vividly because the diner was lit up in the dark Pennsylvania woods like a Grant Wood painting. It was just as bleak and lonely, too.

Bobby and Leanne were still high, and now they were hungry, and this looked like a good place.

They were much too high to notice the vibe of the woman behind the counter as we walked in.

Leanne entered as if she was at the Waldorf Astoria as Wallis Simpson.

She strode over to the counter, wiped down the stool with the hem of her 1940s mink and sat down. Bobby went to the gents', probably to do more coke.

I sat next to Leanne.

The waitress or waitress/proprietor asked us what we wanted. We told her. She went into the kitchen and closed the door. Leanne yelled for some coffee. It was pitch black outside and the wind was blowing. There was no way, I decided, that I was going to end my life here, but I had no control over that.

Suddenly, as if on cue, a large group of white men in orange hunting jackets, carrying their shotguns, poured through the door.

There were big woods out there, too.

Bobby came back and introduced himself to all and sundry in a jolly fashion. Very drag-queen-don't-give-a-damn approach.

He made me remember why I've always liked them, have always admired their courage and sheer madness.

Those hunters didn't know what to make of us.

While I kept my head down, munching on my toast and drinking my tea, Bobby and Leanne got loud as they discussed the Tonys and the Obies and whatever else was going, that they were convinced they would win once New York got a look at them.

The men paid no attention to us, not at all.

I ate as calmly as I could, then suggested that we all get moving before the rush-hour traffic from Greater Philadelphia engulfed us.

We came into Manhattan just as the sun was finding its feet and settling down for the day.

It was an entrance just like the movie – there was the wide expanse of bridges and the ocean and ... the narrowness of it.

I looked back at the buildings rising up behind us.

No, this wasn't like Chicago. Chicago is on the prairie, it's flat and precise.

Manhattan was a hodge-podge; it grew as it grew.

We came down and into Harlem.

I was thrilled. The capital of Black America.

I had never seen a fire escape before, not like those on the buildings in Harlem. Yet it was as if I knew these buildings, this space.

The streets were filled with black people then; I could hear the music of the streets, so different from Chicago.

We were all Southerners there, and Midwesterners, but Harlem was a diaspora. West Indian shops and Afro-Cuban shops, stuff I had never seen before.

I heard reggae and calypso, music you would never hear on the street in Chicago at that time.

I could now understand why, when Miles Davis was asked

in the 1950s why he had not stayed in Paris like so many others before him, he replied that if he had, he would not hear the melody of his people in the streets.

We pulled up in front of a house.

Leanne was going to stay there for a few days.

It was a brownstone, with an arch that led to some vastness out back. I remember this because we all wanted to see that vastness, go out behind and look at it.

So while we waited for whoever Leanne was expecting to come downstairs to see her, we Midwest cornpone-hicks left the car, locked it, and went around the back of the brownstone.

There was nothing behind it but desolation: broken bottles and discarded bags of whatever and old clothes and chairs.

Of course when we returned – it couldn't have been more than ten minutes – the car had been jacked and everything taken except for my suitcase, which they figured belonged in that vacant lot anyway.

We didn't know what to do.

Leanne's friend came down and told us matter-of-factly, after we told her what had happened, that 'folks steal in Harlem'.

Leanne took it reasonably well, seeing that she had lost her valuable coats and her suitcase and just had a shopping bag left. Bobby's stuff was gone, too, except for what he was wearing.

My pitiable belongings, for once, saved me.

Bobby took the wheel, left Leanne with her friend, and drove me down to the Village where Nino lived.

And this was yet another world.

The fire escapes were gone, and what took their place is what I imagined Henry James's fiction was about, and Edith Wharton's. This was the New York City of *Washington Square*.

I had decided that I could not read Henry James, I just couldn't understand his rhythms and his cadences.

Now I could see, now I could hear them in the brownstones and the gentility of Washington Square and Charles Street.

I knew as soon as Nino opened the door that he felt that he had made a mistake. His invitation for me to come to NYC had been accepted with vigour. I was coming lock, stock and barrel.

You don't do that to New Yorkers without ample warning.

I had never been inside of a building with such a narrow hallway.

An old lady stuck her head out and Nino said something to her in Italian.

After that, she promptly closed the door.

Nino's place was basically two rooms, which he used as a small sitting room, a bedroom with an oversized bed, a small bathroom with an old-fashioned claw-foot tub in it, and another area where he kept his piano. I could see that the fire escape had flowerpots on it.

I could also see that the place was pristine; there wasn't a speck of dirt in it. And this wasn't because he had just cleaned it.

He was always cleaning it.

Leanne ought to be living with him. Not me.

Nino stuffed my suitcase in the closet and told me that I was sleeping on the couch and promptly left.

I was hungry and looked in the fridge.

He had some pasta but I was nervous about eating it because I hadn't been invited to. I took the keys that he left on the piano and went out looking for something to eat.

There was a soul food restaurant around the corner where the ladies dressed in plain pink dresses. I ate everything they brought to me, spent about a week's budget and then walked out again.

The street was full of men, beautiful men.

I had never seen men like this before – extremely fit.

Not one of them looked at me.

I was in the heart of the gay community. This was great because I could come home at two in the morning and the street would be full of men, and I felt like they protected me.

Nino composed songs that weren't very good and he sang off key. I'm not quite sure why he didn't know that or why no one had told him.

He had a series of T-shirts with Dean Martin and Frank Sinatra on them – 'Frankie and Dino' – which he wore when he played.

He cooked pasta a lot and taught me how to throw it at the wall until it stuck.

I was able to contribute to the food but I couldn't pay rent. I had to find a job.

Nino had two boyfriends. I called them the 'Day Guy' and the 'Night Guy'.

Nathan was the Day Guy.

If New York Jews, for some reason, lost their template and one had to be reinvented, Nathan would provide it.

Nathan was shorter than Nino, extremely bright, and I'm pretty sure that no one at work, nor his parents, suspected that he was gay. He was a great cook and would also sit and talk to me about the world.

Nino only really spoke to me to make sure that I picked up something, or washed something. I didn't know what to do. I had nowhere to go.

Nino's Night Guy was Bruce.

Bruce worked for the U.N., monitoring the apartheid regime and also, I suspect, helping to get opponents out.

Bruce was from Australia and was a blazing redhead, which, he told me, the Australians called 'blue'. He had been to Jo'burg a few times, but the authorities there found out that he was an implacable opponent of everything they stood for, and threw him out.

Bruce was proud of that.

He had a notebook full of clandestine addresses and phone numbers inside South Africa.

And he knew every South African white man who had a black lover and put them up in his flat when they managed to come to New York.

He was a strict observer of the boycott and tolerated no one in his presence violating it. He hated apartheid and all its works.

He always had fifty-dollar bills, which he gave to Nino. He always had a look of deep melancholy in his eyes.

He told me once that his sister-in-law back in Melbourne had forbidden him to enter the family home; she didn't want her son to come into contact with him.

Bruce's brother didn't want to see him, either, but at least they spoke on the phone at Christmas and his brother had called when their father died.

He was very discreet, but I found this out at a party full of Australian expats from every walk of life, roaring drunk by evening's end, and everyone falling into the drinks table and crashing all of the booze to the floor.

I had never seen such hard drinking before.

Bruce explained to me that this happened because everyone was Australian.

The Australian drag queens were the most outrageous, as were the guys in general, beautifully muscled men who – I came to know – had what Bruce called that little edge so that you didn't confuse them with a straight man.

Bruce took me to Studio 54 in its waning days, where I stood at the top of the winding staircase looking down its curved surface to the glittery, silvery world below.

Once I stood at the edge of a low couch, part of a throng surrounding a tiny woman dressed in white with the most luminous violet eyes I had ever seen. It was Elizabeth Taylor holding court.

He took me to the Mine Shaft, which didn't allow women in the basement.

I waited for him to come up, and instead made friends with the guys at the bar.

While Nathan encouraged Nino into thinking that he had a career in the piano bars of the Village, Bruce took him to the edge.

They picked up men together and brought them home; on those days I stayed away in an all-night cinema until it was light.

I deepened my knowledge of Kurosawa that way.

By day Bruce helped the world stay in touch with South Africa. He gave succour and help to the people there.

By night he went cruising, sometimes for derelicts and the men who were crammed into the school buses that took them to the various homeless shelters on the Lower East Side.

Once we rode the lift to the top of the World Trade Center to look out of the windows on the observation deck.

I talked about how all of us who had come to the Big Apple to 'make it', or 'find ourselves', thought it was all here on this tiny, crowded sliver of land way down below.

He said that's because it is.

I would walk over to the Public Theater not far away and genuflect on its once-a-public-library stairs.

This was the sanctum sanctorum, the holy of holies.

Joe Papp, the head of it, would at least give you a hearing.

His theatre was benefiting from *A Chorus Line* on Broadway

and he could afford to be adventurous. He produced black work and hired black actors. Maybe someday…

I needed a job.

Nino worked in a design office for a woman named Phyllis, who had a sideline in Christmas candy and needed more workers.

But I had to meet her and get the once-over before I got the candy-packing job.

Nino said not to mind that she was a JAP, a 'Jewish American Princess'.

I had no idea what that was, and he didn't seem to, either, he just knew the term, and had been told by her that he had a 'Yiddische kop', which was a compliment.

When I asked Nathan what the characteristics of a JAP were, he simply rolled his eyes and muttered something like: 'My sister.'

The candy-packing job was an assembly line, and I loved the irony of doing what Dad did.

I worked ten hours a day, all the hours I could, so that I could give Nino some rent, stave off the inevitable until I could get on my feet.

I made friends with a woman who came in all the way from Queens and who had the same downhome quality as Mamma.

I told Mrs Solkaris about my writing and how I couldn't do it any more.

She was half-listening.

We had a quota of chocolate Santas to fill.

I kept jabbering and suddenly she said that I was probably trying to conform and that was the problem. That's always the problem. And maybe I was a little ashamed of what I was and what I did.

These were the truest things anyone had said to me for a long time.

Deep down I always thought that you should be doing something else if you're a writer, that you should never say that's what you do, because what people do is shovel ditches, or raise kids, or make cans.

It wasn't real.

I had come from people who worked with their hands, who dug and planted and made things. What did I do?

Because if I was going to continue to do it, I had to have a reason why, find a way to be with my 'inherit'.

Nino, who kept his apartment cleaner than most hospitals and who spring-cleaned every Saturday dressed as Lucille Ball in *I Love Lucy*, with a scarf tying his hair up, and apron, complete with heels – and 'woe betide you' if you rang his bell in the midst of that.

While I, on the other hand, kept my suitcase around me beside the couch.

Couches were (and still are) what I was used to, as well as keeping all my stuff near me.

The clutter that was me was starting to get to Nino.

To get out of his hair, I would walk up to Times Square.

I liked the seediness of it, the closeness of it.

Nothing in Chicago was like that: the peepshows where you could pay and a window would open in a booth and a girl would come up, exposing herself, and then the door would snap shut again.

The booths where you could see hardcore films.

I went in there once because I had been walking behind two men and one had said that the guy in front of them was a cop, off duty, but he could not resist coming to Times Square.

He could not resist the squalidness of it.

Before Christmas, Bruce showed me some lesions on his face.

I had no idea what they were, and neither did he.

He told me that he was always getting antibiotics for something or other but the lesions were interfering with his ability to pick up guys.

He asked me to walk with him on the pier along the Hudson where the trucks were and the men came to be together.

All he wanted was to walk among the boys who lay about on the concrete as if they were on the beach and I knew that he was basking in them. Basking in what he was losing.

This beautiful, complex man was looking at his own mortality, his past, wrapped up in two boys kissing up against a truck.

We watched them like we watched a film, and then moved away to the next couple.

I went with him several times.

We went to a Christmas party on a roof overlooking Central Park.

No one at that party was a native New Yorker.

We had all come to find something.

We had all left something behind.

I was not to know that within a decade they would all be gone – the Boys in Chicago, and Nino and Bruce too.

You don't understand mortality at thirty. You don't understand that it exists.

There was a sheet of paper on the table, a waiter's roster.

I took it, found a pen, and began to write.

I was going to make *1919* better, and maybe write another play.

And suddenly I looked up and there was the big city stretching out before me, blinking and twinkling in the dark. I had arrived; I was here.

I did not know what was out there for me, what lay beyond.

But I knew, then, that I had to honour all of the forces, the people dead and alive who made me, who claimed me.

Who helped to make my parallel life, a life that never deserted me even when I lost it, betrayed it.

It was with me now on this Manhattan roof, and there it was, too, the music of the city, and that music made another city, a parallel one in which I found it possible, for a while, to live.

ACKNOWLEDGEMENTS

My thanks and love always to:

My parents, William Mae and the late Ben Greer, Jr;

My siblings, Lelia, Regina and Ben Greer III;

Their spouses, children and grandchildren;

My dear aunt, Mrs Bernice Sayles;

The Arcadia team, Gary, Karen and Martin;

Ted, my friend, who first met me in some of the years covered by this book and remains my friend today;

Fred, the brother of my heart – and his family;

Young Ilya;

Judith, my agent and my protector;

All those I still love, who are gone;

My ancestors;

My hometown, Chicago, a place you never really leave, no matter how far you go and for how long;

My husband David, who makes it possible in every way.

DISCARDED BY
FREEPORT
MEMORIAL LIBRARY